Bankable Business Plans for Entrepreneurial Ventures

Edward G. Rogoff

To order:
Rowhouse Publishing
1375 Broadway, Suite 600
New York, NY 10018-7060
877-363-9866

Find us on the internet at www.bankablebusinessplans.com

Book design: www.folio-bookworks.com

Library of Congress Control Number: 2007933875

ISBN-13: 978-0-9791522-2-1

Publisher's Cataloging-in-Publication
provided by Cassidy Cataloguing Services, Inc.

Rogoff, Edward G., 1951–

Bankable business plans for entrepreneurial ventures / Edward G. Rogoff; foreword by Jeff Bezos. — Textbook ed. — New York: Rowhouse Pub., ©2007.

p. ; cm.

ISBN: 978-0-9791522-2-1
Includes bibliographical references and index.

1. Business planning — Study and teaching. 2. New business enterprises — Finance — Study and teaching. 3. Business enterprises — Finance — Study and teaching. 4. Entrepreneurship — Study and teaching. 5. Venture capital — Study and teaching. I. Title.

HD30.28.R645 2007 2007933875
658.4/012071 — dc22 0708

Printed in Canada

for
Perry-Lynn, David, and Justine

CONTENTS

FOREWORD

The wake-up call for Amazon.com came in 1994 when I read that World Wide Web usage was growing at an astonishing 2,300% a year. The Web was a small place then, but something growing that fast can be invisible today and everywhere tomorrow.

I chose books as the first-best product to sell online. At any given time, there are millions of books active and in print around the world. The largest physical superstores can carry only about 100,000 different titles and mall bookstores typically less than 30,000. Amazon.com would be able to offer the complete selection—millions of books—not just what would fit on the physical shelves. That basic idea—complete selection—was the primary way that Amazon.com was going to add genuine, important value for customers in its early days.

A little after that wake-up call, my wife and I left New York City and headed to Seattle. In the car, I wrote the first draft of what would become the Amazon.com business plan. I continued to work on it for weeks after we arrived in Seattle—ultimately locking myself in a research cubicle at a local library with peanut butter sandwiches for days on end so that I wouldn't be distracted. The more I worked on it, the better the plan became.

The process of writing down my thoughts improved my thinking, and helped me practice mentally and visualize what we were going to do. To be sure, my primary motivation for writing the business plan was to help communicate the idea of Amazon.com to prospective investors, but, in hindsight, an incredibly important benefit that came from writing the plan was crisper, more innovative, more customer-focused thinking. After months of effort and presenting the Amazon.com business plan to some 60 different prospective investors, I was lucky enough to find about 20 "angel" investors who put in approximately $50,000 each. Raising $1 million dollars is supposed to be hard, and it was. I doubt it would have been possible at all without an organized business plan.

In July, 1995, we opened for business with an office and a 400-square-foot warehouse in the Color-Tile building in an industrial area south of downtown Seattle. Our expectations for early sales were modest, and the business plan called for a long startup period where customers would slowly learn about and adopt this new way of shopping. But we were surprised immediately. To everyone's astonishment, in the first 30 days, with no advertising, we took orders from customers in all 50 states and 45 countries.

At this point, our growth was so much stronger than expected, that most of the details in the business plan were no longer valid. It's probably the rare business plan that survives the first day of the business being open. Nevertheless, the process of writing the plan forces you to think through many different cases. As a result, when something changes, you're better prepared for it.

So while the business plan had called for us to be small, we quickly scaled up as customers around the world discovered Amazon.com and kept coming back. After nine months, we relocated to a 12,000 square foot fulfillment center, and seven months later we occupied a 45,000 square foot facility.

Building on the initial business plan, Amazon.com was able to raise $8 million in venture capital by 1996 and the following year, we went public. Customers kept asking us to sell additional categories of products (they still do this). So we introduced music CDs, DVDs, and videos in 1998. That same year we opened amazon.co.uk and amazon.de in Europe. The following year we added electronics, tools, toys, and software, and we began allowing other people to sell their merchandise at Amazon.com. In 2000, Amazon.com had more than 3 million square feet of fulfillment center space in the United States. And we had also opened sites for France and Japan.

As we gained experience, our business continued to be built on offering customers selection and convenience. In July of 2001, we added a third pillar to our business plan: low prices. We would be the kind of retailer that works relentlessly to lower prices for customers. With growing volume and increasing operational efficiencies, we've been able to share the savings with customers in the form of lower prices—and we're going to keep doing that.

Even though all the details have changed over the years, many of the original concepts outlined in the first business plan remain central to our business. In addition, even though you can't plan on it, we've also been lucky. We're especially grateful to our customers, and if you bought this book (or anything else) from Amazon.com, thank you.

I knew Ed before I started Amazon.com, and I believe his experiences with his own successful ventures and as a professor of entrepreneurship make him an excellent person to guide you from initial idea through the creation of an effective plan that will serve the needs of your customers and investors.

A strong business plan will not only help you locate the early funds you need, but will also clarify your thinking and serve as a starting blueprint for future growth in what is always a changing world.

All the best, and good luck serving customers!

Jeff Bezos
Seattle, Washington
October 2002

PREFACE

Why a Book Just about Writing Business Plans?

This book is written with one central purpose: To enable students to create high-quality business plans as part of their course work or as part of their lives.

The origins of this book are twofold: First, my previous mass market book for businesspeople, *Bankable Business Plans*, was well-received and, although not a textbook, it was adopted by many professors for their college, university and business school courses. Second, as a teacher of both graduate and undergraduate courses in which students write business plans, I recognized a need for a textbook on business plan creation that was clear, yet detailed; succinct, yet comprehensive. *Bankable Business Plans for Entrepreneurial Ventures* is written to fill that need.

My extensive experience in writing my own successful business plans, helping other entrepreneurs create effective plans, and advising funding sources on how to evaluate submitted plans, has taught me that a strong plan is built on a single basic element: it must meet the needs of financial supporters, whether they are bankers, investors, family members, or partners. A strong plan written as an assignment in class or for an actual business concept must be anchored in superior financial performance. I call a plan that is attractive to funding sources a *bankable business plan*.

I have personally raised more than $100 million from angels, banks, and venture capitalists to finance my own enterprises by writing bankable business plans that demonstrated how my ventures met the needs of my funding sources. This book will enable you to increase your chances for success both in the classroom and in the real world.

Since 1992, I have been a professor at Baruch College of The City University of New York, the largest and most diverse business school in the United States, where I created and continue to teach both graduate and undergraduate courses on entrepreneurship and business plan development. As Academic Director of the Lawrence N. Field Center for Entrepreneurship at Baruch College, I have developed programs for entrepreneurs and have advised hundreds of individuals as they established their own ventures. Since my clients have an extremely broad range of business ideas—from New York City pedicabs to a web portal for Africans living away from their home countries—it's important for me to make the language I use to discuss the creation of a business plan as uniform as possible. No matter how you envision your course-created enterprise—as a store, an online service, or a firm that reaches your customers by mail order—I refer to the entity you're creating as your "company." When you plan a business of any sort, you're designing a means of delivering your product or service to a wider group of people. Even if you're planning a sole practitioner's venture, it's helpful to think of the way you organize your concept as a company with you at the helm making decisions and setting a course.

Bankable Business Plans for Entrepreneurial Ventures is based on the way successful business people actually create their ventures: From the general to the specific. The book leads each student on a journey from the conceptual stage of a business idea, to proving the idea's feasibility, to fleshing out the details, and, finally, to creating a compelling written plan followed by an effective in-person presentation.

Bankable Business Plans for Entrepreneurial Ventures presents clear and entertaining examples of business blunders and achievements drawn from the actual histories of well-known companies. The book contains lively and interesting discussions under the titles "What They Did Right" or "What Were They Thinking?" that reveal common business mistakes and uncommon business triumphs.

This book can help every student produce the full array of required financial projections, either manually or through helpful outside resources I've used myself and highly recommend. The book's accompanying Web site, www.bankablebusinessplans.com, offers software for producing plans and contains financial templates for all levels of complexity, enabling students to produce fully-linked financial statements with a minimum of inputs.

Bankable Business Plans for Entrepreneurial Ventures is the only textbook that reveals how to focus on the needs and requirements of financial sources, lenders, and investors first. And it is the only book to guide students in employing the Risk Management Association database—the very formulas most banks use to evaluate business loans. The book includes many discussions of how to apply rapidly developing e-commerce and Internet capabilities to reach new markets, reduce costs, and establish a competitive advantage for any business.

With my knowledge of what makes a successful business plan from the point of view of an entrepreneur, a funder, and an educator, I can pass all the lessons I have learned along to you, the reader of *Bankable Business Plans for Entrepreneurial Ventures.*

By following the process in this book you will guarantee that your business plan, in class or in life, will be as bankable as possible.

Edward G. Rogoff
New York City
July 2007

INTRODUCTION

What They Did Right: Jeff Bezos Writes the Plan for Amazon.com

In 1994, Jeff Bezos was working as an analyst with a Wall Street firm when his boss asked him to look into this new technology called "The Web." Bezos quickly realized that he was witnessing the birth of a new and unexplored industry whose explosive rate of growth had not even begun to be tapped. He envisioned the Internet with a gigantic catalog-type cyberspace store that could sell ten or twenty times more books or CDs than even the largest brick and mortar store could handle. Plus customers would be able to browse through the offerings from the privacy and comfort of their own computers.

Bezos was so intrigued by this possibility that he began dreaming about starting his own Internet business. Although he didn't know exactly what the business would be, he decided to settle in Seattle because of the ample supply of people experienced in the computer and software industries. Bezos quit his Wall Street job and headed West:

> In the car, I wrote the first draft of what would become the Amazon.com business plan. I continued to work on it for weeks after we arrived in Seattle—ultimately locking myself in a research cubicle at the local library with peanut butter sandwiches for days on end so I wouldn't be distracted. The more I worked on it the better the plan became.
>
> The process of writing down my thoughts improved my thinking, and helped me to practice mentally and visualize what we were going to do. To be sure, my primary motivation for writing the business plan was to help communicate the idea of Amazon.com to prospective investors, but, in hindsight, an incredibly important benefit that came from writing the plan was crisper, more innovative, more customer-focused thinking.

It was this plan that helped Bezos raise more than $1 million from 20 "angel" investors who enabled him to found Amazon.com in the garage of his rented Seattle house. It has since grown into the Internet's preeminent retailer with more than $7 billion in annual sales. In 2004 at a price of $50 per share, Bezos's stock was worth more than $5 billion.

Amazon.com has not only grown, it has evolved. What Bezos first saw as an Internet bookseller has regenerated into a giant virtual department store that uses a network of huge, state-of-the-art warehouses that maintain and manage enormous inventories to keep deliveries fast.

Jeff Bezos's story is, in large part, all about the power of writing a plan. This process forced him to think through organizational issues, define his concept, and hone his approach to investors. His business plan obviously worked, but it was never set in stone. As both Amazon.com and the Internet grew, the business plan changed and became the basis for Amazon.com's evolution and it's continued success.

The Bankable Business Plan

You want to start your own entrepreneurial venture. A competitor enters the market first. Financing fails to materialize. The economy weakens. Despite such unavoidable dangers, you can actually reduce risk and increase the probability of success by creating a strong business plan *before* setting up shop. A persuasive business plan can not only establish strategies to manage risk, it can also attract investors and partners who will share your risk. You can test ideas on paper before expending large amounts of money and time. In this book, a business plan that makes an entrepreneurial concept more attractive to potential funders is called a *bankable business plan*. By the time you finish reading this textbook, you will be able to create the most bankable business plan possible.

New businesses require thought and careful decision making because you have to control every aspect of the venture. Your product or service may need to be defined or its characteristics refined. The market may not be fully specified and plans for how to reach customers with a message about your business will have to be created. The management team has yet to be assembled and proven effective. From a financing source's point of view, all these uncertainties, combined with a lack of credible historical financial results, mean lots of risk. Most funding sources that have a lower tolerance for risk will probably be less interested in financing a start-up.

One of the challenges of writing a plan for a start-up business is the need to reduce this perception of risk among your company's potential funders. Strategies for accomplishing this include carrying out research to demonstrate that the market wants your product or service, "benchmarking" or finding a similar business that compares favorably to yours, and starting small so that investment is kept to a minimum until the profitability of the company can be established.

A bankable business plan is a document with a purpose. It can help you test the feasibility of a business concept quickly and inexpensively so you can reject untenable ideas and develop a venture with a greater likelihood of success. It can also help you identify and secure the best financial resources from investors or partners, obtain debt such as loans and lines of credit, and negotiate attractive payment terms. A bankable business plan will direct you in building a strong company team by guiding you to key managers, employees, partners, and consultants. It will also help you establish productive business relationships with customers, suppliers, and distributors. And finally, the business plan will create an operational template for the successful management of your particular venture.

This book will guide you through the step-by-step process of producing this singular "document with a purpose." It is not designed to give you a standard form for a business plan. It is designed to give you the template of the process you will follow to create your own, unique and powerful bankable business plan.

As you read this book, you will learn to:

- **Generate ideas** that can grow into a successful venture.
- **Identify the essential elements** and information your bankable business plan must contain.
- **Choose which purposes of the plan are crucial** to the success of your business.
- **Stress the business issues** that are most important to the people whose support and involvement you need.
- **Construct a business plan** that expresses your confidence in the concept.
- **Convince others to believe in the concept** and participate in your business.
- **Develop credible financial projections.**
- **Make an effective in-person presentation** of your plan at a business meeting.

What Defines a *Bankable* Business Plan?

Bankable business plans will attract the attention and interest of people you want to fund and participate in your venture. Business plans are "bankable" in three critical ways. First, they are unique, quality documents. Second, they provide a crucial step in obtaining financing. And third, they establish the groundwork for business success.

Bankable business plans are exciting, thorough documents, but they don't follow formulas. They are customized to your venture. Trying to copy an existing plan or filling in the blanks on a generic plan will produce a plan that sounds canned, lifeless, and uninspiring. Such a plan will do little to motivate others to participate in your venture. In addition, it will take an experienced banker or investor only a few seconds to identify—and discard—a "formula" plan.

Creating a business begins with conceptualization and continues through implementation. Creating a plan should follow that same process. Bankable business plans are produced by developing ideas, analyzing them thoroughly, testing them against simple criteria, and selecting the best concepts to pursue. Once you have identified the best ideas, you can make the process more specific by researching the market and the competition and by developing effective strategies for implementation

Businesses exist to make money. Since a bankable business plan is written to convince lenders and investors to provide financial resources, the plan must address *their* specific desire to make money.

The 12 Essential Issues

When you are beginning the process of creating a new venture you need to follow several primary principles, called the *12 essential issues*, which will form the foundation of your bankable business plan:

1. Generate Ideas and Define the Business
2. Establish Financial and Personal Feasibility
3. Create a Winning Strategy
4. Analyze Potential Markets
5. Develop a Marketing Campaign
6. Build a Sales Effort
7. Organize the Company
8. Identify Potential Funding Sources
9. Produce the Financial Projections
10. Demonstrate the Entrepreneur's Abilities and Qualifications
11. Present the Plan on Paper
12. Present the Plan in Person

The Entrepreneur's Tool Kit: Use "Thought Experiments" to Test Ideas

For centuries people believed that heavy objects fell faster than lighter objects. Legend has it that in 1612, Galileo performed one of the most famous experiments in history. By dropping objects of different weights from the top of the Leaning Tower of Pisa (which had begun to tilt during its construction over four centuries earlier), Galileo demonstrated that they hit the ground at the same time. Whether or not Galileo actually performed this famous act, he was confident of the results because he had carried out and recorded a ***thought experiment*** beforehand.

A thought experiment is a tool that uses only the mind and its imagination to test an idea. To explore the question, "Do heavy objects fall faster than lighter objects?" Galileo immediately posed another question: "What would happen if a heavy object and a lighter object were connected to each other?" He reasoned that the assumption that heavier objects fall faster made two opposite outcomes possible: 1) the combined object was heavier and thus would fall faster or 2) it would fall more slowly because the lighter object would slow down the heavier object. Galileo realized that this made no sense and concluded—still only in his mind—that all objects must fall at the same speed. So even before he purportedly leaned over the top of the Tower in Pisa to drop objects of different weights, he was sure of the outcome.

Entrepreneurs can use thought experiments just as successfully. In fact, business plans are thought experiments that are written out. Let's say you want to create a business plan to open a dress shop. You will need to employ reasoning and logic to explain how this complex concept would work. Questions that lead to thought experiments in this case might include "Which location under consideration will attract the most customers?" By examining issues such as foot traffic, the neighboring stores, opportunities for signs, and proximity to the demographic groups the store will appeal to, you are basically carrying out a series of thought experiments to help you find the best answer.[3, 4]

A business plan to open a car wash might use thought experiments first to test questions about the hours of operation, pricing, the addition of premium services, or an increase in the number of staff. Thinking through each question in the context of your knowledge and experience will increase the probability of arriving at the best answer and will help you define questions you may want to test through further research.

Issue 1: Generate Ideas and Define the Business

The fundamental reason companies prosper is because they meet the needs of customers, investors, lenders, employees, and suppliers. Each of these groups enters into a relationship with the business for a different reason:

- **Customers** want a good product or service at the right price.
- **Investors** want to earn high financial returns.
- **Lenders** want their loans paid back with interest on a fixed schedule.
- **Employees** want fair compensation, a safe and satisfying work environment, and opportunities for personal and professional growth.
- **Suppliers** want a good customer for their products or services.

You might have noticed that *your* needs do not appear on this list in spite of the fact that you may have many strong personal reasons for starting a business, such as escaping an overbearing boss, not being able to get along with colleagues, or proving to your skeptical father-in-law that you can be a success. Perhaps you have a burning desire to bring wholesome nutrition to the movie-going public with your Bucket o' Broccoli franchise concept, but unless customers will actually purchase your product, your emotional commitment won't mean much to investors or lenders. In fact, they may worry that any noble intentions could actually interfere with your ability to make sound business decisions. Your humanitarian goal of providing a healthy alternative to greasy, salty popcorn in multiplex cinemas may inspire you, but it will not be important to the groups you need to recruit to build your business. Your needs will not play a major role in your final business plan.

So concentrate on the needs of others that your company will meet. What will your product or service enable people to do better, more cheaply, more safely, or more efficiently? Will your broccoli recipe make people's palates delirious with new taste sensations? Will your new paperclip hold paper together more securely? Will your new bubble-gum-scented bubble bath revolutionize the way children agree to take nightly baths?

Think of all the positive benefits your company will provide. Write them down. Admire them. Absorb them into your consciousness. Believe in them. These are the primary motivators that readers of your business plan will respect and value—and these are the benefits that will turn readers of your plan into participants in your business.

Issue 2: Establish Financial and Personal Feasibility

Personal feasibility is a test of whether you have the time, money, and skills necessary to build a successful venture—and whether you are willing to commit them to the business. Besides investing your savings, you may have to use your house or other assets as collateral for a loan. You may have to give up your current job, lose that income and step off a potentially successful career track to become an entrepreneur. You must objectively judge whether you have the skills and knowledge to make this venture a success, and if you don't, how you will obtain them from others. Finally, you need to consider the implications for your family. You may be asking them to invest, to support you financially and emotionally during the process, and to work in the company alongside you. If you can answer all these questions positively, you have established personal feasibility.

Financial feasibility is a test of whether the start-up resources are available for your venture and if the business has the potential for long-term profitability. Whether you want to start a company with 300 employees or a solo business by only adding an extra phone line to your home, you need to make a list of what your start-up expenses will be. Requirements as simple as five hundred file folders and a large cabinet in which to store them need to be listed and their costs estimated.

If you're going to build a better paperclip, you may have constructed a prototype by reshaping paperclips from home, but you'll need a sturdier, more attractive model to show potential investors. What exactly will your paperclip look like? Will you have to acquire large amounts of titanium so your paperclips can be virtually indestructible? What color will they be? How will they be packaged? Do you require money for research and development to further improve on your original prototype? Do you need to hire an engineer to draw up accurate manufacturing designs? Should you patent your invention? Are there federal safety standards for paperclips? Should you allow time to test the materials for durability before you start manufacturing paperclips by the million? How many paperclips do you plan to make at first? All of these represent start-up costs that will need to be paid and for which you must raise funds. If you can't demonstrate that raising these start-up funds is a strong possibility, you have failed to clear the financial feasibility hurdle.

Next, do your homework and establish that the business has a good chance of being profitable. This requires estimating how much revenue your company will have and what its ongoing operating expenses will be. If you plan to open a restaurant, you'll have to estimate how many meals you expect to sell and what the average price will be. You must also determine how much money you'll need to cover expenses such as rent, salaries, taxes, utilities, food, and advertising. If your estimates don't show that revenue exceeds expenses in a relatively short period of time (usually less than a year for a restaurant), then your business will not have proved its ongoing financial feasibility.

Issue 3: Create a Winning Strategy

Although there are millions of types of businesses, there are actually only a few basic strategies that can be applied to make any enterprise successful. The first step in selecting an effective strategy is to identify the *competitive advantage* that your product or service will have in the marketplace. Competitive advantage is the reason customers will choose your products over those of your competitors.

Your competitive advantage may include designing special features not found in rival products. It may entail superior service characteristics such as speedier delivery, a lower price, or more attentive sales people. Perhaps you're establishing an image or brand of exceptional quality and reputation that will bestow a certain status on its users. Or maybe your product or service will create additional profits for your customers' own endeavors.

Suppose you want to open a restaurant that serves squid-flavored pancakes. What will your competitive advantage be? Do you know that the people in your neighborhood devour other squid-based dishes and can't seem to get their fill? Have all the other pancake restaurants in the community failed to include squid-flavored items on their menus? Is squid much cheaper to acquire than other more traditional pancake ingredients, such as bananas? Will that enable you to charge much less for all the items on your menu, including banana pancakes? Will the decor of your restaurant be so enticing to squid lovers that they'll come in to look around and then stay to discover how delicious your squid pancakes are?

You must have a reason why your business will succeed in the marketplace. This is its competitive advantage. Once you've established the competitive advantage, you will be able to select the best strategy to reach your goal.

Issue 4: Analyze Potential Markets

To determine your targeted market, write down the demographics of the people who will use your product or service. How old are they? What do they do for a living? What are their personal values and how do they make decisions? Will your main customers be men, women, children, or teenagers? Is your product or service attractive to a particular ethnic or economic group of people? Will only wealthy people be able to afford it? Will your ideal customer have to live in a certain type of neighborhood, such as a sunny suburb with grass lawns, in order to use your solar powered lawn mower? Answering these questions about the demographics (who they are), geographics (where they live), and psychographics (how they think) of your prime customers will help you establish the clear characteristics of the people you need to reach.

If you're selling soap, you may believe that every dirty body needs your product, but you can't start with the entire world as your initial market. Even if you've developed such a ubiquitous item as soap, you need to identify a smaller, more targeted customer group first, such as children for the bubble gum-scented bubble bath. If your soap only works with pumped well-water without fluoride, you must acknowledge that your intended market has geographical limits. If the major benefit of your soap is its bubble gum scent, your primary customers will probably be children under the age of eight—or rather, their parents, who do the actual shopping. If your soap contains pumice that will remove car grease, paint, and tile cement without toxic chemicals or fumes, your market will be defined by people who work in specific professions, such as mechanics, house painters, and bathroom contractors. To obtain the greatest results from your first expenditures, you want to make sure that you have targeted the best buyers first. The more focused your market, the more realistic, sensible, and convincing your plan will be.

Establishing the size of your potential market is important, too. This will be easier once you've completed the demographic analysis. Then you'll be able to research the numbers. If you're producing soap, you will need to know how many car mechanics, house painters or tiling contractors are doing business in any given community. Or perhaps, how many children in the United States are currently under the age of eight? How much soap will they use in a month or a year? How many other soap manufacturers already have a share of the market? How big are your potential competitors? Do any of them make bubble gum-scented soap? And where do you find the answers to all of these questions?

Identifying your market is one of the critical steps and great satisfactions of starting your own business. You're thinking about the actual people who will use your product or service and how pleased they will be buying it as you are selling it. When you have completed this Introduction and examined Issue 4, you will have solid answers to all of these questions.

Issue 5: Develop a Marketing Campaign

Entrepreneurs, especially inventors, often believe that their business concept is so spectacular that promoting their product or service won't be necessary—sort of a "build it and they will come" attitude, especially if what you're building is the proverbial better mousetrap. One of the most common flaws in business plans is the entrepreneur's failure to describe exactly how customers will be reached and how products will be presented to them. Potential investors, staff, and partners won't be convinced that your idea can succeed until you've established well-researched and effective methods of contacting your customers—and the assurance that once you've reached them, you can convince them to buy your product or service.

Marketing describes the way you will position your product or service within your targeted market and how you will let your potential customers know about your company. Positioning is how you will define your product's competitive advantages in comparison to your competition. Common positioning strategies include low price, superior quality, special features, and design.

Suppose you want to open a financial services business to advise Wall Street investors who wish to buy stocks in the rubber sole industry. You've probably already identified your target market as major New York City based investors interested in rubber sole stocks and your competitive advantage as your unparalleled expertise in rubber sole stocks.

Some of the questions you'll have to ask yourself before you develop a marketing campaign include: What trade journals and newspapers do your potential clients read? Would ads in these publications be worth the cost of placing them? How could you interest a reporter for one of these periodicals in writing a story about your new advisory firm? Is there an organization of rubber sole company investors that you should join? Are there conventions for investors in rubber sole companies that would be worth attending? Will your knowledge of a related industry, such as flip-flop manufacturing, give you more impressive credentials in finding clients? Will direct mailings to investors or posting information on the Internet be useful outlets?

Once you have thought through how you will market your product or service, you will be able to develop a bankable business plan that will help you gain market share, generate revenue, and bring your financial projections into reality.

Issue 6: Build a Sales Effort

The word "sales" covers all the issues related to making contact with your actual customers once you've established how to reach them through your marketing campaign. Sales is the process that occurs immediately before you ring up the item on your cash register or sign the order. To be successful at building your sales effort, you need to establish how you will train your sales staff to approach potential customers. Perhaps you will divide them up so some become experts in selling your bubble gum-scented bubble bath to small, independent retail toy stores, while others concentrate on developing relationships with national retail chains. Will you have a sales force expert in buying television slots on Saturday morning cartoon shows or placing ads on the backs of kid-oriented cereal boxes?

Think about which advertising and promotional efforts you will employ—two for the price of one specials or free coupons inside the boxes of kid-oriented cereals? Where can you locate lists of the greatest concentrations of children under the age of eight? What will you convey to children about your bubble bath that will convince them to ask their parents to buy it? Will you have to follow federal guidelines that require you to stick warning labels on every bottle to keep children from drinking your delicious smelling soap?

As you plan your sales activities, you will also need to answer questions such as: Will you be the only salesperson in the beginning stages of your company? When will you know it's time to hire more sales staff? How do you convince your clients that your sales staff will take care of them as well as you did? What will your basic sales philosophy be—building long-term relationships with a few major clients or developing a clientele of many short-term customers?

You will also need to consider how you will compensate your sales staff—with a base salary plus a commission or in bottles of bubble gum-scented soap? Will you hire full-time staff with full benefits, or part-time staff without benefits? How will you motivate your staff to do the best possible sales job?

Knowledge of your competitive advantage is just as important in designing a dynamic sales effort as it is in developing an effective marketing campaign. You'll need to think about what product or service qualities will be the most compelling to your prospective customers. Then you'll have to devise convincing language that clearly communicates this competitive advantage to your sales staff who will in turn use it when talking to your customers. The most important element of an effective sales effort is having a sales staff that thoroughly understands your business and the needs of your potential customers.

Issue 7: Organize the Company

By the time you've reached this stage of thinking about your potential business concept, you'll probably have a reasonable idea of the number of people you'll need and the skills they'll require to get your enterprise up and running. Keep in mind that your initial plans will undoubtedly change as your business grows. You may need to hire more managers to supervise your expanding staff or to set up new departments to meet new customer demands. Projected growth and expansion for your company should be mentioned in your business plan, but it's not the primary focus. For now you want to secure help in getting started and convince your funding sources that you will become profitable.

Let's imagine that you have been running your grandfather's tuba plant since his death, but the operation is still small and old-fashioned. You have identified a competitor's tuba factory to purchase. Buying the new plant will enable you to bring your manufacturing methods up-to-date and expand your customer base.

Investors will want to know if you're capable of running the show by yourself after you take over the new plant. Do you need to bring in experienced managers right away? Will you keep some of the existing employees or hire all new people? And where will you find these potential employees?

Funding sources will also want to know if any of your partners expect to work by your side or if their obligations are only financial. They may ask how you plan to maintain the trust and cooperation of the employees from both your previous plant and the new tuba factory. And how will you reassure both plants' customers that your new tubas will be as good as, if not better than, the tubas that used to roll off the assembly lines?

Your plan will need to specify the key management jobs and roles. Positions such as president, vice president, chief financial officer, and managers of departments will need to be defined as well as who reports to whom. You may hope to run your company as one big happy family—and it may work out that way—but organizations require formal structures and investors will expect to see these issues addressed in your plan.

Running a manufacturing plant will require you to deal with dozens if not hundreds of employees, but what if you want to create a financial services company?

You will have some of the same issues, such as handling partners who may want to work side-by-side with you on your venture, but you may be the sole full-time employee for quite some time. How will you find the right consultants to advise you? Will you collect a salary? When will you know you need to hire a staff? What skills must they have? How do you recruit them? How will you structure your company so the chain of command and quality control are maintained if the company grows dramatically?

And as soon as you have employees, you need to consider how you will handle their salaries and wages, their insurance and retirement benefits, as well as analyzing the extent of your knowledge of tax issues. As you think about hiring personnel and organizing your workforce, you must also confront your desire and ability to be a good boss. If you haven't contemplated this aspect of your commitment to owning your own business, now is the time to give it serious consideration.

Issue 8: Identify Potential Funding Sources

As your business concept begins to take shape, you can home in on the most likely financing sources. Issues such as the size of your business, the industry it is in, and whether you can provide collateral to a lender must be considered in creating a target list of funding sources. Banks and investors don't share their money because people with interesting business ideas are nice. They follow specific guidelines which are designed to insure that they will make money by lending to or investing in your company. Bankable business plans identify the needs of potential financing sources and demonstrate how those needs will be met.

For the vast majority of entrepreneurs, the well-known, high-profile means of raising money, such as through venture capital companies or by going public, are not viable options. Your own credit, credit rating, and business history are key factors in obtaining financing for your venture through Small Business Administration (SBA) guaranteed loans and other bank credit. Your ability to tap into your personal network of friends, family, and professional contacts is crucial to raising money beyond what your own personal funds or credit can provide. In all of these cases, there are important considerations, such as the potential impact on relationships when family and friends become investors.

When you have completed the process of identifying likely funding sources and writing a bankable business plan that addresses their needs and answers their questions (even before they ask them!), you will have greatly increased your chances of obtaining the financing you need.

Issue 9: Produce Financial Projections

The accuracy of your financial figures and projections is absolutely critical in convincing investors, loan sources and partners that your business concept is worthy of support. The data must also be scrupulously honest, extremely clear, and completely comprehensive. Your assumptions and projections must be supported by independent evidence and comparisons to industry averages.

The actual number crunching portion of your business plan is not the place to talk about your pie-in-the-sky hopes for opening a tuba manufacturing plant in every country around the globe or for convincing theater chains that they should replace popcorn with your company's "Bucket o' Broccoli." This *is* the place to discuss how and why you need certain equipment, how much these items will cost, when you expect to turn a profit, and how much return and other benefits your investors will receive.

More new businesses fail because they simply run out of cash reserves than for any other reason. Investors lose confidence in the entrepreneur and the business and become reluctant to invest more when projections are not met. Had the projections been less optimistic and the investors been asked to invest more in the beginning, they probably would have done so. In most cases, proper planning and more accurate projections can avoid this problem.

Start analyzing your financial information by going back to Issue #2 that covers how to establish financial and personal feasibility. Study the list of the resources you need to start your company and the costs you have estimated. Your business plan should clearly state the amount of funds you need, how soon you require them, and how long before you can start repaying investors. You should also explain what type of financing you hope to acquire, either equity (such as through the sale of ownership shares in your company) or debt (such as bank loans), and if you require capital expenditures to buy equipment or working capital to pay for product designs and market research.

This is also the section of the business plan in which you should provide detailed figures on expected income, cash flow estimates, balance sheets, and future reasonable forecasts for your business. Do you hope to be producing 1,000 tubas a week in five years? Will you be able to lower the price of your better paperclips once you can buy titanium by the ton? Are you planning to open three additional restaurants featuring squid-flavored pancakes?

After you've pulled together all the important financial data, you'll have a clearer picture of how much money you'll need to borrow, how much of your own funds you'll be able to commit, and the amount of investments you'll have to secure. No matter what business you intend to start, you will need to know how to analyze not only projected profits and losses, but actual profits and losses as soon as your first customer walks through your pancake house door or buys a bottle of your bubble-gum-scented bubble bath.

Issue 10: Demonstrate the Entrepreneur's Abilities and Qualifications

The talents, experience and enthusiasm you bring to your enterprise are unique. They provide some of the most compelling reasons for others to finance your business concept. Keep in mind that investors invest in people more than ideas. Even if your potential business has many competitors or is not on the cutting edge of an industry, the qualifications and commitment you demonstrate in your plan can convince others to proffer their support.

Your resume will be included in a separate appendix of exhibits at the end of the plan, so this is not the place to list every job you've ever had or the fact that you were an art history major in college, especially if these experiences have no direct bearing on your ability to start your own business. But it *is* the place to emphasize qualifying skills that may not be readily apparent from your resume.

Say you want to open the restaurant featuring squid-flavored pancakes. Investors won't be initially impressed by your successful career as a commercial airline pilot. They may be much more swayed by the fact that from the age of 13 until 22, you worked after school and on weekends in your father's delicatessen. This information has probably never appeared on your professional resume, which stresses the number of flying hours you have logged and the citations you received for customer satisfaction. But having worked for so long and intimately in a family-owned retail food business indicates that you know how to supervise cooks, run a grill, and order perishable foodstuffs in bulk. You are probably even an expert in the Heimlich maneuver, which with squid-flavored pancakes, may come in handy.

Perhaps before you embarked on your flying career, you joined the Peace Corps and worked in a country that happened to be the world's 4th largest squid exporter. The knowledge you've acquired about the squid business and the contacts you have maintained in your Peace Corps country will enable you to purchase tons of high-quality squid more cheaply and rapidly than any of your competitors.

But don't overlook the impact being a pilot may have on your ability to run a restaurant, especially if those skills are not apparent to your potential investors. You should stress that you know how to supervise a crew of people working together to make a group of customers comfortable, or at least safe. You have undoubtedly handled dissatisfied or enraged customers. Even that B.A. degree in art history may enable you to teach cooks how to make their dishes more appealing to the eye.

If you have partners or staff, you must cover the same issues for them, especially if they bring skills to the venture you don't have. Perhaps one is an expert in state-of-the art hand-held computers that waiters can use to send orders immediately to the kitchen or to tally bills and approve credit card purchases within seconds. Another may be a champion napkin folder who can create caricatures of customers as soon as they sit down at their tables.

Your unique qualifications will separate you from all the other people who have sought funding for specialized restaurants. Boasting about these skills is not hubris; it indicates that you have a highly honed business savvy.

Issue 11: Present the Plan on Paper

A plan that motivates others to support your venture is built around a basic core message: Your business can be successful and you are the best person to accomplish this goal. But it also requires a well-structured format that employs graphic tools such as timelines, charts, and tables, with helpful headers and subheads to make the key points of the plan as accessible as possible. The language throughout the plan must be concise, grammatical, and persuasive. How would you feel about a plan that had a misspelling in the first sentence? Or one that was verbose and disorganized? The entrepreneur who wants to open a restaurant selling squid-flavored pancakes needs thorough research and understandable graphics to establish that people will like his product. Cute cutouts of squid swimming around the margins of his business plan pages may be eye-catching, but they won't do the job.

Before you begin writing the text, create a carefully constructed outline, remembering to cover the first ten essential issues and the needs of your particular readers, whether they are family members, bankers, or investors:

- Begin with an overview of the business, the reason an opportunity exists, and the amount of support you need.
- Then discuss the business environment, including your potential customer's needs, your targeted market, the industry as a whole, and any possible competition.

- Follow by identifying the business strategy that will allow you to develop a strong competitive advantage.
- Next, describe the implementation of your concept through your particular work experience and management skills, as well as the organizational structure you have chosen, and the marketing and sales efforts you will design.
- Finally, add financial materials, such as Projected Income Statements, Balance Sheets, Cash Flow Statements, Returns Analyses, and comparisons to RMA figures or other significant industry data, remembering to adjust your material to each specific funding source.

Don't follow this book's outlines to the letter or let a computer program for business plans dictate the content or structure of your plan. If you do, the resulting plan will look canned and will waste peoples' time by not addressing each reader's specific interests. A bankable business plan is unique to you, your business concept, and the funders you are approaching to support your venture.

Issue 12: Present the Plan in Person

If your business plan is clear, strong, and convincing, investors will want to meet you in a face-to-face discussion that will make or break the deal. Practice and preparation are key. Entrepreneurs must know how to listen carefully, what to say, and when to address the core issues of potential supporters. There is a great deal happening during these interactions. Both sides are judging each other's needs and deciding if they would like to work together. They examine such important topics as financial requirements, management structures, and exit strategies. The merits of the plan are reviewed and often challenged in detail.

Everyone has participated in meetings where people "talk past each other" and nothing of substance is accomplished. You may have witnessed a sales call in which the person doing the selling moves aggressively for a commitment before the other person's important issues have been addressed. Successful entrepreneurs recruit the resources they need to make their ventures soar by stressing the mutually beneficial long-term relationships that are possible with their bankable business plans.

Meeting with potential supporters is similar to presenting your plan to your classmates, an exercise your professors should schedule as part of your course work. Making your enthusiastic pitch about your business idea, presenting your research, explaining your financial figures and answering your classmates' questions all provide a risk-free opportunity to practice your techniques. The better prepared you are, the better you can engage in this critical interaction, and the greater your likelihood of a successful outcome—or a good course grade—will be.

Focus on Research: Does Planning Actually Improve Performance?

An architect would never consider constructing a building without a plan. An architect's plan a way to avoid mistakes, to elicit clients' feedback, and to schedule the resources needed to construct the building. Yet entrepreneurs often build their ventures without formal plans.

In fact, even experts who study the planning process and its effects find it difficult to prove that planning improves business performance because:

- **There is no single definition of planning.** For some businesses, there is a formal and comprehensive system in place to create plans and projections on a regular basis. For other businesses, planning may mean only conceptual discussions of future options with few clear decisions being made.
- **Many plans are created as a requirement of funding sources** such as banks or investors, but they are often not integrated into the management of the business.
- **It is hard to define "success."** Most people think that for a plan to be successful it must lead to a successful business. In fact, a plan is a success if it helps an entrepreneur avoid the mistake of starting a business that fails.

- **It is difficult to know if planning leads to good performance or good performance leads to planning.** Perhaps faster growing and larger firms have more need to develop written plans to give to potential lenders and investors than weak firms do.

Other research has shown the distinctly positive effect planning can have on business performance. Two of the more interesting studies include one by Leslie W. Rue and Nabil A. Ibrahim, and another by Stephen C. Perry. Rue and Ibrahim, surveyed a broad sample of firms with at least 15 full-time employees and asked members of the top management team in each company about their planning processes and how well their firms performed relative to all firms in their industry. Rue and Ibrahim found that while 32% of firms with no written plans performed above average, 54% of firms with more extensive planning processes outperformed their industry averages.

Perry randomly surveyed firms with 500 or fewer employees in the Dun and Bradstreet database and compared them to a sample of firms that had recently filed for bankruptcy. When Perry matched the on-going companies to the failed companies by industry, size, and location, he found that:

- **Most firms, whether successful or not, engage in very little planning.** 63% reported that they engaged in no planning whatsoever.
- **Overall, about 16% of firms reported engaging in a great deal of planning.** Firms that had filed for bankruptcy engaged in planning only about one-third as often as the on-going businesses.

Frédéric Delmar and Scott Shane also tested the impact of planning on performance among 233 new ventures they studied for the 30 months after each firm's founding. Delmar and Shane concluded that businesses that engaged in more planning prior to beginning operations had a greater probability of success. This success resulted from faster decision-making when they were in operation, a better use of resources such as financing, and a greater focus on key activities that were central to success.

Research seems to be heading towards the conclusion that failing to plan is almost a prescription for planning to fail. The challenge for future research is to explore the relationship between planning and performance more fully so entrepreneurs can learn specifically which kinds of planning processes produce the best results for particular businesses.

MARY WILLIS PONDERS HER OPTIONS

For the last ten years, Mary Willis has been the President of Western Hardware Supply, a business that was founded in 1958 by Robert Connor and is now owned by his three children. Western is literally a nuts and bolts business—and a very profitable one. Western owns warehouses in Oregon, California, and Arizona from which it distributes hardware supplies to construction companies, manufacturers, and retail stores. In 2003, Western had $93 million in revenue and $11 million in profits. It has no debt and owns all its facilities and trucks.

For all of Western's success, Mary saw a problem on the horizon: the Internet. Western's customers ordered products by phone, but Mary felt that customers would increasingly want to order items, pay for them, and track deliveries via a Web site. Mary made this argument to the Connor family but they were reluctant to spend much to make this happen, but they did ask her to research the costs and make a specific proposal.

Mary met with companies and consultants who could help build this Web-based capability. She came to the conclusion that about $2 million would be needed for the design of the Web site, hiring staff, advertising the new service, and covering operating losses for 18 months until it would pay for itself. When she proposed this to the Connor family, she was told that she should start the Web site for $100,000 and they would re-evaluate its performance in a year. Mary knew this was a scenario for a disaster because this was just too little money to build a strong site and hire and train a capable team.

Mary reviewed her numbers and came to the conclusion that she would start her own Web-based hardware business for about $5 million, not counting the $200,000 salary she would have to give up. Under this plan, Mary's new company would outsource the warehousing and distribution to more traditional companies like Western and its competitors. This plan would allow her new company to target any market easily and would also give it a "first-mover" advantage in using Web-based technology to serve its market. Mary projected that in three years her new company would have $40 million in sales and $2.5 million in profits.

A banker she met with offered to lend her new company one third of what she raised from investors, which would be about $3.8 million. But he also said that Mary should expect that her investors—if she can find them—would insist on being the majority shareholders, leaving Mary only about 30% of the stock.

Mary has come into her office to ponder her options, study the plans and financial projections she has developed over the last four months, and make a decision.

Case Questions:

1. What are Mary's options?
2. What are the pluses and minuses of each option?
3. Which option do you think will be most profitable for Mary?
4. Which option is least risky and why?
5. Which option is most risky and why?
6. Which option will lead to a company that best matches Mary's requirements as the entrepreneur and operator of the company?
7. Which option should she choose?

End of Chapter Questions

1. Think about a business you might want to start. Review the first 10 of the 12 issues presented in this chapter and rank them in order of how much work remains to be done on each for your company.
2. Choose an existing business you know well and admire. Answer the question: How well did the entrepreneur plan for and manage each of the first 10 issues?
3. What are the biggest challenges in writing a business plan for a new company?
4. In what ways can writing a business plan improve the chance of business success?

NOTES

1. Edward G. Rogoff. *Bankable Business Plans, 2nd Edition,* (New York: Rowhouse, 2007), pp. xv–xvi.
2. Stillman Drake. *Galileo: His Scientific Biography,* (Mineola, NY: Dover Publications, 2003).
3. Sarah Bartlett, "Seat of the Pants: Everyone Says that Before You Launch a Company, You've Got to Write a Business Plan. So How Come So Many Inc 500 CEOs Kill That Sober Exercise?" *Inc.,* October 2002.
4. Leslie W. Rue and Nabil A. Ibrahim, "The Relationship between Planning Sophistication and Performance in Small Businesses," *Journal of Small Business Management,* Vol. 36, No. 4, October 1998, pp. 24–32.
5. Stephen C. Perry, "The Relationship between Written Business Plans and the Failure of Small Businesses in the U.S." *Journal of Small Business Management,* Vol. 39. No. 3, July 2001, pp. 201–208.

CHAPTER 1

ISSUE 1: GENERATE IDEAS AND DEFINE THE BUSINESS

What Were They Thinking? What Went Wrong with Razorfish

Perhaps no company earned more praise more quickly than Razorfish, a Web site design and Internet consulting business founded in 1995 by two childhood friends, Jeff Dachis and Craig Kanarick. In four years they built their business up to $12 million in revenue. While Razorfish had only small profits during those first four years, Dachis and Kanarick realized the huge growth that was awaiting firms which could provide Web services. Credit Suisse First Boston agreed and in 1999 lead a group of investment bankers in taking Razorfish public, raising more than $50 million. In the next two years, Razorfish compiled a list of accomplishments that would have made even Donald Trump blush.

Dachis and Kanarick raised millions more from both the stock market and from private investors, including a joint venture with one of the world's leading advertising agencies, Omnicom. Razorfish engineered 14 mergers and acquisitions of more than $2 billion with companies sporting cool, one-word monikers such as Spray, Avalanche, iCube, Fuel, and Plastic. Razorfish saw its stock soar from $16 per share to $57 per share, giving the company a total value of $5.6 billion. In 2000, Razorfish was #4 on Deloitte and Touche's list of the 500 fastest growing technology firms and Forbes ranked it as one of the 200 Best Small Companies for that year. Dachis and Kanarick built a high-profile board, including the head of the media, communication, and information technology for the prestigious consulting firm McKinsey & Company. They opened offices around the world, built the staff to nearly 2,000 and moved into a swanky new building in Venice, California. But these heady times for the childhood friends would soon turn into headaches.

In 1999, Razorfish had sales of $170 million and lost $14 million. In 2000, sales increased to $267 million while losses increased to $149 million. In 2001, sales fell to $103 million, and losses continued to increase to $184 million. Their problem: Dachis and Kanarick never developed an idea for a ***profitable*** business. They had never done analysis of financial feasibility or developed a business plan that showed Razorfish making money. Expensive acquisitions just pulled the company down because none of the catchy-named firms they acquired was profitable and Dachis and Kararick had no plan to encourage them to work together to create a successful consolidated company.

In 2002, Dachis and Kanarick were eased out the company they had founded. Razorfish stock went from the $57 per share high down to $1.65—and that was after a 30 to 1 reverse split, meaning that the shares had actually lost 99.9% of their value. Razorfish was sold to SBI, an Internet services company based in Salt Lake City, for about $20 million, which was the amount of cash that Razorfish had left.

Few companies spent so much money during the Internet bubble without a plan to create a profitable enterprise. Even if Razorfish's founders failed to create a bankable business plan for expanding their company, you might wonder why so many professional bankers and investors overlooked this critical missing element. Funders are only human and can have their heads turned by the promise of enormous business success in spite of their training to prefer careful planning and conservative projections. But investors in many high-growth industries also have very short investment horizons and often plan to sell their stock before the bubble bursts. In the face of gold-rush industries such as the Internet in the 1990s, projections were simply hard to make and optimism was hard to control.

How to Develop Ideas

Ideas for businesses evolve in a variety of ways. Many entrepreneurs develop their concepts by analyzing trends, the marketplace, or the current competition. Some take an existing idea and replicate it, or, better yet, improve upon it. Still others are inspired by a creative "brainstorm." Here are examples of how a few well-known entrepreneurs developed ideas for their ventures:

- **At school.** Fred Smith was a student at the Harvard Business School when he came up with an idea for an overnight delivery company. He wrote a business plan based on the concept for one of his courses and, although his professor gave him a C, the idea was a success. The company he founded was Federal Express.

- **At work.** Two young engineers at Hewlett-Packard approached their bosses about developing a personal computer the size of a typewriter. Their bosses didn't like the idea, so Steve Jobs and Steve Wozniak left and founded Apple Computer, Inc.

- **At the unemployment office.** After being fired from the building supply firm Handy Dan Company, Arthur Blank started his own business and called it Home Depot.

- **At home.** In 1937 Margaret Rudkin, a Connecticut homemaker, began baking bread without additives because her son was allergic to store-bought bread. People liked her bread so much she starting selling it and Pepperidge Farm was born.

- **At the gateway to a new country.** Many immigrants start their own businesses because they lack the language skills to work in large American organizations. Others believe that major companies won't give them the best opportunities. Among the most successful are Vinod Khosla from India who founded Sun Computers, Charles Wang from China who founded Computer Associates, and George Soros from Hungary who founded Soros Fund Management, one of the largest pools of capital in the world.

- **At the peak of career frustration.** During the 1950s, Mary Kay Ash was an extremely successful salesperson for several different companies, but she believed that she was never promoted to sales manager because she was a woman. She quit and founded Mary Kay cosmetics to empower women to sell products and build an organization of salespeople they recruit themselves.

- **At the peak of customer frustration.** Chester Carlson was a patent lawyer who was exasperated by the available methods of duplicating patent applications, contracts, and other legal documents. His options were to copy by hand, use carbon paper, or make mimeograph copies—all of which were slow, cumbersome, and messy. In 1938, Carlson wondered if he could adapt photograph technology to create a machine that would make copies. Nine years later his initial "copy machine" had been rejected by twenty companies, including Kodak, when the Haloid Corporation of Rochester, New York, bought Carlson's technology. After 13 additional years of research and development, the Carlson and Haloid company introduced the first commercial copier. Weighing in at 2,000 pounds, it was not just a huge machine, it was also a gigantic commercial success. Carlson and Haloid eventually changed their name to Xerox and fundamentally changed how offices operated.

As you can see from these examples and probably from people you know, many entrepreneurs use their knowledge, skills, experience, enthusiasm and frustration as starting points for their ventures. If you speak English, Japanese, and French, a translation business could be a natural extension of your knowledge. If you are an accomplished accountant, starting your own firm is a good option. The more you bring to your venture, the stronger your business will be. The more experience you have in an industry, the more contacts you will develop. The broader your skill set, the more you can save by not hiring outsiders. The more enthusiasm you have for the business, the more you will motivate others to work with you. The better your judgment, the more confidence funding sources will have in your company's chance of success.

So think about your experience, knowledge, skills, interests and frustrations, and ask yourself: What business would benefit the most from my talents? Table 1.1 lays out a systematic way to ask and answer these questions that will help you develop potential business concepts.

TABLE 1.1
PERSONAL INVENTORY AND RELATED BUSINESS

	Your Response	Businesses that Fit Well with this Strength
Your work experience		
Your greatest areas of knowledge		
Your skills		
Your interests		

Once you have an idea for a business, you need to expand on it and create further options. The next exercise, Table 1.2, will help. On the left-hand column is the question you need to answer. In the middle column is a rather offbeat example. Fill in your responses in the right-hand column.

TABLE 1.2
IDEAS AND OPTIONS GRID

Step Number	Question	Example	Your Response
1	What is your idea?	Open a caterpillar ranch.	
2	Describe the product or service you will sell.	Caterpillars.	
3	What ways could you change the product or service to: A. Give it more status. B. Make it less expensive. C. Expand the product line. D. Fill orders faster. E. Find a way for it to be patented or copyrighted. F. Create a strong name brand.	A. Have Queen Elizabeth appear in the commercials that run in the Super Bowl. If she won't do them, try Prince Charles. B. Outsource production to Asia. C. Add butterflies and moths to product line. D. Breed caterpillars faster. E. Create new varieties through genetic engineering and patent the process. F. Call it "Royal Caterpillar Company"	
4	A. Who is the prime market for your product or service? B. Can you modify the product or service to appeal to different groups by age, gender, ethnicity, or geography?	A. People who like to watch caterpillars crawl up their arms. B. Bigger caterpillars could appeal to older people because they wouldn't have to put on their glasses to watch the caterpillars crawl up their arms. Some people might prefer caterpillars that are trained to stay still because they could wear them like jewelry.	
5	A. How will you package or deliver the product or service? B. How could you change that to make it more appealing to the target markets?	A. Wrapped in a paper napkin. B. Crystal jewel boxes.	
6	A. What do similar products or services do differently than you are proposing? B. Would it make sense to adopt any of their approaches?	A. Ants are delivered in plastic farms. B. No, because caterpillar farms would be too large to ship.	

Develop as many individual ideas as possible and keep one on a separate piece of paper. Then expand every idea into as many variations as possible. As you read this chapter and the next chapter that deals with feasibility, place your ideas into three distinct stacks:

1. Clearly not feasible.
2. Feasible, but not that interesting or exciting to you.
3. Feasible *and* exciting to you. This is the stack of ideas that merit the most attention.

How to Search for Ideas

Not all ideas spring from the entrepreneur's mind. Many business concepts are found through searching, a process that takes place in many ways, such as speaking with friends, reading business publications, or networking. Professor James Fiet of the University of Louisville has analyzed this search process and has developed guidelines for productive systematic searches that will cost the least and take the shortest amount of time. Among his guidelines are:

- Plan your search. Don't just rely on random discoveries.
- Focus the search among sources that you know well, such as family, friends, colleagues, and the networks to which you and they belong. Other good sources are trade shows, government data, such as patent information. and agency reports.
- Put in the effort to find information about your competitors and your industry that is not publicly available. It may come from people who work in the industry, vendors to the industry, or professionals, such as lawyers and accountants, with experience in your industry. Obtaining this information takes more time, but is worth it.
- Value specific information more highly than general information because it is more likely to come from people who are very knowledgeable and may lead to an idea that you can act upon.
- Estimate the likelihood of success for various search activities and focus first on the ones you believe will be the most productive.

Expanding Your Ideas and Options

If you are like many entrepreneurs, you may already have a number of ideas that interest you. Write them down, but don't reject or make judgments about them. Think about ways you could modify or improve them and write these suggestions down, too. But be patient because this process of *creative thinking* takes time—often weeks or longer.

As you begin the process of developing ideas, ask yourself the following questions:

- Where are there underserved markets—especially *growing* underserved markets?
- What businesses, products, or services am I most interested in?
- What businesses, products, or services am I most knowledgeable about?
- What products or services have frustrated me as a customer and have inspired me to find ways to improve upon them?

And as you think about the answers, do the following:

- Keep a pad and pencil, PDA, voice recorder, or phone with a record feature handy so you can jot down thoughts that come to you while you're doing everyday chores such as waiting in the grocery line, taking a walk, or watching a movie. To make sure they don't forget ideas, some people send even themselves e-mails or voicemail messages to keep a record.
- Vary your environment by going for a walk, to a museum, or to the gym. This is a method that's been proven to stimulate new ideas.

Creative thinking cannot be accelerated by working at it more intensively. It is a process that flourishes when it is given time. Research indicates that this may happen because most creative thinking is accomplished by the right side of the brain, which works more intuitively and less analytically than the left side. Even dreams can provide creative ideas and solutions to everyday problems. So sleeping on a problem and trying to remember your dreams may actually help the process of creative thinking.

Focus on Research: Following Your Passion Will Probably Lead to the Most Successful Business

Although your needs are not important to potential investors, lenders, and partners, your love for the work you want to do and your ability to attract others who have a similar sense of devotion is important to your venture's success. Professor Teresa M. Amabile of Harvard University has studied creativity and has come to the conclusion that people are most creative when they love what they do. ***Intrinsic motivation*** is love of work, in contrast to ***extrinsic motivation,*** which includes financial rewards, competition, and directives from an employer. Laboratory studies have provided strong evidence of the greater power of intrinsic motivation. For example, students who expressed more interest in the creative activity of making collages did better than those who expressed less interest, or those who performed the task for financial rewards only.

Amabile has concluded through her research that three components are essential to individual creativity:

1. **Expertise.** Knowledge, experience, or technical skills are the foundation from which one searches for answers. People with greater expertise simply have more options to explore and an enhanced ability to sort the feasible ideas from the impossible ones.

2. **Creative Thinking.** Some people, because of their personalities, backgrounds, or experience, have a greater ability to engage in creative thinking. Research shows that characteristics such as independence, self-discipline, perseverance, and the ability to tolerate ambiguity correlate with engagement in creative thinking.

3. **Intrinsic Motivation.** Amabile describes people with high intrinsic motivation as "driven by deep interest and involvement in the work, by curiosity, enjoyment, or a personal sense of challenge."

Amabile has found that a strong focus on and support for creativity is essential for organizations that need to be innovative in order to survive. This implies that entrepreneurs should concentrate their efforts in areas of their own expertise and interest. As managers of ventures that need to foster creativity in order to maintain their competitive edge and cope with rapidly changing environments, entrepreneurs must establish a culture and management style that supports creative thinking in others.

Refining the Idea

Once you have a general idea of what your business should be—such as a seafood restaurant, a consulting firm, a men's clothing store, or a medical practice—you still have much work to do to before defining precisely what your business will be. Although later chapters will help you design your business in greater detail, this is a good time to think in preliminary terms about what market your business will serve, how it will be different from its competitors, and whether or not something similar has been tried before—and what the results were.

This is also a good time to involve friends, family, and experts in reading your plan to give you honest feedback. Their comments, criticism, and ideas will allow you to make the plan more convincing to its most important readers—investors and lenders.

Exercise: Creating and Refining Your Idea

Write a one-page (or shorter) description of your business idea. Give it to friends, family, and experts who will provide you with honest reactions. Before you call them for their responses, take some walks, go to the gym, and listen to music. These are all proven techniques to help you develop new thoughts about your idea. Then modify your one-page description to reflect any of their suggestions you wish to adopt as well as your own new thoughts. You now have a description of a business idea that you can test for feasibility.

Expanding the Idea

Michael Mikalko, a business author and consultant, created a technique he calls SCAMPER, an acronym for the questions to ask when looking for new ideas.[16] SCAMPER stands for:

Substitute. Can you substitute resources, processes, or people?

Combine. Can you combine the business or parts of it with other businesses?

Adapt. Can you adapt any business functions or capabilities to other functions or to serve other markets?

Modify. Can you modify product attributes such as size, color, packaging, or price to make the product more attractive?

Put. Can you put the business or its product to another use?

Eliminate. Can you eliminate some elements of the business or its products without reducing any advantages?

Reverse. Can you reverse goals or procedures to create improvements?

For the manufacturer of expensive stereo speakers, the SCAMPER analysis might look like this:

Substitute. Use plastic rather than wood or chip components rather than circuit boards.

Combine. Bundle the speakers with stereo components and sell them together.

Adapt. Create a model for outdoor use.

Modify. Change the shape or size of the speakers.

Put. Sell technical services, such as product testing, to audio equipment manufacturers.

Eliminate. Reduce the product line to best-selling speakers.

Reverse. Buy speakers from other manufacturers and only do marketing and distribution.

The goal of this process is to identify a few good ideas among the many that result from this technique, so don't eliminate any possibilities until the SCAMPER analysis is complete and you are ready to evaluate all the options.

A comprehensive list of techniques that inspire creativity can be found at
`www.mycoted.com/creativity/techniques/index.php.`

The Entrepreneur's Toolkit: Group Brainstorming Tools and Exercises

Brainstorming is a tool that can maximize creative thinking by solving a design problem, naming a product, or developing a business idea. The process works like this:

1. Select a group of people of different types, experiences, and knowledge.
2. Bring them together in a relaxed setting where you will not be interrupted.
3. Engage in some fun exercises such as coming up with ideas to improve a business everyone knows. This will get their creative juices flowing.
4. Establish the rule that no one can express negative judgments about any one else's idea.
5. Give the group a question such as: "I want to start a seafood restaurant in town. What qualities would make it successful?"
6. Designate someone who can write quickly to list on easel pads all the ideas so everyone can refer back to them.
7. Have people work individually several times during the brainstorming session to write down their ideas and report them back to the group.
8. After the brainstorming session, go through the list and select the best and most realistic ideas.

Brainstorming can be used to develop an idea from scratch, to refine an idea, or generate a strategy to vie with a competitor.

A variation of brainstorming is "rolestorming" in which each member of the group is assigned an identity and asked to come up with ideas from that person's point of view. For example, the roles of customers, suppliers, or competitors could be used, or fictional characters, such as the superheros Batman, Wonder Woman, and Superman.

Ideas Are Just the Starting Point

There are two sayings: "Implementation accounts for 90% of success" and "The devil is in the details." The first means that your business will succeed or fail based upon how well you manage it, and the second implies that small issues can cause big problems. A great concept is just a starting point. Before opening a diner, an entrepreneur must make decisions about location, name, decor, menu, and prices. Then the right people must be hired, a marketing campaign undertaken, and financial systems instituted. Once the diner opens, the entrepreneur must manage the staff, make sure that customers have a good dining experience, and order food in adequate, but not wasteful, amounts.

In the following chapters you will develop ideas and then identify the best ones before you create a detailed and bankable plan that will become your roadmap to implementation—and success.

IS THERE A FEASIBLE WAY TO START A HEALTHY FOOD RESTAURANT?

Barbara and Noah Williams are devoted to their healthy lifestyle and they enjoy promoting it to others, Barbara as a nutritionist and Noah as a personal trainer. They are constantly amazed by the lack of modestly priced restaurants that serve healthy food and dream about opening one. They began to cook up various scenarios for their business, talk to industry experts, and fantasize about diners testing their recipes.

Initially, Barbara and Noah planned a fast-food restaurant that could expand to hundreds of locations through franchising. They eventually rejected this idea because they learned of the large investment required and the difficulty of franchising a business that hasn't yet opened one single location. So they planned an upscale take-out store focusing on organic, vegetarian, and low-calorie foods, which they felt could do well in a busy downtown location in their large mid-western city. Then they thought about opening an upscale, elegant restaurant.

Although Barbara knows about food values and individual meal preparation, neither she nor Noah has any food industry experience. After talking to a friend who is a banker, they became quite discouraged over their inability to borrow money until their business had a proven record of profitability over several years. They met with a restaurant consultant who agreed to one meeting without charging them. She told them that the food is just part of creating a successful restaurant. Location, pricing, atmosphere, and service were equally big factors.

Unwilling to abandon their concept, the couple decided to re-design their business from the beginning. They would carefully define the customers they would serve and develop a concept to meet their needs. They would use the consultant's formula in which food represents about 25% of the cost of running the average restaurant. This means that once they design the menu and price the food, the restaurant will have to charge four times that amount in order to be profitable.

Without the hope of bank financing, Barbara and Noah resolved to lower their costs as much as possible, but they needed strategies to accomplish that. Their conversations with the banker and restaurant consultant had introduced a strong element of reality into their thinking, so they decided to use a small home equity loan to finance the business, which they hoped to keep as low as possible. Once this strategy was in place they could create a food business that met their healthful standards and could become profitable quickly with as little investment as possible.

Once they were finished with this process, they had a concept that was feasible both as a business and for them as entrepreneurs.

Case Questions:

1. What are Barbara and Noah's strengths and weaknesses as entrepreneurs who want to open a restaurant that offers healthy food?
2. What are their options for the types of healthy food restaurants they could open?
3. Rank these options based on how risky each is, how much start-up capital they will need, and how difficult the restaurants will be to operate.
4. What recommendations would you make to Barbara and Noah?

End of Chapter Questions

1. Choose any three well-known businesses. Research how each business started, including who the founding entrepreneur was, what his or her motivation was for starting the business, and what he or she felt was the original concept for the business.

2. Choose an existing business and develop ways that the company and its products can be expanded or changed using the SCAMPER technique.

3. Once you have completed the SCAMPER technique, put together a group of three or four people and goes through the SCAMPER technique again using group brainstorming.

NOTES

1. "Hot Stock: An Equity Profile," *National Editions: Financial Post Investing*; May 11, 1999, p. D3.
2. "Razorfish Named Fourth Fastest Growing Technology Company in North America by Deloitte & Touche," *Business Wire*, November 16, 2000.
3. "200 Best Small Companies," *Forbes*, October 2000.
4. Razorfish, SEC Filings, 1999–2002.
5. David Shabelman, "SBI nets Razorfish for $8M," *The Daily Deal*, November 23, 2002.
6. Katie Hafner, "Fred Smith: The Entrepreneur," *Inc.*, July 1984, p. 38.
7. Owen W. Linzmeyer. *Apple Confidential: The Real Story of Apple Computer*, (San Francisco: No Starch,1999).
8. Bernie Marcus and Arthur Blank with Bob Andelman. *Built from Scratch : How a Couple of Regular Guys Grew the Home Depot from Nothing to $30 Billion*, (New York: Times Business, 1999).
9. "Pepperidge Farm Celebrates 50th Anniversary," PR Newswire, September 17, 1987.
10. Ronnette King, "Mary-Kay, Cosmetics Icon Mary Kay Ash Dies," *The Dallas Morning News*, November 23, 2001.
11. Nanette Byrnes, "A Dogged Image Maker," *Business Week*, June 7, 2004, p. 18.
12. James O. Fiet. *The Systematic Search for Entrepreneurial Discoveries*, (Westport, CT: Quorum Books, 2002).
13. Bruce Bower, "Whole-Brain Interpreter," *Science News*, February, 24, 1996, Vol 149, Issue 8.
14. Teresa M. Amabile, "Motivating Creativity in Organizations: On Doing What You Love and Loving What You Do," *California Management Review*, Vol. 40, No.1, Fall 1997, pp. 39–58.
15. Teresa M. Amabile, B.A. Hennessey, and B.S. Grossman, "Social Influences on Creativity: The Effects of Contracted-For Reward," *Journal of Personality and Social Psychology*, Vol. 50 (1986) 14–23.
16. Michael Mikalko. *Tinkertoys*, (Berkeley: Ten Speed Press, 1991).

    Michael Mikalko. *Cracking Creativity*, (Berkeley: Ten Speed Press, 2001).
17. Alex F. Osborn. *Applied Imagination*, 3rd Edition, (New York: Scribner's, 1963)
18. Vincent R. Brown and Paul B. Paulus, "Making Group Brainstorming More Effective: Recommendations from an Associative Memory Perspective," *Current Directions in Psychological Science*, Vol. 11, Issue 6, (December 2002), pp. 208–212.

CHAPTER 2

ISSUE 2: ESTABLISH FINANCIAL AND PERSONAL FEASIBILITY

What Were They Thinking? Iridium Falls to Earth

In the 1980s Motorola designed a satellite system to provide phone service anywhere, all the time. The new phone company, dubbed Iridium, raised $5 billion: $1 billion from Motorola, $1.1 billion from banks, $800 million from the sale of bonds, and the rest from public and private sales of stock. To break even, Iridium estimated it needed more than 300,000 subscribers who would pay $3,000 to purchase the phone and $7 per minute to use it. To fill the first wave of expected orders, Iridium manufactured 200,000 phones. In 1997, Iridium launched its service by sending 66 satellites into orbit around the globe. Two years later, with losses equaling its start-up costs of $5 billion, Iridium filed for bankruptcy.

Some attributed this massive failure to the change in both technology and the market between Iridium's inception and implementation. It's true that by the mid-1990s, terrestrial-based cellular phone service was well established with smaller phones at lower prices, but Motorola had been a leader in building cheaper, smaller, more feature-laden cellular phones, so the fault didn't lie there.

When Iridium went into default on its loans, it was still far from its break-even point of 300,000 subscribers: It had 6,009. A feasibility analysis would have shown that Iridium had only a few competitive advantages from the start and that those were shrinking fast. It would have also revealed that the Iridium concept had even far more competitive *dis*advantages. The Iridium phones were about the size of a brick, weighed about as much, and needed to be outside for their antennas to work. They were not the kind of phones reporters in war zones were likely to use, let alone businesspeople with important calls to make.

Iridium failed because it tried to build a business without establishing that it could achieve profitability.

When you have idea that you wish to pursue, the next step is to test if the venture is feasible. Assessing feasibility enables you to reject ideas that have little or no hope of being developed or of being profitable, so you can focus on creating a business with the greatest chance of success. A feasibility analysis is not a full business plan with detailed financial projections, specific marketing plans, decisions on legal and organizational issues, and research on the market and the competition. When you have concluded that your idea is, in fact, feasible, then Chapters 3-12 will take you through the process of creating that detailed plan.

There are three possible answers to the question "Is this business feasible?":

1. Yes, it is feasible and I should proceed with a full business plan.
2. No, it is not feasible and I should reject this idea and work on another business idea.
3. I don't know, and I have to continue to work on the plan until enough evidence is developed that it is or isn't feasible.

The purpose of this chapter is to make sure you clear the hurdles to prove the feasibility of your business. Surmounting each hurdle requires successfully answering three fundamental questions:

- **Feasibility Hurdle #1: Is this business right for me?** Answering this question assesses if you have the right skills, knowledge, and abilities to establish this business. The question also asks if this business meets your own personal and financial needs.
- **Feasibility Hurdle #2: Can I obtain the resources required to start this business?** A time-travel vacation business that could send people to any location at any time in history would be a sure success. But can you obtain the time-travel technology to make this business a reality?
- **Feasibility Hurdle #3: Can this idea become a profitable business?** To be successful for the long term, a business must make profits. A vacation resort on Mars or bicycles with jet engines could not be profitable because the prices would have to be so high that virtually no one could afford them.

Personal and financial feasibility are often closely linked because, along with time and expertise, the entrepreneur's contributions to the business often include personally providing financing or having the ability to obtain financing from others.

Feasibility Hurdle #1: Making the Required Personal Contributions

There are several key questions that must be answered positively to establish the personal feasibility of the business:

- Do you have the financial resources required and are you willing to commit them to this venture?
- Are you ready to pledge collateral, such as a home, that lenders may require to make a loan?
- Are you willing to commit the necessary time?
- Do you have the skills and knowledge for this venture?
- Is your family willing to make sacrifices, such as sharing in the financial risks of the venture and coping with the amount of time you must spend on the business?

- Are you willing to step off your current career track to become an entrepreneur?

While these questions may seem to require simple "yes" or "no" answers, this is not actually the case. To answer most of these questions you must devote time to serious thought, discussions with family and friends, and looking at issues pessimistically.

What Do You Want from Your Venture?

The goals that are driving you to establish your new venture will be as individualized as you are. The two most basic issues in exploring your goals are 1) what you want the business to provide you, and 2) how you will prioritize your goals. Here are some of the goals that people often set when starting their own businesses:

- **Financial goals** such as making money, earning a profit when the business is sold, or garnering benefits such as insurance or tax-deferred pension plans.
- **Family goals** such as owning a business that offers a way to employ relatives or enable them to work together.
- **Lifestyle issues** such as owning a business that requires a limited time commitment or offers personal flexibility, or a desire to bring the kids to work, have long vacations, or work in a field with a strong social or personal agenda such as fitness, health, or education.
- **Professional growth** such as the opportunity for career development or to face new challenges.
- **Social goals** such as carrying out research to cure a disease or providing a service to an underserved group.

Below are two worksheets, Tables 2.1 and 2.2, to help you establish your goals for your new venture. The first asks you to fill in several goals in each category; the second asks you to select and rank the top five. Many entrepreneurs would like to achieve every goal they set, but most goals must be balanced against each other. Uncovering which goals are the most important is essential.

TABLE 2.1
WORKSHEET FOR LISTING YOUR GOALS

Type of Goal	Your Specific Goal
Financial (such as earning current income or building an asset for future sale):	
Family (such as creating opportunities for family members):	
Lifestyle (such as being able to work part-time or working in a specific industry):	
Personal (such as bringing an idea to reality or working in a particular industry):	

TABLE 2.2
WORKSHEET FOR RANKING YOUR TOP FIVE GOALS

Rank	Goal
1.	
2.	
3.	
4.	
5.	

Is There an Entrepreneurial Personality?

Many people believe that there is an entrepreneurial personality characterized by an appetite for risk-taking, a drive to innovate, a desire to be rich, and the willingness to be tested by challenges and struggles. Certainly there are people like this. Entrepreneurs such as Ted Turner and Richard Branson exemplify these characteristics in both their business and personal lives.

- Ted Turner proved he was an innovator by being the first to put a local television station, WTBS in Atlanta, up on satellite so that cable television systems around the country could carry it. He also took a great risk in starting CNN, the first all-news television network and later in purchasing the film library of MGM, which became the programming core on the cable channel Turner Classic Movies. On a personal level, Turner was a champion sailor, competing in and winning the America's Cup.
- Richard Branson challenged a variety of large enterprises, such as British Air, when he founded Virgin Airlines, the major music companies with his Virgin label, the global soda manufacturers with his own cola, and the established cellular telephone giants with his own brand. He has also been a world-class balloonist, several times attempting, albeit unsuccessfully, the risky task of flying a helium balloon around the world.

But this does not mean that one cannot be a successful entrepreneur without these characteristics. In fact, experience and research, much of it done by Professor Robert Brockhaus of St. Louis University, demonstrate that people of any personality can be successful entrepreneurs.

The real question for an entrepreneur is not "Do I fit the profile of an entrepreneur?" but *"How can I create the right match between myself and a venture?"* For example, suppose you are introverted and very reluctant to approach new people to sell your company's services. You can compensate for this by hiring a sales team with those abilities. Your bankable business plan must show how all the necessary skills and talents are present either in you alone or in your team as a whole.

The process of performing this analysis is achieved in four steps:

1. Define the skills, ability, and personality characteristics that are required to make the business a success.
2. Measure yourself to see if you are qualified.

3. Define the gaps between what you have and what you need.
4. If necessary, refine your management team to ensure that they will have all the skills, abilities, and personality characteristics to succeed.

Table 2.3 below shows what such an analysis looks like for Bob Bartok who is planning to start a piano moving company in Lompoc. Bob worked for a piano moving business for ten years in Portland before relocating to Lompoc. In Portland, he started as a helper, became a job foreman, and later worked as a supervisor in the business office.

TABLE 2.3
MATCHING THE VENTURE'S NEEDS, THE ENTREPRENEUR, AND THE ENTREPRENEUR'S TEAM: THE LOMPOC PIANO MOVING COMPANY

What's Needed	Does Bob Have It?	If Not, Where Will He Obtain It?
Industry Knowledge	Yes	Ten years experience in this industry has taught Bob a great deal.
Product Technical Knowledge	Yes	Bob knows a lot about pianos.
Industry Professional Network	No	He is new to Lompoc and needs to hire someone who knows musicians, schools, and performance halls in Lompoc.
Financial Skills	No	Bob is comfortable with computer systems for accounting, but not with producing statements and tax returns. He plans to hire the firm of Block and Knox in Lompoc that specializes in small businesses to do these.
Selling Skills	Not Sure	Bob did a great deal of customer service in Portland and thinks he probably can sell, but he wants to make sure the local person he hires has these skills.
Management Skills	Yes	Bob believes he is a good manager.
Social and People Skills	Yes	Bob wants every office employee and team supervisor to have these.
Negotiating Skills	Yes	Bob did a lot of negotiating in Portland.
Language Skills	No	Lompoc has a large group of Hungarian speaking musicians. He wants the office assistant he hires to be fluent in Hungarian.
Professional Licenses	No	Bob doesn't have a moving license yet, but it is not difficult to obtain and he has already applied for it.
Decision Making Skills	Yes	Bob feels comfortable making decisions but he plans on creating an advisory board to give him frank feedback.

Measuring Personality Characteristics

Since entrepreneurs come in all types and backgrounds, there is no test that will tell you if you have what it takes to be an entrepreneur. However, certain standardized tests have proven to be valid and reliable measures of personality characteristics. The most common ones are the Myers-Briggs Type Indicator ® *(MBTI®)* and the Strong Interest Inventory. These tests are very useful to entrepreneurs who want to understand themselves and develop strategies for successful and satisfying careers. Since these tests usually require the interpretation of a trained professional such as a psychologist or career counselor, they can be expensive. However, many career centers, human resource departments, and counseling centers offer them to students and employees at no cost.

The Myers-Briggs Type Indicator ® (MBTI®) measures personality on four scales:

1. Extroversion-Introversion measures whether people have a focus on others or on themselves.

2. Sensing-Intuition measures how people take in information. "Sensing people" focus more on facts and "intuitive people" focus more on patterns.

3. Thinking-Feeling describes the decision-making processes that are focused either on analysis or on the impact they have on others.

4. Judging-Perceiving determines whether people are orderly and rigid in dealing with their environment or are more flexible and spontaneous.

Based on these four scales, the MBTI® can predict your likely strengths and weaknesses as an entrepreneur. This information can help you focus on your strengths, work on your weaknesses, and add needed members to your team.

The Strong Interest Inventory has six scales that reflect various themes in your work interests:

1. Conventional, with an interest in analysis, executing defined processes (such as accounting), and preferring to work in formally structured organizations.
2. Enterprising, with an interest in managing and selling.
3. Artistic, with a preference for creative activities.
4. Social, with an interest in helping or teaching others.

5 Realistic, with an interest in fact-based analysis and execution, such as construction.

6. Investigative, with an interest in doing research and analyzing the results.

Again, these measures can be compared to averages, but more importantly, they allow you to see how your abilities match the needs of your venture, to define a company culture that is a good match with your personality, and to select partners and employees who best match your style.

There is a test available through Consulting Psychologists Press that combines the MBTI® and the Strong Interest Inventory with a special focus on entrepreneurs. While it cannot tell if you are qualified to be an entrepreneur, it can identify your strengths, weaknesses, and style and show you comparisons to data about existing entrepreneurs.

The Home-Based Business Option

What do Amazon.com, Microsoft, Hewlett-Packard, Pepperidge Farm, Lillian Vernon, and Playboy all have in common? They were all started as home-based businesses. In fact, of the approximately 10 million businesses in the U.S. about half are home-based. Some will grow beyond the home while others will happily remain at home. All home-based businesses require a significant personal commitment by the entrepreneur and his family.

The most common home-based businesses include individuals working as contractors, lawyers, and accountants, as well as jobs in sales, real estate, daycare, insurance, and farming. If you are considering a home-based business, there are many advantages which should be stressed in your business plan, including:

- Having low overhead costs that make the business more competitive.
- Being able to draw on the help of family members as needed.
- Saving time by not having to commute.

Potential disadvantages should also be addressed to reassure investors that you are aware of them and have strategies to minimize any problems they might cause:

- Having many distractions that could interfere with work.
- Not having space to hold business meetings.
- Needing to be a "self-starter" to deal with lack of office structure.

- Appearing small and less established to customers, suppliers, and partners.

There are a variety of strategies to deal with home-based business disadvantages. You can obtain access to conference space for meetings by reserving rooms at local hotels or convention centers. Creating a dynamic Web site can make your business look as big as any competitor. Communication technology such as voicemail, pagers, call forwarding, and email can provide excellent service and make you appear as professional as even the largest competitor. Quality printed materials such as business cards, stationery, and brochures will make your business appear professional. Finally, establishing a separate, quiet, private work space that minimizes interruptions will be a must for a serious home-based entrepreneur.

Feasibility Hurdle #2: Obtaining the Required Resources

In this section you will establish the availability of the resources you will need to start your business venture. Completing this step diligently is important because it will help you quantify exactly what you need. When you have researched and enumerated the resources your business will require, you will have established the groundwork for defining the financial feasibility of your business.

In the introduction to this book you were asked to state the concept of your business and to define it in terms of what it will accomplish for others, including investors, lenders, customers, employees, and suppliers. Now it is time to focus on satisfying the needs of your investors and lenders by estimating the financial requirements for starting the business and how much of that amount you are likely to obtain.

Initial costs vary drastically with the exact nature of your business. Establishing a metal fabricating company that uses multimillion dollar metal-shaping machines, a fleet of trucks, and a 200,000 square foot building will require lots of research into various options and details. To establish a home-based computer consulting business you may only need a computer, an Internet connection, a phone, and some office supplies to get started.

Key Expense Categories to Research

You must calculate two types of costs: The funds needed to start your business—called *start-up capital requirements*—and the cost of running your business—called *operating expenses*. Start-up capital costs include items items with a long lifespan, such as restaurant equipment, and filing cabinets, as well as expenditures you need to make prior to initiating operations, such as raw materials for manufacturing.

There is no better way to develop expense estimates than to actually go shopping for what you need. In many industries there is often a big gap between asking price and final price. In other industries, obtaining actual costs for items, such as raw materials, data, or skilled workers, may be much more difficult than you expected. Because this step is meant to establish feasibility and not include all the detail that will go into your business plan, you can think of these as "back of the envelope" calculations—reasonable and conservative, but still rough estimates. So you do not need to research every cost completely at this time, but you should look carefully at the following three categories, which are typically the largest: real estate, employees, and advertising and promotion. Estimates of these three categories will be used to calculate the basic amount of financing you will need for both the capital requirement to start your business and the annual operating expenses.

Real Estate Costs

Real estate costs can be either a capital requirement if you plan to purchase a location or an operating cost if you plan to rent space. You may not be able to make that decision until you can compare the two options, especially since there is often a large gap between bid and asking price in real estate. Start with newspaper ads, but don't stop there. Call agents and arrange to see available spaces. Discuss what a final price is likely to be and research actual recent sales of comparable properties in similar locations. After you have seen a number of properties and talked with several agents, you will understand pricing and the tradeoffs on location and amenities. This can be a time-consuming and tedious process, but it will pay off when you actually sign a lease or buy a property.

Employee Costs: Salaries and Benefits

The costs related to hiring employees are generally categorized as operating expenses, but some costs—such as moving people to your location or offering bonuses—may represent capital costs. Your ability to find and retain quality employees can be one of the major determinants of your ability to deliver a quality product or service to your customers. Because salary costs are a major expense for most businesses, this is another estimate you cannot trust to "winging it." To obtain accurate salary estimates, you need to talk with employment agencies, employees who do similar jobs at other companies, and managers of companies who handle hiring. You can also check the Occupational Outlook Handbook from the Department of

Labor (at www.bls.gov/oco/home.htm) for salary information on different types of jobs. These steps will help you develop bankable knowledge of likely employment costs and the availability of qualified workers.

Attracting good employees is one issue; keeping them is another. Establishing attractive employee benefits includes providing government programs such as Social Security and Workman's Compensation, as well private health insurance, pension plans, stock options, and life insurance. Some of these are mandatory by law, and all are typically categorized as operating expenses.

Employee benefits are a very technical, complex, and highly regulated area, which may make it difficult for you to estimate these costs. Employee benefits include private health insurance, pension plans, stock-option plans, life insurance, and government programs such as Social Security and Worker's Compensation. The best solution to the problem of estimating these might be to obtain the services of a benefits consultant, a financial planner, or an accountant, but you can also visit the Web sites of the Social Security Administration, the IRS, and the Small Business Administration for some guidance.

You need to decide what benefits you'll offer and how the costs will be divided between the company and the employees. If you're hiring people such as fast-food workers, who view their jobs as temporary before they move on to better positions, then it's best to provide minimal benefits and make their current pay as high as possible. If you're hiring people who see their jobs as long-term career moves, then you should offer long-term benefits, such as pension plans and stock options. Analyzing this expense will enable you to compile a description of the benefits you expect to offer and a cost per employee expressed as a percentage of each salary, a fixed amount per employee, or a combination of the two.

Advertising and Promotion

For many new and established businesses, especially retail enterprises, advertising to attract new customers is an important part of the initial plan. At this stage of your research you must think about advertising and promotion both as a capital cost (because you might schedule some advertising before you open) and as an ongoing operating expense. You will read about detailed marketing campaigns in Chapter 5, but at this point you need to consider two major issues: First, how will you find your customers, and second, how often your message must reach them.

To answer the first question, find out if there are particular magazines or newspapers that your targeted audiences read, and which radio stations they are likely to listen to. If you don't already have a list of potential customers, can you purchase one? From the answers to these questions, you can create a simple budget for reaching your market. As for how often your message must reach your customers, you need to remember that repetition is the essence of advertising. You will need to purchase multiple ads, send multiple mailings, and make multiple sales calls before your message is heard by a large share of your target audience. When researching these initial costs, be certain to budget enough funds to achieve this critically important repetition.

Creating Estimates for the Financial Resources Required to Start and Operate Your Business

Once you have completed researching the real estate, advertising, and employee costs along with other expenses specific to your business, you can create one estimate of the financial resources required to start your business and another for the annual expenses needed to operate your business.

The estimate for start-up costs should include all the costs you have identified plus a generous margin for error: 25% and above is often standard. The estimate for yearly operating costs should also include a generous margin for error and an estimate for how long it will take you to break even and then become profitable, since any losses must be covered by money that you provide yourself or raise from others. Most businesses do not break even until at least two years of operation, even though revenues continue to grow.

The total amount of financing your business will require is the sum of the start-up costs plus any losses the business will incur until it becomes profitable. The following worksheet (Table 2.4) provides a way to organize these estimates.

TABLE 2.4
WORKSHEET FOR ESTIMATING MAJOR START-UP FINANCING REQUIREMENTS

Start-Up Cost Category	Cost
Up-Front Expenses:	
Real Estate (deposits, down payments, legal costs, renovations)	
Employee Costs (salary prior to opening, training costs, relocation costs)	
Advertising and Promotion prior to opening	
Others	
TOTAL UP-FRONT EXPENSES (1)	
Yearly Operating Expenses:	
Real Estate (maintenance, taxes, rent, mortgage)	
Employee Costs (salary, benefits, taxes)	
Advertising and Promotion	
Other Costs Specific to Your Business such as shipping, raw materials, fees, utilities, supplies, or royalties)	
TOTAL ESTIMATED ANNUAL OPERATING EXPENSES	
Time until business breaks even in percent of year	
TOTAL ESTIMATED OPERATING EXPENSES UNTIL BREAK-EVEN (2)	
TOTAL CAPITAL REQUIREMENTS: UP-FRONT EXPENSES PLUS OPERATING EXPENSES UNTIL BREAK-EVEN (1 + 2)	

ESTABLISH THAT THE START-UP FINANCING IS OBTAINABLE

Each funding source has its own needs. Banks must be paid interest. Investors want ownership shares in your company. Suppliers want to know that you will be a good long-term customer for them. Family and friends may consider loans or investment rather like gifts to you—or maybe not. Now you need to look at Table 2.5 for each of the following possible sources of start-up financing and fill in the amounts you *conservatively* expect to obtain from each.

TABLE 2.5
FUNDING SOURCES WORKSHEET

Funding Source	Amount
You	
Family Members	
Friends	
Investors	
Bank Loans	
Suppliers (in the form of credit extended to your business)	
Customers (in the form of prepaying orders)	
TOTAL POTENTIAL FUNDING (1)	
TOTAL START-UP FINANCING REQUIRED (2) FROM TABLE 2.4	
DIFFERENCE BETWEEN REQUIRED AND POTENTIAL FUNDING (1 - 2)	

If the total estimate from your potential funding sources equals or exceeds the start-up financing requirements, you have cleared the second feasibility hurdle. If it falls short, you have to revisit the business concept or change some of the ways you anticipate starting and operating your business.

Feasibility Hurdle #3: Demonstrating that Your Business Can Be Profitable

Once you've determined your start-up costs and your likely sources of available capital, you will need to establish how your business will make money for you, your investors, and lenders. To do this, you will have to estimate revenue, which is influenced by factors such as the economy, your competitors' response to your concept, and the effectiveness of your marketing and sales efforts. Here are some suggestions:

- **Anchor revenue projections to reality.** Methods for doing this include supplying lists of potential customers, by pretesting your products or services through surveys or focus groups, by comparing your product's features and price to the existing competition, and by comparing your revenue projections to industry averages or to specific businesses that you have researched.

- **Be conservative in the extreme.** After you have created projections that you are certain approximate reality, cut them mercilessly. Here's a rule of thumb: When revenue projections seem ludicrously low to the entrepreneur, they are usually approaching reality!

- **Costs are easier to estimate if you detail them.** This requires a tremendous amount of work. Putting in the effort early in the process will save you huge amounts of time later on.

Remember that because companies differ greatly you may need to change some of the categories to make them reflect your venture more accurately.

You can create revenue estimates three different ways:

- By estimating the number of customers and how much you expect them to spend.

- By "benchmarking" your estimates against average revenue for similar companies.

- By multiplying the expected price per unit times the number of units you expect to sell.

Create estimates using all three and compare them. If there is a huge difference among them, try to figure out why; then revise your estimates. If the revenue estimates are "in the same ballpark," then pick the lowest one to use in the profitability test.

Compare the revenue estimate with the yearly operating expense estimate you made earlier. If the business becomes profitable shortly after starting, you have passed this hurdle. As a rule of thumb, it is nearly impossible for companies to have significant annual losses for longer than three years and still survive. If you cannot clear the financial feasibility hurdles, return to your concept and see if there are ways to start smaller, reduce the required start-up costs, increase revenues, or in some other way change your strategy so that the company can become profitable sooner.

THE ENTREPRENEUR'S TOOLKIT: CUSTOMER-BASED REVENUE ESTIMATING

Revenue is one of the most important—yet most difficult—estimates to make. Revenue projections for existing companies are usually made by taking last year's revenue and increasing it by some percentage, but this is not possible with a new venture. Sometimes industry averages or the entrepreneur's experience in a comparable business can be used as reference points. These are valuable sources, but another tool, called Customer-Based Revenue Estimating, is more accurate, creates more credible projections, and is more likely to reveal flaws in assumptions. It works like this:

- **Estimate traffic.** This is the number of people who will enter your store, visit your Web site, attend presentations, or be called on by you and your sales staff.
- **Estimate the closing ratio.** This is the percentage of people who will actually purchase your product or service. The closing ratio can vary greatly depending on the type of business you will establish. For retail stores, a closing ratio of about 50% is reasonable, while for Web site visitors 10% is considered an excellent percentage of actual purchasers.
- **Estimate the average order size.** This could be the average bill in a restaurant, the average purchase in a store, or the average commission earned by a real estate brokerage.
- **Multiply traffic by the closing ratio by the average order size.** For example, if you estimate traffic for a month at 1,000, the closing ratio at 25%, and an average order size of $50, your estimated monthly revenue will be 1,000 x .25 x 50 or $12,500. For businesses that are highly seasonal or experiencing rapid growth, you may want to do this multiplication at various periods of the year separately.

To accomplish Customer-Based Revenue Estimating you will need to research what is typical in your industry, complete actual percentage counts in similar businesses, or talk with salespeople who have sold similar products. You should be sure to show your estimates to people who are highly experienced in your industry because they will be able to judge how reasonable your figures are. These calculations will also serve as an excellent supplement or appendix to the financial projections in your plan. Unfortunately, many entrepreneurs let optimism guide their preparation of these figures, so be sure to make your estimates very conservative.

PLANNING FOR A PROFITABLE EXIT

A *business exit* occurs when the owners sell or close their company. Although thinking of an exit strategy when you begin your venture may seem odd, it is a necessary step. While you do not need to have an exit strategy in order to establish financial feasibility, a successful exit is how many companies earn most of their profits. Some ventures, such as real estate, are generally easy to sell because there are clear ways of establishing value, there is usually a large pool of potential buyers, and financing is readily available. Other businesses, such as consulting firms or professional practices, are more difficult to value because the owner or key employees may be crucial to business performance, and the group of interested buyers may be small.

You need to think through the possible exit strategies for your business. The components of this strategy include:

- Who the most likely purchasers will be.
- The market value of the business at the time in the future when you anticipate selling.
- The likelihood that the sale will be made for a single cash payment or paid over time.

From these factors you will be able to estimate how much the business will sell for and on what terms the sellers will receive their payment.

There are some factors that can make selling a business difficult or even impossible. Regulatory barriers, such as a license that requires government approval before it can be transferred, labor agreements, or golden parachutes for executives that mandate big payouts when a company is sold can all create delays and even prevent a business from being sold. Environmental issues, such as inspections and testing to certify that there are no potential liabilities from toxic materials, may take months and entail huge expenses before a company can be sold.

Confirming Entrepreneurial Feasibility

You have now completed the analyses to clear the three financial and personal feasibility hurdles:

- You have defined the personal commitments in terms of time, financing, skills, knowledge, and abilities that you need to make for this venture to be successful.
- You have established what the resources are that you require to start your venture and you have confirmed that these resources are obtainable.
- You have demonstrated that the company can be profitable through operations or through an exit strategy.

Now you are ready to take an in-depth look at strategic issues, which will be covered in the next chapter.

Focus on Research: The Issues of Being in a Family Business

Family enterprises are the most prevalent business form in the United States. Family businesses run the gamut from providing daycare for a few children at home to corporate giants such as the Ford Motor Company and Johnson & Johnson. The 1997 National Family Business Study surveyed households throughout the United States and found that one in ten contained at least one person who owned a family business. It also revealed that more than 80% of American businesses meet the definition of a family business—in which family members run the business and own more than 50%. This means that more than 40% of all business income in the United States is generated by family businesses.

A 1996 study compared a sample of 118 businesses that employed two or more family members with a sample of 113 similar ventures that did not qualify as family businesses. Although this study was not as broad as the 1997 National

Family Business Study, the results showed that the major goals for all businesses, whether family businesses or not, are making money, allowing the owners to live how and where they like, and making contributions to society by providing a valuable product or service.

The 1996 study also revealed that family business owners had a greater focus on using their companies to achieve family goals, such as creating wealth for their families or building a business that their children can run. They also reported having greater conflict between their businesses and families, but generally felt that they were able to manage these problems. Respondents revealed that their businesses benefitted from their family members' involvement and that hiring non-family members would probably cost more.

In the final analysis, family-business owners feel that their ventures are better off for the contributions that their family members make. They also appreciate the opportunity to accomplish both family and business goals in the same entrepreneurial effort.

JOHN TEJADA DECIDES TO OPEN A HOME OFFICE

John Tejada worked for Scales Construction and Development in Tucson for more than 20 years. He started as a helper on job sites during summers while he was in college. Robert Scales, the founder and President, was impressed with John and offered him a full-time job after John graduated with a B.A. in Architecture. Over the next 20 years, John worked as a job-site foreman, estimator, and project manager. Although Scales Construction focused on residential development, they also served as the general contractor on commercial projects such as strip malls, schools, and small office buildings.

John enjoyed the varied nature of the work, the ability to be outside an office during much of the work day, and the opportunities the Scales company gave him to expand his skills. Last week, Mr. Scales informed the staff that he had decided to retire and would be selling the business to The Corbett Group, a much larger development company. Corbett announced that they would not be keeping any of the staff from Scales.

John decided that it was time to go out on his own. He had good skills and knowledge of the construction and residential development businesses. He knew many people in the industry who he felt would be a good source of projects. To keep his costs low, at least while he was getting started and working on his own, John wanted to open a home office by converting his guest room. His wife was supportive of the plan and offered to help the business three or four hours a day, but she was concerned about how effective a work environment it would be given that they had a 12-year-old daughter and a 9-year-old son.

John needs to create a plan of very specific strategies to make his home-based business successful.

Case Questions:

1. What is the best way for his wife to contribute to the business?
2. How can he make his business look established and professional to clients?
3. What technology, such as computers, telephones, beepers, and wireless Internet, could he use to make his business more efficient while improving service to clients?
4. Should he keep to a fixed work schedule, including being away from the house when his children come home from school?
5. How will he manage if additional people are required to work as estimators, architects, project managers, or bookkeepers?
6. Where will he hold client meetings?

End of Chapter Questions

1. What do you think are the most important personal characteristics for an entrepreneur to have?
2. What are the three tests for proving the feasibility of a venture?
3. Think about a business you are interested in starting. What are the key areas of expenses and investment that will need to be researched?
4. What are the major methods that can be used to estimate future revenue?

Note: All financial estimate worksheets are available as spreadsheet downloads from www.bankablebusinessplans.com.

NOTES

1. Christopher Price, "A Sobering Tale for High-Risk Investors: The Satellite Phone Industry," *The Financial Times*, September 29, 1999, p. 6.
2. CNNfn Digital Jam, Interview with Armand Musey, Analyst with Banc of America Securities, March 17, 2000, 7:30 PM.
3. "Court Orders $300 Million Paid to Banks by Motorola," *New York Times*, January 9, 2002. Section C, Column 1, p. 9.
4. Robert Brockhaus, "Risk Taking Propensity of Entrepreneurs," *Academy of Management Journal,* Vol. 23 (July 1980), pp. 509–520.

   Robert Brockhaus, "The Psychology of the Entrepreneur," in C. Kent, D. Sexton, and K. Vesper (Eds.), *Encyclopedia of Entrepreneurship*, pp. 39–56. (Englewood Cliffs, NJ: Prentice-Hall, 1982).

   Robert Brockhaus, and P.S. Horwitz, "The Psychology of the Entrepreneur," In Donald L. Sexton and R. Smilor (Eds.), *The Art and Science of Entrepreneurship*, pp. 25–48. (Cambridge, MA: Ballinger, 1986).
5. Judy M. Chartrand, Fred H. Borgen, Nancy E. Betz, David Donnay, "Using the Strong Interest Inventory and Skills Confidence Inventory to Explain Career Goals," *Journal of Career Assessment*, Vol. 10, No. 2 (March 2002), pp. 169–190.
6. R. Bryan Kennedy, "Using the Myers-Briggs Type Indicator in Career Counseling," *Journal of Employment Counseling*, Vol. 41, Issue 1, (March 2004), pp. 38–45.
7. Consulting Psychologists Press, Inc. *Strong and MBTI Entrepreneur Report*, www.cpp.com/products/mbti/index.asp
8. John Renner and Carol Dunne. *The Insightful Entrepreneur*, (Palo Alto: Consulting Psychologists Press, 1999).
9. Ramona K. Z. Heck and Kay Stafford, "The Vital Institution of Family Business: Economic Benefits Hidden in Plain Sight," In G. K. McCann & N. Upton (Eds.), *Destroying Myths and Creating Value in Family Business* (Deland, FL: Stetson University, 2001), pp. 9–17.
10. Paul and Sarah Edwards. *Working from Home*, 5th Edition, (New York: J.P. Tarcher, 1999).
11. Ramona K. Z. Heck and Kay Stafford, K., Ibid.
12. Myung-Soo Lee and Edward G. Rogoff, "Research Note: Comparison of Small Businesses with Family Participation versus Small Businesses without Family Participation: An Investigation of Differences in Goals, Attitudes, and Family/Business Conflict," *Family Business Review*, Vol. 9, No. 4, (Winter 1996), pp. 423–437.

CHAPTER 3

ISSUE 3: CREATE A WINNING STRATEGY

WHAT THEY DID RIGHT: HOW FILLING THE NEEDS OF TAXPAYERS HAS CREATED SUCCESSFUL BUSINESSES AND ENTIRE PROFESSIONS

No matter how inconvenient and burdensome the IRS is to most Americans, alert companies have been able to capitalize on the market it has created. What began as a short-term tax during the Civil War has morphed into a morass of rules, exceptions, and complications that fill tens of thousands of pages of the Internal Revenue Code, occupy thousands of accountants and lawyers, and drive most taxpayers to the edge of insanity.

The first income tax was passed in 1862 when the North faced a $505 million war debt and was having trouble borrowing money from banks who feared the Union might not survive the conflict. The tax was levied at 3% on annual income between $600 and $10,000, and 5% on income over $10,000. There were no tax credits, and only one loophole: a provision that income on bonds was taxed at a low rate of only 1.5%. After the Civil War ended, the income tax expired. But in 1913, Congress established it again and it has been with us ever since.

What started as a one paragraph law in 1862 has now become so complex that 25% of Americans use professional tax preparers to file their tax forms. The cost to taxpayers is twofold: they pay the salaries of the IRS employees and then shell out fees to hire experts to prepare their tax returns. Joel Slemrod, a professor at the University of Michigan, has studied the cost of income tax compliance and estimates it at $80 billion annually, which falls disproportionately on low-income earners. Among specific groups who bear the largest share of these costs are recent immigrants, people with low levels of education, and individuals with little time or willingness to spend on deciphering their tax returns.

H&R Block, a small accounting firm in Kansas City, grew to become a leader in meeting this need after they saw how many of their small-business clients asked for help with their personal taxes. H&R Block developed a strategy to open up storefront locations that would be visible, accessible, and not intimidating to potential customers. Today the company has over 10,000 locations and $4 billion in revenue.

The institution of an income tax has been a huge boon to lawyers, accountants, and tax preparers who are hired to interpret, haggle over, and manage this vast system. In fact, entire professions, such as tax lawyers, tax accountants, tax appraisers, and tax preparers have been spawned by this system. The application of technology to filling this need has also produced successful companies that sell software products such as Turbo Tax to help taxpayers, as well as professionals, automate some aspects of the daunting task.

The lesson? A good strategy is to let the government—or someone else—create a need that you can fill.

You have developed an idea and you have satisfied yourself that it is feasible. Now you start the process of filling in the details. This chapter helps you select a winning strategy for your company by analyzing the type of industry you have chosen, the competition you will face, regulations you may have to follow, and the market you will serve. You will learn that general strategies such as "I will have the best product or service" are not nearly as powerful, convincing, or bankable as the strategies outlined in this chapter. As you read this chapter, think about how you can use these concepts to analyze your competition, which is a major method of developing a powerful strategy for your business.

Goals are what you hope to achieve with your business, such as profitability, improved market share, or a lucrative sale of your company. Strategy defines *how* you will reach those goals through actions including advertising, cost control, and product characteristics and enhancements. Here are a few important points about strategies:

- Strategies are outwardly oriented, focusing how your company will interact with its environment—customers, competitors, suppliers, and the government.
- Good strategies are specific, simple to implement, reasonable, and provide the blueprint for building the results you want.
- Winning strategies help your company achieve a strong and long-lasting competitive advantage in the marketplace. A competitive advantage enables you to attract customers, price products or services so you earn a profit, and build a valuable business—but it should be difficult or impossible for other firms to duplicate.

The Two Basic Strategies

There are many different strategies to choose from, all of which are greatly affected by the quality of your team members, the accuracy of your timetable, and the availability of resources. However, all strategies fall into two fundamental categories: *Low cost leadership* and *differentiation.*

Low-Cost Leadership

Everyone likes to pay the lowest price possible for any product or service, so companies that can offer their customers lower prices have a very strong competitive advantage. One master of low-cost strategies is WalMart, which uses its huge buying power to negotiate lower prices from its suppliers and then manages its operations so inexpensively it can set prices well below its competitors and still make a profit. Another is Toyota, regarded as the lowest-cost manufacturer of cars. This advantage enables Toyota to increase market share by lowering prices while still remaining profitable, thus forcing competitors to lose money if they match Toyota's prices.

Many entrepreneurs launching new businesses think they will be able to execute a low-cost strategy, but most find out otherwise. It is often difficult for a new business to operate more efficiently than existing companies that already know their market, are profitable, and have experienced and knowledgeable staff. In addition, existing businesses usually have more access to financing than start-ups.

DIFFERENTIATION

Designing a product or service precisely to match the preferences of your customers makes your business attractive and sets it apart from your competitors. Think of all the options you have when you decide to book a hotel room. Hotels differentiate themselves with such qualities as location, room size, amenities, luxuries, reputation, sports facilities, image, style, and level of service. Motel 6, for example, is geared to the bargain traveler who isn't interested in amenities, but the company is successful because their product appeals to a sizeable, yet very specific, group of customers. Your business plan must define your target market and state how you will differentiate your product or service to appeal to your potential, specific customer group.

Identifying a Competitive Advantage

To be successful, every company must have some competitive advantage over its competition. Competition is the enemy of profits: It is great for customers, but bad for business. Competitive advantage is the barrier that keeps competition at bay. The stronger the competitive advantage, the more profitable and less affected by competition your business is likely to be. For example, a *patent* or *copyright* prevents anyone else from using your product without your permission. Velcro and Post-it-Notes are protected by patents. Software, music, and books are protected by copyrights. Another competitive advantage is a *government granted monopoly*, such as a cable television franchise, which prevents anyone else from entering the same business in your geographical area. An *effective monopoly*—such as Microsoft's Windows operating system, which is not only protected by copyrights on the software, but also by its emergence as the *de facto* standard in personal computers—virtually assures that new customers will purchase the company's product.

Other competitive advantages rely on your customers' perception of your product. These include being a name brand, having a positive image, a strong reputation, or a position as a high-status product. While these competitive advantages may take years to build, they can also be created quickly for new businesses through marketing strategies such as advertising, promotion, and word-of-mouth.

A great brand name or a strong reputation can also be a sizeable competitive advantage. For example, Oreo cookies and Jell-O occupy a prime position in people's minds for a particular category of product. New products such as Lucky Jeans, Fubu, Atkins' diet foods, and Linksys created strong brands very quickly by having the right product and great marketing.

High status is also a desireable competitive advantage. Products such as Rolex or Rolls Royce separate themselves from their competitors, command high prices, and generate high profit margins. Many small, local retail businesses also have strong brand names and excellent reputations, such as long-established neighborhood restaurants, banks, and bookstores.

Speed in delivering a product or service is another powerful competitive advantage. From Clipper Ships to FedEx jets, customers have always valued speed. Other companies built using speed as a key strategy include Domino's Pizza, Dell Computer, and many Web-based ventures, such as job-search site Monster.com, which enable customers to find the information they want more quickly than the paper-based systems they replaced.

Great service, such as an unparalleled *distribution system,* is another powerful competitive advantage. Pepsi and Coca Cola are virtually everywhere. It would take a new competitor millions—perhaps billions—of dollars and many years to build a distribution system that connects with customers throughout the world as well as Pepsi or Coca Cola. Their new products, such as Dasani bottled water from The Coca-Cola Company or Aquafina from The Pepsi Bottling Group, can take advantage of these companies' huge distribution networks. New companies without distribution systems will likely need a plan to outsource distribution to existing firms. Great service such as provided by a plumber, electrician, or a car dealer are essential elements of their competitive advantages.

Weak competitive advantages also abound, such as electronics or appliance retailers that sell the same products as their competitors and are forced to compete on price and reputation for service. Many food retailers, sometimes owned by the same parent company, have weak competitive advantages and must compete based on location differences. In New York City, for example, there are thousands of take-out pizzerias often within a block or less of each other, yet they are generally very successful because the demand for pizza and customer preference for a convenient location are so strong.

Because competition drives down prices and profits, building the strongest possible competitive advantage becomes the main tool to erecting a barrier that keeps competition at bay.

Ultimately, consumers take all the characteristics of your product and service—along with its price—and judge whether they are getting "value." A product or service delivers good value when its cost relative to its characteristics are—in the customer's view only—better than the alternatives. *Consumer Reports* rates products and identifies those that deliver good value by deeming them "Best Buys." These are the products that offer the best characteristics and features for the price.

Intellectual Property Issues

Intellectual property, such as patents and copyrights, represent a major class of assets and a powerful source of competitive advantages for business. Given the growth of computer-based technologies, such as the Internet, cell phones, and digital files, along with the general growth of knowledge-based businesses, such as databases, there is a great likelihood that your business plan will include a strong role for intellectual property. Intellectual property law evolved because, unlike physical objects, intellectual property is easy to copy and its actual ownership is difficult to prove. It is hard to steal a locomotive, but it is easy to steal its design. The main types of intellectual property are:

Patents

Patents represent a legal right to prevent someone else from using the design and technology of your invention. Machines, processes, objects, designs, and new varieties of plant life can be patented. To obtain a patent, the invention must be non-obvious, useful, and new. The application for the patent must disclose the details of the invention which are then available to anyone who wishes to see them. The advantage of patents is that they can produce a stream of income in the form of licensing fees if others want to use your invention. The negative is that the process is long and expensive, requires disclosure of the details of your invention, and demands that the patent holder find and stop infringement on the patent (or charge a fee for its use.) Many patents do not hold up to legal challenge. Depending on the type of object or process being patented, patents are granted for a total of 14 to 20 years from the date they are filed.

Trade Secrets

Trade secrets are for inventions such as devices, processes, and formulations, as well as for information that is of value to the company. To be classified as a trade secret, the item, process or information must be non-obvious to people in the field, have value, and be treated as a "secret." This means that rigorous policies are maintained through confidentiality or non-competition agreements with employees, that the trade secret is not available to others, and that key documents that relate to the trade secret are clearly marked. The positives of trade secrets compared to copyrights or patents are that they are inexpensive, they don't have a fixed time period of protection, and they don't require public disclosure. The negative is that someone else can patent something similar to your trade secret and can then collect a fee from you for infringing on his patent.

Copyrights

A copyright is the exclusive right to print, copy, distribute and sell works created by artists and authors such as books, recordings, scripts, paintings, and other types of design and art work. To secure a copyright, the work must display the word copyright or the symbol © along with the date. Copyrights run until 50 years after the author's or artist's death.

Trademarks, Service Marks, and Trade Dress

A trademark is a name or design used to identify an organization or product. A service mark functions the same way but for a service. McDonald's is a service mark, while Big Mac is a trademark. Service marks and trademarks can be registered with the Patents and Trademarks Office, which is signified by using an ® after the name. The term trade dress describes the unique style of a retail business, including design, decoration, lighting, and attire of the employees. Many retail businesses, especially large chains, such as TGI Friday's restaurants, work to establish a unique trade dress and then defend it if copied.

Strategic Analysis

Strategies are how your company will achieve its goals, covering issues such as competitive advantage, management and financial capabilities, and product characteristics. It is important to understand the strategic strengths and weaknesses of your proposed business. This will not only help you improve your long-term strategies, but will also enable you to present your concept persuasively in your business plan. Three excellent tools for evaluating businesses are the Resource-Based Approach, Porter's Five Forces, and SWOT Analysis. The Resource-Based Approach focuses on the company's internal capabilities; Porter's Five Forces assesses the external environment; and SWOT Analysis examines both the internal and external factors, but in a somewhat simpler way.

The Resource-Based Approach

Organizations can be seen as the sum of their human, financial, and organizational resources. This set of resources becomes the means by which companies develop the capacity to accomplish their goals, from building products to creating films. The greater an organization's resources and the better these resources can be combined into strong capabilities, the more a company can develop and implement a strategy to achieve its goals.

Robert M. Grant, a professor at Georgetown University and a leading thinker on business strategy, designed a framework for strategic analysis that identifies a company's resources and capabilities, then develops a strategy based on this analysis to establish a strong competitive advantage. This approach can also reveal gaps in resources, which when filled could improve the company's capabilities and, in turn, its strategy. Seeing how additional resources can change strategy or how different strategies can change the types and amounts of resources required will help you home in on the best mix of strategy and required resources. This approach is very well suited to entrepreneurial ventures because one of the major tasks of an entrepreneur is to recruit the resources needed to bring a plan to fruition.

Table 3.1
The Process of Preparing a Resource-Based Strategic Analysis

Step 1	Identify Resources	– Identify resources your business currently has. – Appraise resource strengths and weaknesses relative to competitors. – Identify better ways to use current resources.
Step 2	Define Capabilities	– Identify your business's capabilities. – Evaluate capabilities relative to competitors. – Define the resources needed to sustain each capability.
Step 3	State Competitive Advantage and Assess its Strength	– Define your company's competitive advantage. – Judge the strength of each competitive advantage in terms of its ability to be sustainable over time. – Judge the strength of each competitive advantage in terms of its ability to create revenue and profits.
Step 4	Create a Strategy	– Select a strategy that best uses your company's resources, capabilities, and competitive advantages.
Step 5	Identify Resource Gaps and Actions to Fill Them	– Identify resource gaps that if filled would lead to a stronger competitive advantage and a more effective strategy. – Define actions to recruit those resources. – Take those actions. – Return to Step 1 and begin analysis again.

Here is how this process might look for Connie Chon, who wants to start Pickle World, a 100,000 square-foot superstore that sells a wide variety of pickled foods of every type from tomatoes to fish. Connie trained as a chef in France, has owned several successful restaurants, and has $400,000 to invest in this new venture. The budget for starting Pickle World is about $7 million.

Table 3.2
A Sample Resource-Based Strategic Analysis: Connie Chon's Pickle World

Step 1	Identify Resources	– Owner has extensive food and business experience. – Owner has $400,000 to invest.
Step 2	Define Capabilities	– Connie knows more about pickles than anyone. – Connie has a great recipe for pickled pigs feet. – Connie can tell a great pickle just by smelling it.
Step 3	State Competitive Advantage and Assess its Strength	– Pickle World will carry 15,000 types of pickles. The largest supermarkets carry only a few hundred. – People will probably travel from around the world to shop at Pickle World. – Pickles have long shelf-lives, don't need refrigeration, and everyone loves them.
Step 4	Create a Strategy	– Variety of pickles and friendly service will be how Pickle World will differentiate itself.
Step 5	Identify Resource Gaps and Actions to Fill Them	– Needs $6.6 million in financing and location near international airport for those traveling from other countries to shop at Pickle World. – Needs business partners. Everyone Connie has talked to so far about joining the founding management team has just walked away shaking their heads.

Porter's Five Forces

In 1980, Harvard professor Michael E. Porter published a seminal book, *Competitive Strategy: Techniques for Analyzing Industries and Competitors*, in which he argued that five forces determined long-term industry profitability. Entrepreneurs prefer to establish their companies in industries that are fundamentally profitable, and funding sources are also attracted to industries, such as real estate, that are generally profitable, rather than industries, such as airlines, which are fundamentally unprofitable.

The five forces that Porter identified are:

1. **The character of the rivalry between competitors,** which can run from subdued to vicious.
2. **The height of barriers to entry** that determine how easily new competitors can enter the industry.
3. **The extent to which there is a threat of substitutes** that give customers alternatives from other industries.
4. **The amount of bargaining power suppliers have,** which they can use to raise their prices and thus lower the profitability of the companies they sell to.
5. **The amount of bargaining power customers have** to negotiate lower prices or additional features that will reduce revenue and lower the profitability of the companies they purchase from.

Porter argues that the most profitable industries have two or more of these forces working in their favor. Of course, in the long term anything can change. For example, an industry with few competitors could attract new competitors who are lured by the industry's high profits or because new technology makes it easier and cheaper to enter the industry. The presentation of this analysis in your business plan can be useful if it helps explain the attraction of the industry and the conditions that make your particular strategy a good choice.

FIGURE 3.1
ASSESSING THE HEALTH OF COMPETITION: PORTER'S FIVE FORCES FRAMEWORK

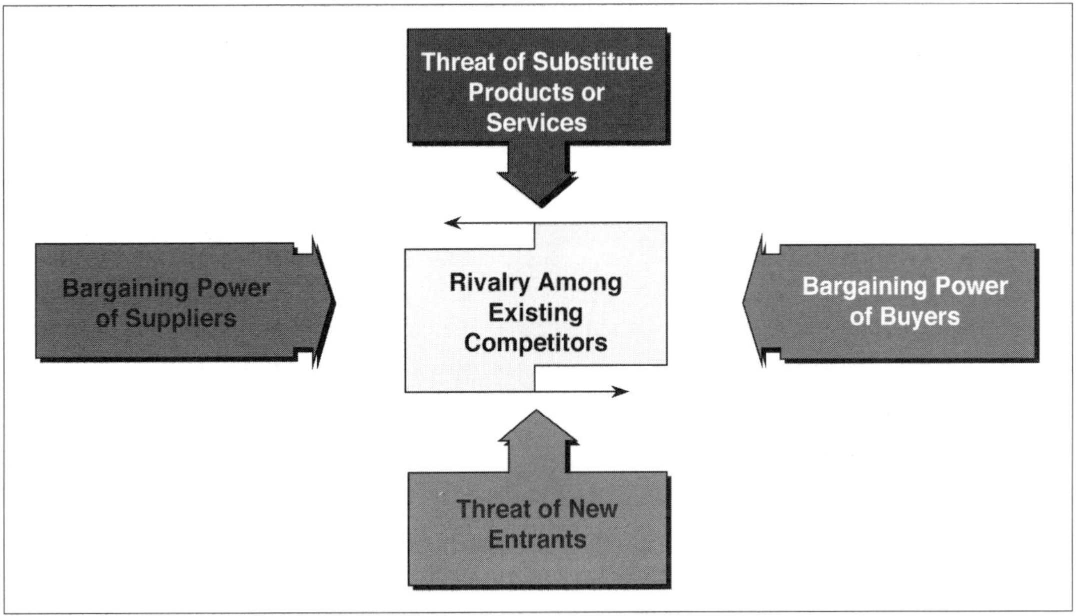

SOURCE: M.E. PORTER, COMPETITIVE STRATEGY: TECHNIQUES FOR ANALYZING INDUSTRIES AND COMPETITORS (1980).

SWOT ANALYSIS

An effective tool in evaluating a business idea is a SWOT analysis. an acronym which stands for **S**trengths, **W**eaknesses, **O**pportunities, and **T**hreats. Strengths and weaknesses relate to the organization's internal capabilities, such as good relationships with key customers and strong technical skills, or inadequate warehouse facilities and poor sales staff. Opportunities relate to external issues such as underserved markets in adjacent communities, a change in regulations, or a current competitor who could be bought out. Threats are also external, such as a change in traffic patterns that could make it more difficult for customers to find your store, or a potential increase in sales taxes that could send customers to an adjacent state.

Your SWOT analysis does not have to be scientific or rigorous, but it's a good way to organize your thoughts about strategy. Including a SWOT analysis in your business plan will show potential investors and lenders how you will address your company's pluses and minuses. Reasonable funders will not expect you to run a business free of weaknesses and threats, but they will expect you to show how you will manage these potential problems and minimize their impact.

TABLE 3.3
SWOT ANALYSIS CHART

	Pluses	**Minuses**
Internally Focused	Strengths	Weaknesses
Externally Focused	Opportunities	Threats

One way to develop specific strategies is to take the strengths, weaknesses, opportunities, and threats that are enumerated in the SWOT Analysis Chart and create specific strategies that link them. This can be done using a TOWS (this is SWOT spelled backwards) Strategic Matrix. For example, in the TOWS Strategic Matrix below (Table 3.4) strategy A would be specifically designed to minimize or even eliminate weakness 1 and to handle threat 1. Strategy K would be designed to make the most of strength 2 to take advantage of opportunity 2. Not only might working from a TOWS Strategic Matrix enable you to develop specific strategies, it will also help you gain a good overall view of which strengths are the ones to build on and which weaknesses are important to eliminate or minimize.

TABLE 3.4
TOWS STRATEGIC MATRIX

	Weaknesses 1. 2. 3.	**Strengths** 1. 2. 3.
Threats 1. 2 3.	Strategies A. B. C	Strategies D. E. F.
Opportunities 1. 2. 3.	Strategies G. H. I.	Strategies J. K. L.

The Entrepreneur's Toolkit: Pulling Together a Comprehensive Strategic Analysis

This chapter presents specific approaches to crafting a strategy to match your business needs, but it is also possible to take a more comprehensive approach. Use the following exercise to create a bankable business plan which employs several different strategies:

1. Identify the type of industry your company is in.
2. List all the strategies that apply to that industry.
3. Research and list the regulatory barriers in your industry.
4. Define your company's competitive advantage.
5. Subject your business strategies to a resource-based analysis, SWOT analysis, and an evaluation using Porter's Five Forces.
6. Create a list of the pluses and minuses of each strategy (from step 2) and rank them in overall attractiveness.
7. Select the strategy most likely to make your company profitable for the long term.
8. List ways your competitive advantage could be made stronger.
9. Identify the resources and capabilities your company will need to strengthen its competitive advantage.
10. Develop a plan for recruiting those resources.

Industry Analysis as a Tool for Crafting an Effective Strategy

Many people believe that only ventures in rapidly growing industries can be successful, but there are effective strategies for all types of industries, even stagnant or declining ones, if the *right* strategy is used. Investors and lenders recognize five categories of industries: Emerging industries, maturing industries, stagnant and declining industries, fragmented industries, and industries with dominant leaders.

Let's review the nature of these five categories and the specific strategies that are likely to lead to success in each industry.

Emerging Industries

Emerging industries are the gold rush opportunities that spring up quickly and attract a great deal of attention and investment in the early phases of their development. Examples include the Internet during the 1990s, housing construction immediately following World War II, and the automobile industry after Henry Ford's inventions and innovations. While emerging industries grow rapidly, they are also burdened with a good deal of competition and uncertainty. Let's look at the pluses and minuses of doing business in an emerging industry:

Pluses of Emerging Industries:

- There is a rapid rate of growth as new customers enter the market.
- It is easy to enter the market, even for people without experience, because no one has experience.
- There are no established leaders, as in mature industries, who need to be overcome, making the playing field nearly level for all competitors.

Minuses of Emerging Industries:

- Many of the technologies and standards are unclear and may not be clarified for a long time. If you were a software company early in the personal computer revolution, no one knew which operating system would become dominant. If you decided to write your software for an operating system other than Microsoft's, then you probably put yourself out of business. Similar struggles exist today with digital systems for the distribution of music, books, and cellular phones.
- Although the ease of entering the market is listed as a plus above, it can also be a negative if you are one of the first to establish a business in an emerging industry. When companies in Web site design began to develop, the low barriers to entry kept prices and profit margins minimal as new companies and individuals flooded the market and priced their services low in order to build client bases quickly.

- Lack of information about your competition can leave you in the dark about how to price and market your product or service. You may not even know who your competitors are, what products they are developing, or how well they are selling, all of which can make it difficult to manage decisions about your own business. As a result, you may not realize that your market is too limited or your price too high until it's too late and your business fails.
- Buyers may delay purchasing products in an emerging industry because they want to see if a dominant technology arises or if prices will drop dramatically as manufacturing costs fall. You may have done this yourself with a piece of equipment such as a digital camera or a big-screen television. This reluctance on the part of buyers to purchase immediately can create big problems for companies in emerging industries.
- Needed resources can be hard to find and you may have to pay more to procure them. During the California gold rush in 1849, there were reports of prospectors paying more than $100 for a shovel that usually retailed for 50 cents. During the peak of the Internet boom, high school students who could program in HTML, the language used for Web sites, were offered jobs at Web site design companies for $100,000 per year.

As these examples show, because resources such as financing, components, and raw materials can be expensive, if available at all, it is often better to sell *to* companies in emerging industries than to *be* one.

Strategies for Emerging Industries

Certain strategies are best for emerging industries. First, create a bold, *win early* strategy. This is what both Amazon.com and 3Com, the maker of the Palm Pilot, used in their emerging industries. The concept was to grow as quickly as possible to make themselves the brand name. Next, be the best. Sony, Hewlett-Packard, and Cisco Systems are companies that established new performance standards for their products, putting distance between themselves and their competitors.

Another strategy is to superserve niche markets. Define and develop customer groups by geography, application, pricing, or marketing. Both Computer Associates, which owns many niche software products, such as computer security and accounting, and Symantec, which owns niche software products for personal computers, have used this strategy successfully. Neither one of these companies competes directly with the big players like Microsoft, but they each identified markets that were too small for Microsoft to pay much attention to.

Picking the winning technology as soon as possible is also a valuable strategy. If you have a company that produces computer screens and televisions and you decide to focus on CRTs rather than flat-screen technology, it is likely you will soon be out of business.

And, finally, build brand loyalty, especially with consumer products. Given all the competition and uncertainty in emerging markets, the faster you can build a brand that customers recognize, the sooner you will be constructing some protection from your competitors. Brand loyalty is a powerful tool for grabbing and maintaining customers.

Entrepreneurs in emerging industries must be prepared for well-financed outsiders to move in aggressively. After gaining dominance in Operating Systems, Microsoft has systematically entered the word processing, e-mail, spreadsheet, and database software markets, often destroying all competition in its path. Huge companies such as Time Warner, Comcast, and AT&T had the stability and finances to wait for the cable television industry to develop into a large-scale, viable business. When the cable television industry proved itself to be attractive, these large companies bought thousands of small, local cable television operators.

If your business is in an emerging, high-growth industry, you should think about what happens to your venture and your investors when the giants awaken. Will you sell your company to the big guys? Do you have a battle plan to withstand their onslaught? Or do you expect to cash in early and be lounging by your Olympic-sized swimming pool before this occurs? Whatever you expect, you must cover future possibilities in your plan.

Maturing Industries

As an industry matures, its rate of growth slows. This is happening today in the personal computer industry and the Internet Service Provider (ISP) industry. It occurred recently in the retail-location video rental business and, during the 1960s and 1970s, in the automobile industry. Growth typically slows in maturing industries in several ways. The first sign is that demand slows. While the industry may still be growing, the rate of growth of demand for the products or services is beginning to diminish. This usually makes competition rougher because the same number of companies are fighting over fewer new customers.

Demand can slow because buyers are smarter. Buyers become more sophisticated and demanding as they gain experience with new products or services. Perhaps when you bought your first DVD player you didn't know enough to check if it could fast forward without blanking the screen, but you certainly figured this out by the time you made your next purchase. As demand slows, excess supply begins to appear and it usually takes time for manufacturers or suppliers to adjust their production. When supply exceeds demand, some suppliers start to cut prices to push their products out of inventory, which can reduce both market prices and profit margins.

Consumers become aware of the *switching costs* in maturing industries. As customers develop purchasing and usage patterns, they become reluctant to switch to different products and different suppliers because they don't want to learn new systems, abandon what they have already bought, or take the risk of changing to a product that might be worse. High switching costs are a major competitive advantage in established companies.

Another issue in mature industries is that international competition increases. Foreign competitors who have lower labor costs or higher government subsidies can enter a market during a maturing period and provide tough price competition. After a few years of domestic DVD player sales, a low cost Chinese manufacturer entered the U.S. market and underpriced the competition by nearly one third.

Because competition often results in price cuts, profits can suffer. Companies that are weak financially can fail or become takeover targets.

When supply exceeds demand, profit margins diminish, and weaker companies face failure. During this trend a maturing industry usually enters a phase of consolidation in which bigger companies buy smaller companies and some smaller companies combine to form larger ones.

Strategies for Maturing Industries

The major strategic options in maturing industries are:

- **Reduce cost.** Once profits are pinched by lower prices, companies must strive to maintain profitability by reducing costs. Ways of doing this include paying closer attention to efficiency, eliminating costly product features, and curtailing the product line so the company saves on manufacturing costs. Motorola dominated the cellular phone industry during its early years, but later new, foreign competitors entered the market. Ultimately, Motorola was forced to trim its product line to reduce its manufacturing and marketing costs.

- **Focus on large customers.** Steady customers with large orders can be served more efficiently than small customers who purchase in limited and sporadic quantities. The large orders of major customers usually make it easier to maintain price competitiveness because, even with a small margin, a large order can be significantly more profitable.
- **Expand to new markets.** As existing markets become saturated and it becomes more difficult to remain profitable, you can expand into new markets with less competition and newer, less sophisticated customers.
- **Purchase rivals.** One way to reduce competition is to purchase your competitors. This strategy is sometimes called a *roll-up*, which describes the buying of many small businesses to form a much larger company. This has occurred recently with media companies, accounting firms, hospitals, and car dealerships.

Think about well-known, recently founded companies and see if you agree that their current strategies are a closer match to those in maturing, rather than emerging, industries. Although Amazon.com executed strategies for emerging industries when it opened for business—namely to get big fast and seize a strong market position—the company has since applied mature industry strategies to reduce its costs by focusing on efficiency, expanding its market to include more countries served and more types of products sold, and concentrating on better service for bigger customers. Similarly, Apple pioneered an entirely new type of product with the iPod. But after experiencing rapid growth and great brand recognition, Apple began to focus on new designs and serving customers better by creating a system to sell them digital music over the Web.

Stagnant or Declining Industries

There are successful strategies available even for industries that are experiencing zero growth or whose markets are actually shrinking. The mattress and pillow industries had been stagnant for many years until new products, such as allergy-proof bedding and the use of high-tech foams, revitalized them. After decades of decline, the candle industry saw significant increases once successful upscale retail candle stores were established in major cities.

Strategies for Stagnant or Declining Industries

Three strategies work best in stagnant or declining industries:

- **Focus on niches, especially growing niches.** In addition to allergy-proof products, the bed and pillow industries have focused on people with back and neck problems, a growing group as the American population has aged. They also focus their advertising on magazine, newspapers, and television shows that reach wealthy older audiences.
- **Differentiate and innovate.** The candle industry has been revitalized by innovative new designs such as long-lasting candles and the addition of various scents.
- **Reduce cost wherever possible.** Cost reduction is always a good strategy because it allows a company to stay profitable even if it needs to cut prices. In the bedding industry, for example, companies began selling to customers through catalogs, thus avoiding the overhead of maintaining retail locations. This reduced costs and enabled companies to target consumers who were too busy to shop and wanted fast delivery of these bulky items.

Fragmented Industries

Industries with many competitors, none of which has a large market share, are called fragmented industries. Highly fragmented industries include restaurants, lawn care companies, building contractors, and florists, most of which focus on local markets. Fragmented industries are generally easy to enter because they require low levels of investment, which accounts for the constant stream of new competitors. It is also very difficult for businesses in fragmented industries to become more efficient as they grow. General Motors, in a non-fragmented industry, can make a million cars a year with a lower cost per car than if it makes 1,000 cars. But restaurants, plumbers, florists, or other fragmented industry companies can't benefit from these types of efficiencies, called economies of scale, as they grow. In fact, it can become more expensive for these companies to provide their services as they grow. For example, a pizzeria owner who wants to open an additional restaurant in another neighborhood may save some on bulk food purchases, but the new pizzeria needs the same number of waiters and cooks per customer in order to maintain the same level of service and quality of food as the original store. The new pizzeria may even need its own manager, which the original store didn't have because the owner was present.

STRATEGIES FOR FRAGMENTED INDUSTRIES

The best strategies for fragmented industries include:

- **Focus on the local market.** Because of the characteristics of fragmented industries, one rarely sees regional plumbing companies or regional florists. The successful businesses remain focused on building clientele in their local markets.
- **Specialize.** As fragmented industry companies specialize they are able to gain competitive advantages, maintain strong prices, and become more profitable. Bakeries that concentrate on elaborate wedding cakes, health clubs that focus on using personal trainers, or lawn care companies that specialize in sports fields are all examples of this strategy.
- **Create "formula" facilities.** When companies in fragmented industries want to expand, the best strategy is to create simple, standardized, formula facilities. Successful examples of formula facilities include Kinko's (now part of FedEx), McDonald's, Dunkin' Donuts, and the UPS Stores. The strategy of creating formula facilities also lends itself quite easily to franchising.
- **Keep costs down.** Fragmented markets are by definition very competitive. Only companies that control their costs can withstand the constant onslaught of new competitors who try to gain a foothold by underpricing the competition.

Industries with Dominant Leaders

Successful industry leaders such as Microsoft, Toyota, and McDonald's stay on the offensive by consistently striving to improve their operations and efficiency and by bringing out new, more popular products. They constantly promote and advertise to fortify their brands and only reduce prices to maintain their market share as a last resort. When they do it right, as these three companies have, they are tough competitors. But not all market leaders do it right. Before being purchased by SBC Communications in 2005, AT&T had withered to a shadow of the untouchable giant it once was through a combination of uncontrollable problems, such as regulatory changes that opened up the door to new competitors, and missteps, such as giving up its technological edge. Kmart, the successor to the venerable Kresge Department store company, filed for bankruptcy in 2002 because its older, smaller stores and weaker management couldn't keep up with competition from WalMart, Target, Kohls, and others.

Strategies for Competing with Dominant Leaders

You can develop a business plan to take on the big guys and win by following strategies that focus on the long term, by taking risks, and by knowing the market.

- **Focus on the long term.** Large companies tend to focus on their quarterly financial performances because this is how Wall Street evaluates them. As a result, they can miss the long-term trends or be reluctant to invest in long-term projects. The music industry refused to focus seriously on the impact of digital music until Internet-based, file-sharing services such as Napster began to hurt them significantly. Traditional music companies have subsequently begun to buy and build digital services to catch up.
- **Take risks.** Corporate managers are, well, corporate. They can be rather bureaucratic and reluctant to take risks that might endanger their careers, the next big bonus, or a desired promotion. New York City Mayor Michael Bloomberg took a risk and made himself a billionaire by competing with the financial reporting systems owned by large companies. He built a better system that now dominates this industry.
- **Know the market.** Corporate managers tend to believe that they know the market better than their customers do. In what was one of the worst business decisions of all time, Western Union turned down the option to purchase Alexander Graham Bell's telephone because they didn't think enough people would use his contraption. Pursue your belief in what will sell. If the big guys don't agree with you, think of Alexander Graham Bell.

Weaknesses among big company executives create what has been rightly called the *attacker's advantage*. It can be a very potent strategy. So if you are a David and want to confront a Goliath, don't despair. With the attacker's advantage based on a long-term focus, your knowledge of the market and your willingness to take risks, you can still compete with the big guys.

It is important to match the strategies you use to reach your business goals with the characteristics of your specific industry. Be sure your strategies are outwardly focused and geared to your best competitive advantage. Make certain that they will impress potential investors and lenders as being the most effective means to achieve your business goals—and theirs.

Your Most Powerful Partner—The Government

Every business must function in an environment of government regulation. If you think otherwise, consider areas such as taxes, employee benefits, construction, or contracts, to name a few. One of the major tasks in analyzing the market of your venture is to identify the key regulatory restrictions that will make an impact on your business.

If you are opening a restaurant, you may require a license, your employees may need mandatory training in food handling, there could be noise and kitchen emission regulations, and you might have special fees and taxes to pay. Any business that requires construction will have to deal with zoning regulations, obtain a certificate of occupancy, and comply with literally hundreds of building codes. Although your architect or contractor may take care of many of these issues, you must ascertain if any regulations could interfere with your plans to construct a building of a certain size, provide for adequate parking, or remain open during the hours you anticipate. You must, therefore, budget for the licensing fees, taxes, and the costs of compliance in your business plan.

There may be changes in regulations that could affect your business, so you will need to speak with government officials, lawyers, politicians, and other business people to learn about current and possible future regulations. There is the case of the mid-western entrepreneur who planned to open a new restaurant on a main street leading into town. The owner didn't do his research with local officials and a few weeks after the business opened, the city changed the traffic patterns in town and the number of cars passing his restaurant dropped by more than 60%. Three months later the restaurant closed.

Many regulations, perhaps most regulations, are actually good for business. Tough licensing standards act as barriers to entry, keeping new competitors at bay. Government granted franchises—such as cable television, broadcast stations, or street vendor hot dog stands—often amount to government protected monopolies. Complex regulations and licensing requirements that are expensive to follow, such as those for day-care centers, schools, and financial services firms, are, in effect, protective barriers to entry for those businesses that have cleared the regulatory hurdles.

In industries such as education, health, and transportation, regulations provide for huge government expenditures that become the main source of income for thousands of companies. Recently enacted tougher accounting and governance standards have forced most firms to spend more on auditing and regulatory reports. This, in turn, has created a boom in business for large accounting firms and securities lawyers. Your research and your plan should explore the ways that government regulations may actually help to protect your company.

Government Regulation Creates Winners and Losers

Some industries would not exist without government regulation while others exist largely because of government regulation. There are industries that help individuals and businesses comply with government regulations, including legal (tax lawyer, real estate lawyers, etc.) and financial (cost accountants, tax accountants, auditors, etc.), as well as companies that set up and monitor systems for regulatory compliance at schools, hospitals, and public events. There are even companies that inspect and test government required fire extinguishers.

Some businesses are prohibited through government regulation such as restrictions on sugar, ice cream, and most cheeses imported into the United States. Restaurants and bars that allow smoking are slowly being forced into non-smoking facilities because of local laws and ordinances.

Government licensing can act as a strong barrier to entry through many, even surprising, requirements. Everyone is familiar with the licensing of doctors, lawyers, and accountants. These professions, like many industries, mount strong lobbying efforts at all levels of government to protect them from competition. But they are hardly alone. Look at Table 3.5 which lists a small but surprising sample of professions that require licenses in certain states.

TABLE 3.5 PROFESSIONS REQUIRING LICENSES

State	Licensed Occupation
West Virginia	Carpet Installer
Florida	Ceiling Tile Installer
Massachusetts	Movie Projectionist
Florida	College Math Teacher
California	Paperhanger
California and New Mexico	Drywall Installer
Louisiana	Florist
California	Upholsterer
Alaska and Maryland	Make-up Artist
Connecticut	Windshield Installer

It seems difficult to imagine that there is a public interest reason to protect consumers from unlicenced florists or upholsters. These rules exist more to protect the people who are currently in these professions from new competitors, making them "winners" and potential members "losers."

IT'S A FAST-CHANGING WORLD

Companies must constantly reevaluate their strategies in light of changes such as new competitors, advances in technology, and regulatory shifts, as well as in political and economic trends. Each alteration in the business environment can affect the supply of materials, the labor force, marketing strategies, consumer demand, and costs at every step of the company's operation.

Serious implications of these changes are:

- Entrepreneurs and their companies need to be constantly surveying the environment for changes that could affect them.
- Changes are good for those businesses that take advantage of them and are dangerous to those who ignore them.
- Business plans must be revised as changes require.

Focus on Research: What Many Businesses Do Right—Copy a Proven Success

Steven Schnaars, a professor of marketing at Baruch College, has studied companies that copied their competitors and found that imitation was not only the sincerest form of flattery, but an excellent business strategy as well. By developing detailed case histories for 28 products, including automated teller machines, calculators, and microwave ovens, in which the imitators surpassed the pioneers, Schnaars was able to identify important elements of first-mover advantage, as well as the equal, if not greater, advantage of being an imitator. His study also revealed the conditions that create the best opportunities for copy cats.

The credit card industry offers several good examples of imitators surpassing the pioneers. Although department stores had been offering credit cards since the 1930s, in 1950 Frank McNamara developed Diner's Club, a card that could be used in different types of stores and restaurants, as well as for travel services. Diner's Club developed the basic model of credit card companies: They charged the retailer a percentage of purchases and charged the consumer an annual fee. Diner's Club did the tough ground work of signing up retailers and changing the public's attitudes towards buying on credit. By 1960, Diner's Club boasted 1.25 million cardholders.

Although some other companies, such as Carte Blanche, tried to challenge Diner's Club, most lacked the financial resources to spend heavily on marketing and were sold to competitors. But Diner's Club also encountered some basic problems as a pioneer. The company incurred heavy costs while marketing the credit card concept to retailers and consumers, and developed cash flow problems that continually plagued the company, especially during its period of rapid growth. In 1958, American Express entered the credit card market with its huge financial resources based primarily on its traveler's check business, its large database of customers, and its established name brand. Within a few years, American Express had outstripped Diner's Club and became the market leader. While Diner's Club continues to exist as a part of Citicorp, it never again became the dominant force in the industry.

Another example is the microwave oven, which was invented in 1942 by Raytheon, a highly innovative technology company and a successful defense contractor. Raytheon introduced the first commercial version in 1946 and four years later marketed the first counter-top models, priced at $1,875 (about $20,000 in today's dollars). By 1968, through manufacturing improvements, prices had been reduced by 70% and Raytheon, under the Litton and Amana brands, had the microwave market virtually to itself. But then Japanese manufacturers entered the industry with a great deal of experience making and marketing conventional ovens. They also had a competitive advantage with lower production costs and a willingness to sell at lower margins. During the next 20 years, Raytheon's market share fell to below 10%.

Schnaars concluded that imitator success follows particular patterns:

- Imitators often exploit the long period from development to commercial success that many new products and services encounter. During this time, they are able to catch up with technology, develop new strategies, and apply the lessons learned from the pioneer company's mistakes.
- Successful imitators take advantage of the work the pioneer has done to create demand among customers, then they enter the market and are able to obtain customers much less expensively.
- Pioneers are subject to inertia arising from their confidence in their product, an inability to see new trends, and an unwillingness to replace or improve the successful products they have developed before their competitors do it for them.
- The major effect of pioneers is to open the door for large, established firms. Apple created the personal computer, but only retained about 3% of the market after IBM established its competitive products that used Microsoft software. The first commercial jet aircraft were built by the Canadian firm deHavilland in the 1960s. After they proved the product was viable, larger companies such as Boeing and McDonnell-Douglas entered the market and eventually dominated the industry.

The lessons are clear. While there certainly are opportunities for first-mover pioneers, imitation is a real and often successful strategy. For first movers to be successful in the long run, they must carefully control costs to compete with new entrants who may have low cost structures and need to grow rapidly to maintain their position as the market leaders. In addition, they have to change and improve their products as they learn what the customers want or to match competitors, and remain financially strong enough to accomplish all of their goals.

CASE ON POINT

JOEY'S CHILIBURGER FACES A STRATEGIC CROSSROADS

Joey Pitino opened his first chiliburger store eight years ago when he decided to leave a job as a financial analyst for an insurance company and become an entrepreneur. His plan was to open a store that served great chiliburgers, fries, and sodas. He set his prices below and quality above the major burger chains. Customers could eat in the simple but attractive store or order take-out at the counter or from a drive-through window. His first store was an immediate success and over the next five years Joey opened two more in similar, nearby suburban neighborhoods. To his amazement, Joey's three stores soon had annual revenues of nearly $1.5 million and profits of $375,000. Because he had started his business with his savings and it grew with profits, Joey had no debt and no partners.

Joey felt he was now at a crossroads. He could leave his company unchanged and probably continue to earn a great income, but he was concerned that competitors might emerge and lure away customers. Joey also felt that he could expand beyond the three stores as much as his financial and management abilities allowed, which would probably be at the rate of about two new stores per year. An owner of a fast-food franchise had asked Joey if he had plans to franchise. Franchising would allow Joey to collect a one-time fee when he sold a franchise and then earn ongoing royalties based on each franchise's revenues, but it would require large upfront legal fees and move him from selling chiliburgers to selling franchises. Joey's lawyer recommended that he diversify out of chiliburgers with new stores focused on healthy fast-food alternatives.

When he thought about which strategy made the most sense, Joey had trouble describing the industry he was in and its characteristics. Was he in the fast food, burger, or chiliburger industry? While the burger business might be mature, Joey felt that the chiliburger industry was growing rapidly.

Was his competitive advantage price, quality, name brand, strong reputation, or the local character of his stores? He didn't know how well any of these competitive advantages would hold up in the face of new competitors.

Joey felt he had to take a deep breath, get some perspective on the situation, and figure out what, if anything, he should do to insure his business the greatest chance for success for many years to come.

Case Questions:

1. What are Joey's strengths and weaknesses as an entrepreneur?
2. What are Joey's Chiliburger's strengths and weaknesses as a business?
3. What are Joey's options at this point?
4. What is your recommendation for what Joey should do? Why?

End of Chapter Questions

1. What is strategy?
2. What is competitive advantage? Give examples of competitive advantages.
3. What are the two basic types of strategies that will help a business obtain a competitive advantage?
4. What are the three types of strategic analysis that can help entrepreneurs understand their competitive position?
5. What are the basic types of strategies that work best in different types of industries?

NOTES

1. John F. Witte. *The Politics and Development of the Federal Income Tax,* (Madison: University of Wisconsin Press,1985).
2. Robert M. Grant, "The Resource-Based Theory of Competitive Advantage: Implications for Strategy Formulation," California Management Review, Vol. 33. No. 3, (Spring 1991), pp. 114–135.
3. George Stigler. *The Essence of Stigler,* edited by Kurt R. Luebe and Thomas Gale Moore, (Stanford University: Hoover Institution Press, 1986).
4. "Protecting an Innocent Public from Untrained Flower Arrangers," *Forbes,* April 26, 2004, p. 36.
5. Steven P. Schnaars. *Managing Imitation Strategies: How Later Entrants Seize Markets from Pioneers,* (New York: The Free Press, 1994).

CHAPTER 4

ISSUE 4: ANALYZE POTENTIAL MARKETS

What Were They Thinking? The Introduction of the "New Coke"

Coca Cola was first concocted by a druggist in 1885 and for over a hundred years maintained a commanding lead over its nearest rival, Pepsi Cola, in distribution, market share, and profitability. By the beginning of the 1980's, however, Coke began losing market share to Pepsi. Halfway through the decade it was a virtual dead heat between the two reigning colas. Coca Cola executives felt that it was time to re-evaluate the 100-year-old Coke formula. To explore ways to regain their former popularity, the company undertook a major research project, which had remarkably contradictory results:

- In blind taste tests, most people preferred Pepsi.
- In taste tests in which the two colas were identified, most people preferred Coke.

- In focus groups, consumers said that Pepsi could be improved.
- In focus groups, consumers felt strongly that Coke could not be improved[1]

While consumer research was being pursued, laboratory tests were also conducted to determine if the Coke formula could be improved. The outcome was a new formula that beat Pepsi overwhelmingly in blind taste tests. Based on these studies that focused on the product's recipe, Coca Cola decided to change the 100 year-old-formula of Coke and call it "New Coke." On April 23, 1985, more than 10 million cases of the New Coke were delivered to stores.

The response from consumers was staggeringly negative. Newspapers carried stories of people stockpiling the "Old Coke" before it was discontinued[2]. Coke fans were quoted as saying how terrible—indeed, even unpatriotic—it was to change Coke. Less than three months after introducing the New Coke, the company went back to the old formulation[3] and has continued to outsell Pepsi[4]. In 2003, the U.S. market share for Coke was 18.5% with a 11.9% share for Pepsi[5].

In hindsight, the mistakes Coca Cola made included:

- Drawing too strong a conclusion from research that was actually contradictory.
- Failing to ask consumers how they would feel if the formula were changed and if the old formula were no longer available.
- Missing the real trend, which was Pepsi's ability to win over young consumers, a market they had successfully wooed and won through its enormously effective "Pepsi Generation" advertising campaign.

The overarching lesson of Coca Cola's mistake is that while research is a great tool, it also has its limitations. Companies can never know with absolute certainty how consumers will react to a product. Coke executives started out believing that they were losing market share because of the product, not its marketing. They then designed and interpreted their research to prove themselves right. It took consumers to prove them wrong.

There are three aspects of a marketing plan that fall under the heading "more is better." These are research, targeting, and testing. The more of each you do and provide to your potential funders, the better and more convincing your plan will be—and the more likely your business will succeed.

Your marketing strategy begins with a carefully researched, highly specific description of your target market. If you're building welding tools for use in manufacturing and modifying cars, you need to research potential customers and the competitive products they currently use. Based on this, you will be able to create a list of the companies that need your product, as well as the names of the people at each company who make the purchasing decisions. Finally, you can actually test for market acceptance of your product by speaking with people in the industry.

If you're selling poles for pole vaulters, you can research the colleges and universities that train pole vaulters and the coaches who decide which poles to buy. From this information, you can create a list of potential customers, and test your concept by speaking with coaches and athletes.

If you're opening a clothing store for teenage girls, you should research this market by collecting industry and consumption pattern data, and by researching the stores that currently sell in the geographic areas you are considering. Based on this research, you will be able to define your potential market by demographic characteristics such as age, geography, income, and race. Finally, you can test your concept by interviewing teenage girls who are in your target group, and actually asking them if they would shop at the kind of store you envision.

How to Research Your Potential Market

Your plan may specify millions of customers or only ten, but no matter how many you expect to have, you must learn a great deal about them. You will find some sources for consumer data later in this chapter if you are targeting a broad market, but you can also commission or carry out your own research to test potential consumer reaction to your concept. As discussed later in this chapter, you can accomplish this through phone surveys, in-person interviews, or consumer focus groups. This can be very expensive if you hire a professional research company, so try to invest some of your own time by speaking directly with members of your target group.

The smaller and more tightly defined your target market is, the more likely your plan will grow into a successful business. Identifying the most likely purchasers of your product or service will produce the greatest returns on your marketing expenditures, so make the target definition as specific as possible.

Narrowing and describing the target market will help you tailor your marketing campaign effectively and efficiently. Research can define your target market in some of the following ways:

- **Geographically,** so you can locate near your customers, position yourself against the neighboring competition, or advertise to reach customers efficiently.
- **Demographically,** by factors such as age, gender, and ethnicity, so you can focus your marketing efforts and make your product or service appealing to your customers. Age, gender and ethnicity provide powerful ways to describe virtually any market because tastes, media usage and consumption patterns usually vary greatly by demographic groups.
- **Psychographically,** so you can determine your customers' values and attitudes and understand how your market thinks and feels about your product or service. If you know that most people who like your line of exercise equipment consider themselves serious football fans, then you know you can reach them by advertising on televised games or in sports magazines and catch their attention by using a football player as a spokesman.
- **Seasonally,** so you can focus your marketing efforts when buying is most likely to occur. Seasonal patterns are a powerful tool in understanding your market and planning how to reach them. For example, it is not unusual for December sales to exceed 25% of the annual sales for many stores and categories of products, such as toys. Some florists do 15% of their yearly business on Valentine's Day.
- **Based on buying patterns,** such as knowing products or services that tend to be bought at the same time, so you can tie your marketing to theirs. Battery manufacturers run joint marketing programs with flashlight companies, and some even market flashlights themselves. It is likely that the success of satellite radio companies will depend on the effectiveness of their joint marketing programs with car manufacturers—just as Motorola's success in the 1940s depended on its first great product, the car radio.

Understanding buyers' motivations enables you to design your marketing so it appeals to your potential customers. If you have a business that manufacturers glassware, it would be useful to know if customers will buy your product for their vacation homes, from the bridal registries of young engaged couples, or as a basic to purchase anytime because of its blend of functionalism, design, and price. Knowing that customers believe your product can bestow status—as Rolls-Royce cars or Rolex watches do—will help you make the right decisions about designing, packaging, pricing, and marketing.

Researching Your Competitors and Their Marketing Efforts

You must also understand your competition and their marketing in order to determine how you will position and market your own product or service. For each competitor you can:

- Collect their printed or Web site promotional materials.
- Record their broadcast advertising and estimate their advertising expenditures.
- Develop a profile of their customers based on industry research, interviews with experts, or by simply watching and recording the characteristics of people who enter their stores.
- Create a comprehensive study of their product line, including each product's characteristics, target market, and price.
- Create a corporate history that details each competitor's marketing history, including both the successful and failed strategies they have employed.

Reviewing the history of your industry will help you understand the major trends. For example, the food industry witnessed significant changes due to the rise in dual income households. Increased income reduced the demand for traditional food products that require lots of preparation time and increased the demand for prepared foods that can be put on the table quickly. Our aging population has encouraged the health club industry to offer low impact exercise equipment that works the cardiovascular system, but is gentle on aging joints. Understanding the history and trends in your industry will help you position and market your business effectively.

Information about pricing, profit margins, bank lending practices, and investor commitments can be enormously useful in building your financial projections. You will learn how to create a detailed financial model in Chapter 9, but at this point, know that information based on actual research will always instill more confidence in your projections than assumptions based solely on your own judgment.

Test Before You Launch

You will increase the effectiveness of your marketing strategy if you actually test your concepts first. A successful test will also greatly increase the confidence potential investors will have in your plan. This test could take the form of a small mailing to prospective customers asking them if they would order your product once it's available, or making sales calls on prospective customers and seeing their reactions.

Remember that your plan must convince readers of the efficacy of your idea. There is a Harvard Business School case study on the startup of *Parenting* magazine, which shows the plan that the founder of the business, Robin Wolaner, used to attract investors. The plan is thorough and sensible, but the most convincing part is the results of the test mailing to young parents describing the magazine and asking them to subscribe. These results clearly showed that a larger mailing would attract enough subscribers to make the magazine successful, which is exactly what happened. In the *Parenting* magazine case, the mailing was itself a significant expenditure. If your budget doesn't allow for that, there are still many alternatives:

- **Arrange to put sample products** in stores to see how they sell.
- **Make sales calls on prospective clients or customers**, and ask them if they will commit to buying as soon as your business is up and running.
- **Interview potential customers** and industry experts to solicit their opinions of your business idea.
- **Study the performance** of close competitors. This can include counting the foot traffic into their stores, estimating their revenue from public databases such as Dun and Bradstreet, or from private sources such as lawyers, accountants, or past employees.
- **Run your own research program** with focus groups, consisting of approximately a dozen consumers in your target group, at which you discuss your proposed products or services.

- **Talk to customers** of a business you are planning to buy to find out how satisfied they are with the products or services they currently receive, and what ideas they have for improvements.

Careful testing will give you useful information about how the market will view your product or service, and it will add considerable credibility to your plan.

Focus on Research: Is Business-to-Business Advertising Different from Consumer Advertising? The Value of Analyzing the Content of Advertisements

Most people believe that business-to-business advertising differs in important ways from consumer advertising. They perceive it as being more rationally based, more concerned with customized services and products, and addressing more complex issues.[6] If this is true, then the content of advertising aimed at business-to-business markets would likely be less emotional, with a strong focus on technical benefits and price.

I.W. Turley and Scott W. Kelley,[7] professors of marketing at the University of Kentucky, set out to test these notions by analyzing the content of ads that ran in leading national business magazines, and then comparing the messages of ads aimed at consumers with the content of ads that were targeted to businesses. This type of analysis, called "content analysis," is a very inexpensive, yet effective way to quantify differences in written documents such as memos, annual reports, or advertising.[8]

Content analysis is carried out by reading the text of an ad and breaking it down into components, such as frequently used words and themes, as well as having readers make judgments about the overall impression it gives[9]. Using a similar approach, it is possible to study the messages your competitors are sending. This may give you a great deal of insight into how they are trying to convince consumers to buy their products.

When Turley and Kelley carried out content analysis of consumer and business-to-business advertisements to see if, in fact, the appeals were different, their findings were surprising. Although business-to-business ads were generally more rational and consumer ads were generally more emotional in their appeal, both categories focused on claims of product quality, price information, and Web site addresses in equal amounts.

This study is important for entrepreneurs who are trying to define their markets precisely and market to each potential customer group in the most cost effective way possible. The reasons are twofold: 1) It demonstrates that for products and services sold to both consumers and businesses, virtually the same message can be delivered to both groups; and 2) it shows how a simple research technique can be used to define and understand how your competitors are crafting their message to various markets, and to test whether you should follow their marketing approach or take a different—and perhaps better—one.

Library Resources

Plan on spending at least one entire day in the library, preferably a business library. Electronic databases have revolutionized the process of research, and making the time to read material carefully will turn up useful information. The specifics of your industry will determine which resources will be the most fruitful.

Look for industry-related magazines, newsletters, and journals as well as databases. General business publications such as *The Wall Street Journal*, *Forbes*, and *Business Week* cover almost every industry and frequently profile individual businesses within a particular field. Academic journals may not make the most entertaining reading, but they publish articles about a vast number of subjects, including studies which may use samples of businesses in your industry and contain relevant research.

Business Resource Centers

There are many government supported business resource centers. Small Business Development Centers (SBDCs) are part of the federal Small Business Administration (SBA) and they maintain useful information about local markets, access to data on virtually every industry, and sample business plans. Many state and local governments have business resource centers for the purpose of encouraging businesses to locate in their areas. Staff members are often very knowledgeable about data sources on the local economy and business environment.

The Web—Useful but not Comprehensive

The good news is that there is a huge amount of information available on the Web. The bad news is that you cannot make the Web the keystone of your research efforts. In the next section, you'll find a list of the most useful sites, including the SBA and the United States Census Bureau. Industry associations in your particular field may also maintain helpful sites. Beyond that, you are venturing into potentially dangerous areas.

Keep in mind that virtually every Web site is installed by a person or organization with an agenda to sell something, influence government policy, or publicize someone. The facts and data are secondary to this purpose. In addition, the sources of the data are often not stated, and, even if they are, an independent Web site may not be playing by the same rules as established, well-respected data sources you can find in the library—for free.

Demographic, Industry, and Company Databases

Some databases available on the Web or through business libraries are especially valuable because their data is of high quality and breadth and can be customized to serve individual business plans. These sources include:

- *The United States Census Bureau*, `www.census.gov`, carries out billions of dollars worth of high-quality research on populations, industries, employment, and ethnic groups, most of which is available for all localities throughout the United States. The Census Bureau also publishes many industry reports that are available on their Web site.

- *The United States Small Business Administration* maintains a large site at `www.sba.gov` that has a great deal of industry-specific information and links to many other sources. It includes industry reports, financing worksheets, and background on government programs. It is somewhat cumbersome to navigate, but worth the time. Some of the same information is available more directly through another SBA site called the U.S. Small Business Advisor at `www.business.gov`.

- *The Survey of Consumers* carried out by the University of Michigan has interviewed at least 500 U.S. consumers per month since 1946. The survey asks consumers how they view their own financial situations, how they regard the economy both in the long and short term, and the likelihood of their purchasing homes, large household items, and vehicles. Their Web site is: `www.sca.isr.umich.edu/main.php`

- *Choices II* (formerly called *Simmons*), and *Mediamark Reporter* (MRI), provide statistical data from an annual survey of 25,000 adults, and can be used for target marketing, media planning, and strategic advertising. The statistical data covers demographics, attitudes, product usage, and media exposure. It is available through business libraries that subscribe to its online database.

- *Statistical Abstract of the United States* is a gateway to over 250 statistical publications and sources from government and private organizations. It is available at `www.census.gov/statab`.

- *American Statistics Index* (ASI) and *Statistical Reference Index* (SRI) are gateways to over 1,000 statistical publications of private and state government sources. *The Index to International Statistics* (IIS) is a similar gateway to 2,000 titles from 100 international intergovernmental organizations. All of these require subscriptions to access, but most business libraries have them.

- *The A.C. Nielsen Company* and *The Arbitron Company* produce media and consumer studies, including their well known ratings systems for both television (Nielsen) and radio (Arbitron). Some of these reports are available through subscribing libraries in print or online form.

- *The Encyclopedia of Associations* published by Gale-Thomson is available in book form or on the Web through libraries that subscribe to it. It is a good place to find out if your industry has an association that might publish industry background information.

- *Thomson Register of American Manufacturers,* also published by Gale-Thomson, is available in book form or free on the Web at www.thomsonregister.com. If you are looking for potential suppliers for your business, it is an efficient place to begin.

- *Hoovers.com,* at www.hoovers.com, provides company and industry data and various useful links. Some information is provided at no charge; other data is provided on a fee basis.

- *Financial and Operating Results of Department and Speciality Stores,* published by the National Retail Merchants Association, is an annual presentation of detailed financial information on member retail stores that provides useful guidance and comparisons.

- Other ways to search the vast array of government offerings include the *Catalog of Federal Domestic Assistance* at www.cfda.gov, the *Government Printing Office* at www.gpo.gov, FedStats at www.fedstats.gov, *First Gov* at www.firstgov.com (which also offers state and local information), and the *National Associations of Counties* at www.naco.org/counties.

- *The Securities and Exchange Commission* site, at www.sec.gov/edgar.html, provides fast access to all public company filings. Information on public companies in your industry can provide good background or comparisons with your own plans. *Quicken* (www.quicken.com) and *CNNfn* (www.cnnfn.com) offers current and historical financial information on publicly-owned companies.

- General business background information is available through www.factiva.com which is the site for searching the *Reuters* and *Dow Jones* business publications. *LexisNexis* at www.lexisnexis.com offers data from public records, newspapers, and magazines. *Standard and Poor's* has various industry reports at its site, www.standardandpoors.com. You can use all three of these sites for free at a library that subscribes to these services, or for a fee you pay yourself on the Web.

- *Kompass* at www.kompass.com provides product and contact information for 1.7 million companies throughout the world. It is searchable using their own product classification.

- *Economy.com* at www.economy.com/freelunch offers links to nearly a million sources of economic and financial data on industries, consumers, and government statistics.

- Many libraries offer information directly over the Web, or provide links to business references. Among the better ones are:
  - *The Library of Congress* at http://lcweb.loc.gov
  - *U.S. Public Libraries on the Web* at http://sunsite.berkeley.edu/Libweb/Public _ main.html
  - The New York Public Library at www.nypl.org
  - *The American Library Association* guide to Best Business Web sites at www.ala.org/rusa/brass/besthome.html
  - *The Librarian's Index to the Internet* at www.lii.org/

With so many sources of quality data available, you can make your business plan both bankable and convincing.

The Entrepreneur's Toolkit: Interviewing Techniques, Focus Groups, and Survey Research

Entrepreneurs collect a great deal of information about their concepts through many one-on-one conversations with potential customers, partners, funders, and industry experts. Being able to engage in conversations that lead to *the exchange of the greatest amount of truthful information on topics of importance to the other person* is the goal. Here are some guidelines for holding productive interviews:

Interviewing

- **Listen, don't talk.** You may be so enthusiastic about your idea that you cannot control your urge to speak, but every minute you talk is a minute less that you are learning from the person whose opinion you're soliciting.

- **Keep your opinions to yourself.** The purpose of the interview is to find out what someone else truthfully thinks about your idea. People have a natural tendency to agree with each other, so when you communicate your opinions, the responses you hear tend to be biased.
- **Prepare a list of questions.** You will have a great deal to think about during the conversation, but you want to remain focused. A list of questions will keep you from becoming distracted or wandering away from your topic.
- **Have a list of questions, but not a script.** The conversation may go off in many unexpected, but productive directions which might uncover important information. If you rigidly stick to a list of prepared questions, you will not uncover this significant, but unexpected information.
- **Take notes or record the interview.** Don't expect to be able to reconstruct the conversation later from memory. People are usually flattered that you want to remember their exact words and will not mind the presence of a tape recorder—if you ask first—or a notebook and pencil.
- **Pick the right spot.** Places with few distractions, such as conference rooms, are best. If you meet in someone else's office or in a restaurant, signal your commitment to reducing interruptions by turning off your cell phone and leaving it on the table.
- **Give it enough time.** It is impossible to predict how long an interview will take, so budget time generously and tell the other person how much time you will need. For the vast majority of interviews, 30 minutes is a reasonable amount of time.
- **Phone interviews are just fine.** There are pluses and minuses to phone interviews. It is easier and cheaper to reach people by phone rather than by traveling to a meeting. Many people are more comfortable disagreeing with someone over the phone than in person. On the minus side, it is harder to build an attitude of trust between people on the phone, interruptions are difficult to avoid, and the person you are interviewing can readily end the call.

Focus Groups

The focus group or consumer panel is an easy and inexpensive way to carry out quality research on almost any subject. Focus groups typically consist of a group of 10 to 20 people who sit around a table and discuss topics present before them by a moderator. They are not a replacement for survey research, in which interviews with many people reveal answers that are more representative of a larger population, but focus groups can provide an excellent way to learn how consumers think about a product, what language they use to describe it, and how they react to specific concepts. Focus groups can also help define the questions you might want to use later in a survey[10] and they can uncover the subjects that consumers feel most strongly about[11]. Typically, the process runs like this:

- **A set of research topics are developed,** including consumer opinions about various businesses, their reactions to new concepts, and their thoughts about specific marketing campaigns.
- **A group of participants are recruited** who fit a profile of people most likely to be knowledgeable and helpful. This might include people who are heavy users of the product you are researching or who fit the key demographic group of your target market.
- **The focus group has a moderator** who will pose questions and solicit more information from all group members. The moderator must be completely non-judgmental, obtain opinions from all of the group members equally, and raise topics of concern to the business being discussed.
- **The sponsor of the focus groups is not directly revealed** because this could bias responses. Usually the participants are told a research company is doing work for a business, the identify of which has not even been revealed to the group moderator[12].
- **Focus group members are usually paid** for their participation. These payments typically vary from $20 to $100 depending on the difficulty of recruiting participants and how much time the focus group will take.

- **The groups meet in a central, well-known location** such as a hotel or conference center.
- **It is good to run several groups** because group opinions can often be steered by a small number of participants or even by one individual with a strong opinion[13].

Survey Research

Survey research that reaches a large sample of people is generally a complex, time-consuming, and expensive process. But it is also probably the best way to research your market. The process follows these steps:

- **Create a sample of the population** you wish to survey. This could be a phone, e-mail, or address list, or a list of street corners to stand on and ask people to participate.
- **Design a formal questionnaire** that is long enough to cover the issues you need addressed, but short enough so that people will participate. When questionnaires take longer than 20 minutes, response rates drop. The questionnaire has to include scales such as "a great amount" to "none" or number scales from 1, meaning "strongly disagree" to 7, meaning "strongly agree."
- **Enter the data that is collected** in an easily-tallied data-analysis software system.
- **Run an analysis of the answers,** including comparisons among various groups.
- **Use a large enough sample** so that the results are meaningful on a statistical basis.

While carrying out survey research is usually regarded as off limits to all but a few new ventures—those with lots of money— it is possible for a hard-working entrepreneur to produce meaningful results at a reasonable cost.[14, 15]

CASE ON POINT

MOUNTAIN MAN DECIDES TO OPEN A BOXING GYM

After a successful amateur boxing career that including being a Golden Gloves and state champion, "Mountain Man" Martin Snow, a native of Brooklyn—a city with nary a hill—faced the decision about whether to become a professional. Martin decided he would probably have a longer, healthier, and happier life if he retired from the ring and put his enthusiasm for boxing into teaching the sport in his own gym. Martin realized that virtually all boxing gyms scared away most prospective customers who simply wanted to have fun, learn about boxing, and get a healthy workout. Martin's idea was to open a gym that would reflect the colorful history of boxing, but make everyone from serious boxers to male and female business executives feel welcome and comfortable.

After Martin looked at a suitable space, the enormity and risk of this undertaking hit him like a right uppercut. The landlord was asking $8,000 per month and wanted a three-month deposit because it was a new business. The space had been used as a warehouse for a stationery supply company so it needed extensive work to be converted into a gym. Bathrooms, showers, locker rooms, ventilation systems, and lighting had to be installed. Necessary purchases were major, including boxing rings, punching bags, aerobic equipment, and weights. Martin would need a computer system for tracking and billing customers, and his staff would require training to use it effectively. But he didn't have a staff or know how many people he would actually need.

Martin had no idea how many customers he could entice into the gym or how he should market his concept to attract people. He hadn't a clue as to how much he could charge or how to structure his fees. Should he offer a yearly membership with additional costs for training in small groups or individually? All the boxing gyms Martin knew only trained people who wanted to be serious boxers, but his market would be quite different—he just didn't know how to reach them.

As Martin pondered his situation, he really didn't know what questions to ask first, or second, or third. He felt strongly that his concept would work, but he didn't know how to refine the idea and prove to himself and others that it could be a successful business.

CASE QUESTIONS:

1. How should Martin research the potential market geographically and demographically?
2. If you were to run a focus group with potential clients for Martin's boxing gym what questions would you ask them and what issues would you want discussed?

End of Chapter Questions

1. What characteristics of a marketing plan will help lead to a successful business?
2. How can markets be segmented to help an entrepreneur define a target market?
3. What types of resources and databases are likely to be most valuable for researching your business idea?
4. How can entrepreneurs use interviews, surveys, and focus groups to learn more about their markets?

NOTES

1. Thomas Oliver. *The Real Coke, The Real Story*, (New York: Random House, 1985).
2. James Barron, "Fans of Old Coke Say the New Is Not In," *New York Times,* June 12, 1985. p. A16.
3. Kenneth N. Gilpin, "'Old' Coke Coming Back After Outcry by Faithful; Old Formula of Coke Is Being Revived," *New York Times,* July 11, 1985. p. A1.
4. Robert M. Schindler, "The Real Lesson of the New Coke: The Value of Focus Groups for Predicting the Effects of Social Influence," *Marketing Research*, Vol. 4, No. 4, (December 1992), pp. 22–28.
5. Chad Terhune, "PepsiCo Sees Rise in U.S. Market Share," *Wall Street Journal.* (Eastern edition). March 5, 2004. p. A.12.
6. Philip D. Cooper and Ralph W. Jackson, "Applying a Service Marketing Orientation to the Industrial Services Sector," *Journal of Services Marketing*, Vol. 2, No.4, (July, 1988), pp. 67–70.
7. I.W. Turley and Scott W. Kelley, "A Comparison of Advertising Content: Business-to-Business versus Consumer Services," *Journal of Advertising,* Vol. XXVI, No. 4, (September 1997). pp. 39–48.
8. Barbara B. Stern, "What Does an Ad Mean? Language in Service Advertising," *Journal of Advertising*, Vol. 17, No. 2, (July 1988), pp. 3–14.
9. Harold H. Kassarjian, "Content Analysis in Consumer Research," *Journal of Consumer Research*, Vol. 60, No. 3, (July, 1977), pp. 58–68.
10. Edward Fern, "The Use of Focus Groups for Idea Generation: The Effects of Group Size, Acquaintanceship, and Moderator on Response Quantity and Quality," *Journal of Marketing Research*, Vol.19, No. 1 (February, 1982), pp. 1–13.
11. John A. Ledingham and Stephen D. Bruning. *Ten Tips for Better Focus Groups, Public Relations Quarterly*, Winter 1998-1999, pp. 25–28.
12. Angela Sinikas, "Getting the Most out of Focus Groups," *Total Communication Measurement* Vol 2, Issue 4, (April 2000) p. 11.
13. Holly Edmunds. *The Focus Group Research Handbook*, (Chicago: The American Marketing Association, 1999).
14. Peter M. Nardi. *Doing Survey Research: A Guide to Quantitative Methods*, (Boston: Allyn and Bacon, 2003).
15. Floyd J. Fowler, Jr. *Survey Research Methods,* 3rd Edition, (Thousand Oaks, CA: Sage Publications, 2002).

CHAPTER 5

ISSUE 5: DEVELOP A MARKETING CAMPAIGN

WHAT THEY DID RIGHT: HARLEY-DAVIDSON RISES FROM THE ASHES

From the time the company produced its first motorcycle in 1900, Harley-Davidson quickly grew to become one of the major manufacturers of motorcycles and one of the great American name brands. Yet by 1981 the wheels were just about to wobble off the Harley-Davidson company. Its market share had crumbled to a mere 3% in the face of competition from Japanese manufacturers of lighter, more reliable, and cheaper motorcycles.[1]

The Harley-Davidson reputation was being eroded by the failing quality of its motorcycles and by the unsanctioned use of its name and logo. As *Forbes* reported in 1983, "When your company's logo is the number one requested in tattoo parlors, it's time to get a licensing program that will return your reputation to the ranks of baseball, hot dogs, and apple pie."[2]

AMF, the sports-oriented conglomerate that had owned Harley-Davidson since 1970 and absorbed more than $50 million in losses, decided to call it quits. They put Harley-Davidson up for sale. A management team led by Vaughan Beals bought Harley-Davidson from AMF and refinanced the company with $81.5

million in debt and equity financing from Citicorp, which enabled the company to invest in design, operating, and marketing improvements.

With the help of politicians from its home state of Wisconsin, Harley-Davidson won a five-year increase in federal tariffs from 4% to 45% on imports of motorcycles from Japan. The company argued that it needed this help to get back on its feet and place its cost structure and product quality in line with its Japanese competitors.

Beals confronted the operating issues by improving morale and creating functioning management systems. Quality improved, costs declined, and the brand name was treated—and protected—as the valuable asset that it was. Over the next decade, demand for Harley-Davidson motorcycles dramatically increased and often pushed retail prices above the sticker price. A line of carefully chosen and controlled consumer items, such as leather jackets, were selected to carry the Harley-Davidson name, many of which were sold in stores built into the dealerships. The profile of customers changed accordingly. By 1990, *The Wall Street Journal* reported that 60% of Harley-Davidson customers were college educated, and one of every three customers was a professional.[3]

The financial transformation was nothing short of incredible. The company went from sales of $210 million and a loss of $25 million in 1982 to sales of $1.1 billion and profits of $54 million in 1992. By 2003, Harley-Davidson had almost $5 billion in revenues and profits of $760 million. The company's stock had gone from $7 per share in 1990, when it went public to repay venture capital investors, to $60 per share in 2004. The turnaround was complete.

Harley-Davidson's remarkable recovery defines the power of brand names. After years of neglect and mismanagement, there was little of value left in the company but the Harley-Davidson name. But that name was the foundation of the strategy the new management used to reconnect with customers and polish the company's tarnished image. The turnaround created dramatic improvements in operations, finance, and marketing, but without the strong brand name, it could not have happened.

Many entrepreneurs believe that the superiority of their products or services will attract all the customers they will ever need. But the only businesses with excellent products or services that survive are those that define their markets carefully, create an effective plan for reaching them, develop an efficient means for distribution, and set a price that customers are willing to pay. You have already defined what your company will do, what its fundamental strategy will be, and you have researched the market you hope to reach. The next step in creating a bankable business plan—and often of business success—is deciding how to reach your customers and sell them your product or service through a strong marketing campaign.

Every bankable business plan must include an effective marketing strategy in which you describe how you will reach your customers and what you will say to them. This is the portion of the business plan that convinces lenders and investors that you will be able to gain market share, generate revenue, and bring your financial projections to fruition.

Marketing describes the way you will position your product or service within your targeted market and how you will let your potential customers know about your company. There are several highly successful companies that are based on little more than a strong marketing campaign. Nike, the shoe and athletic-wear giant, owns no manufacturing plants and only a few stores and warehouses. It contracts with factories around the world to make its products, which are shipped directly to retailers such as WalMart and Macy's. Nike creates the brands, markets the products to potential customers to create demand, and arranges for distribution to retailers. Instead of owning supermarkets for shoes, Nike is a super marketer of shoes.

Real estate companies such as Century 21 do not own the properties they sell, they don't provide financing, and they don't build houses. They are, in effect, contract marketers for people who do own houses and want to sell them. Most retailers are marketing organizations. They manufacture little or nothing of what they sell. The key to their success is finding a good location, creating an attractive atmosphere, choosing the right mix of products to sell, pricing their items competitively, and delivering excellent service. These are all marketing functions.

The 4 Ps of Marketing

Strong marketing plans are based on what are termed the 4 Ps:

1. The **product** or service you will sell.
2. The **price** you will charge.
3. The **place** you sell from, or how your product or service will be distributed.
4. The **promotion** and advertising you will employ to communicate with potential customers.

Let's examine each of the 4 Ps in greater detail:

PRODUCT

Your plan needs to present compelling reasons for why customers will want to purchase your product or service. Some of the most convincing reasons are:

Convenience. Domino's Pizza is built entirely on making it easier and faster to eat pizza through a superior delivery service. Cellular telephones deliver convenience by eliminating the wire so their customers can carry their phones with them.

New Functions. It is rare when a completely new product emerges, but don't let that discourage you. Thomas Alva Edison succeeded with the light bulb and the record player. More recent revolutionary products include e-mail, PDAs, DVD players, and iPods.

New Applications. Many people have built successful businesses by simply finding one more use for a computer during those idle hours when it sits on someone's desk. Video games, calendar functions, and spreadsheet programs are new applications for an existing product. The Sony Walkman was developed as a pocket memo and dictation machine for businesspeople, but found a much bigger application and audience by playing music.

Improved Performance. A product may be more attractive to customers by being nosier (motorcycles), quieter (dishwashers), smelling better (deodorant), or not smelling at all (deodorant). Successful marketing is based on improving the performance or characteristics of a product in the minds of consumers.

Quality. Consumers usually have a strong opinion about what constitutes quality in a product or service. Food with better ingredients, cars that are reliable and have a "solid" feel, or stereo systems that sound more like live music are all examples of how quality can be perceived and promoted.

Status. Rolex, Jaguar, Dom Perignon champagne, Versace, and Sub-Zero are all products marketed, in part, on their status appeal, which means that the prestige of the product rubs off on the purchaser.

Packaging. How a product is packaged draws attention and sends a message to consumers. Big packages, such as jumbo plastic laundry detergent jugs, shout "value." Small packages, such as concentrated laundry detergent in recyclable cardboard boxes, stress "convenience" and "environmental responsibility." Pharmaceutical companies often repackage medications in "extra strength" formulas, which are really just two pills squeezed into one, thus creating new life for old products.

Appearance and Styling. The automobile industry has thrived for decades on minor styling changes to create demand for new cars. Flashy fins in the 1960's didn't change the function or performance of the car—just the appearance. They also made last year's models look out-of-date. Now that computers are commonplace, styling is playing a more significant role. Does a see-through computer case turn you on? Is gel toothpaste a new product or just a styling change?

High Switching Costs. Many products achieve dominance because the time and money involved in changing to a new product are high. Microsoft benefits from this advantage because customers don't want to endure the time-consuming and risky process of changing their computers to a different operating system.

Remember that you don't need to have a revolutionary product to create a successful product. In fact, it may be just the contrary. Entrepreneurs with truly revolutionary ideas often have trouble recruiting the resources they need. Alexander Graham Bell had a great deal of trouble recruiting investors to back his newfangled device, the telephone. Then he had significant difficulty getting businesses and individuals to adopt it. Sometimes the most compelling product idea is one that employs a widely-used and accepted product, but which only changes slightly or becomes easier to obtain. John D. Rockefeller, the founder of what is now ExxonMobil, didn't invent oil; he set up a system to control its manufacture and distribution. Ray Kroc, who built McDonald's, didn't invent hamburgers, fast service, or even the orginal McDonald's; he took an existing business and grew it dramatically.

PRICE

Pricing your product or service is an important element in your plan that investors, bankers, and partners will scrutinize carefully. There are many approaches to pricing because price has strong effects on demand, consumer perception, competitive position, and company profitability. Just as your marketing plan must fit within your business plan, your approach to pricing your products must reinforce your marketing plan.

One major approach to pricing is to vary price during the product life cycle:

- When a new product is first introduced, a high price can be set to "skim" the most eager buyers. This market skimming strategy is often used in consumer electronics and fashion. After those customers who are willing to pay the most have been served, the manufacturer wants to appeal to a broader market and lowers the price.

- An alternative strategy, called *market penetration pricing,* prices on new products are set low to capture the largest possible market share quickly. Store-opening specials and introductory offers to sign up for services such as cable television are common examples of this strategy.
- Older products in declining industries are sometimes priced at high levels because they have little competition. Vacuum tubes, buggy whips, and century-old style fixtures for Victorian houses are all available, but at high prices.

Another pricing approach focuses on the competition: see what they charge and set your price around theirs. If you want your product viewed as higher quality, you might charge somewhat more. If you want to attract those buyers who are sensitive to price, you might charge somewhat less. Some industries have relatively standard "keystoning" formulas for product markups: Along the supply chain in the clothing industry, for example, manufacturers, distributors, and retailers may all have typical markup formulas.

Since businesses exist to make profits, it is certainly reasonable to set a price that will result in maximum profits. This involves finding the right number between a high skimming price and a low market-penetration price that makes the company as profitable as possible. This price for maximum profit will vary for different businesses or products based upon the company's capacity, and the additional cost of producing each unit, which is called *marginal cost.*

Another strategy is to divide the market into segments and set different prices for each. The goal of this strategy is to charge each segment the most it will pay. Airlines do this by charging a low price to vacation travelers who book early, and a very low price to passengers on standby, and a much higher price to business travelers who make last minute arrangements. The lowest prices go to tour operators who buy in bulk for groups.

Switching costs also figure in setting prices. Hewlett-Packard printers have been able to maintain a very high market share and be very profitable. The printers are high quality and competitively priced. When the consumer starts spending on expensive replacement cartridges, he realizes the full cost of the printer. Hewlett-Packard, however, prices the cartridges below the point at which most consumers would invest in a new printer. The initial price is competitive, but once switching costs become a factor to consumers, Hewlett-Packard's price is actually relatively high.

Most people assume that a lower price is always better, simply because we are so conditioned to look for lower prices as consumers. But before you select a low price for your product or service, think about some of the implications:

- **It is much more difficult to raise prices than to lower them.** If you price your product too low and can't make a profit, you may not be able to raise prices quickly enough to save your business.
- **Low prices sometimes send a message of low quality to buyers.** Do shoppers expect to find high-quality products in 99¢ stores?
- **You need to make a profit.** Quite simply, your business plan won't work if you can't earn money. Choosing a price that will attract customers in droves won't be enough if you don't show a profit.
- **Selecting too low a price may hurt your ability to be profitable** without proving to be a big competitive advantage. If you have a patent, copyright, or license that protects you from competition, you may be able to charge more without your competition being able to match your prices.
- **Price may not be a big part of your competitive advantage.** Some other product characteristic or part of your service delivery may be the major competitive advantage of your business. Picking too low a price could hurt your bottom line without generating much additional revenue.
- **Price is the key factor for marketing commodity-type products** such as rice, chemicals, or bank savings accounts because purchasers see few differences of quality. Companies that sell such products often focus their marketing appeal based on service, location, or delivery, but being the low-price producer remains the most important determinant of their success.

The task in planning price is to make it an integral part of your venture's overall strategy. This includes the position you want your product or service to occupy in consumers' minds, the financial implications, the supply issues and the competitive advantages. There is no one right price all the time, but there is a best price for your product or service at any particular time.

Place

Where you open your business or how you distribute your products, is often overlooked in the marketing campaign portion of a business plan. When an industry consultant once announced to a packed convention audience that "publishing is fundamentally a distribution business," people were shocked. What about great books, glowing reviews, beautiful stores, and word-of-mouth? Well, he explained, those are important elements, but they mean little if the books aren't in the stores when customers want to buy them. If too few books are distributed, no one can buy. Too many books, and the store and publisher end up deeply discounting the title, placing it in the remainder bin and losing money.

Consider the impact place and distribution will have on your marketing campaign by thinking about these questions:

- How will your customer obtain your product or service?
- How do your competitors distribute? Do they use wholesalers and distributors as middlemen?
- Have your competitors "locked up" all the established distribution channels, making it hard for you to reach your customers?
- Is there an alternative distribution channel available, such as the Internet, discount retailers, or direct-to-consumer advertising that could give you an advantage?
- How will you manage distribution so that you know where your products are and what areas are experiencing shortages?
- How will you focus your distribution? The most likely markets, certain geographic areas, or areas where your competitors are weak?

Your Web Site

Just about every business needs a Web site, and your Web site should be an integral part of your bankable business plan. Your investors, partners, lenders and anyone else who reads your plan will want to know that you will take full advantage of the opportunities afforded by the Internet. There are a vast number of options for your venture's Web site. The costs vary just as widely. Your plan for your Web site should include these elements:

Define your Web site's purpose. Your Web site can be informational to communicate your company's location, its history, or the services you provide. The site might also be designed to service existing customers by allowing them to make appointments or check their accounts. The site could be a virtual store which handles selling functions directly. Alternatively, the site might be intended to convert prospects into customers by promoting your business and encouraging them to call or visit your physical location.

Commit to a professional design. People will judge you and your business based on your Web site, so it must look professional and make a strong first impression. Web sites are great tools for new and growing businesses because even small businesses can look big on the Internet. But that also places a burden on you to have a site that is just as professional, credible, and well-functioning as your competitors. Creating that Web site requires a team that includes a designer, who lays out the site for function and gives it a visual style, and a programmer who will convert the design into computer code. Stating your intention to create a strong site and identifying who will be the members of your online team should be part of your bankable business plan.

Maintain a system for tracking. Every click on a Web site by every visitor is recorded and tallied. This provides a great trove of information that you can use to measure the performance of your site, see how visitors are navigating the site, and help you to improve it. Your home page functions are your store window and the better they are, the more people will enter this virtual store to explore, learn, and buy. The company that hosts your site can track all these patterns and allow you to access this data whenever you want. Your bankable business plan should discuss specifically how you will employ the information about your site's performance and how committed you are to updating and improving your site continuously.

Market your site. There are literally billions of Web sites, so your bankable business plan must include a marketing campaign for "driving traffic" to your site. People find Web sites through search engines such as Google and Yahoo!, by bookmarking them from previous visits, from links at other sites, and by learning about them from advertising. Putting your Web site's address on all your printed materials and on all retail store signs, as well as mentioning it on radio and television ads, and negotiating links from other sites will greatly improve the effectiveness of your Web site.

Develop e-mail campaigns. Building a list of the e-mail addresses of your existing and potential customers opens up the door to marketing via e-mail. While people detest uninvited e-mail or spam, e-mail from businesses they have invited or approved is highly effective and inexpensive. Your marketing plan will benefit from specific ideas for using e-mail as a tool. You will be able to track the percentage of people who open your e-mail, how many potential customers click through to your site from your e-mail, and how many of those actually make a purchase.

Promotion

Promotion is how your potential customers find out about your product or service. Promotion might include advertising, news coverage, placement in retail stores, direct mail, word-of-mouth, or dozens of other ways of creating awareness that will lead to demand for your product. Good promotion plans should be specific, with clearly stated goals, and should hold your expenses accountable for the results they produce.

Coupons, free samples, free trial periods, volume purchase discounts, in-store displays, manufacturer's rebates, financial incentives to distributors, contests, and premiums are all examples of sales promotions. During its period of major growth, AOL distributed millions of CDs that gave customers thousands of free hours if they simply tried AOL. Frequent flyer miles and coupons for products sold in supermarkets have become standard promotional tools in their respective industries. Here are some basics that can create an effective promotion plan:

Be specific. Your promotion plan must be precise and detailed. If you intend to use coupons to promote your product, you must explain the terms of the coupon, decide on how it will be distributed, and determine how many coupons you expect to get back.

State your goals. Explain what you expect to accomplish and why you are using this particular means of promotion. Having a product booth at a convention attended by many of your customers is a clear, focused way to reach your market. Many companies that have booths at conventions put on special promotions just for purchases made at the convention to encourage customers to buy before the convention ends.

Hold your expenses accountable. By establishing goals and a system of measurement, you can hold your promotional expenses accountable for the results they produce. If you expect your newspaper ads to bring people into your clothing store, then you need a way of measuring traffic—before, during, and after the ads appear in the paper. With coupons you also need a way to track how many have been distributed and how many are being redeemed. This will allow you to adjust your strategies and prevent you from wasting money on promotional efforts that fail to produce results. It will also impress the readers of your plan.

Create a Central Message. A critical element of an effective marketing campaign is a simple, clear, central message about your product or service. Consumers probably can't list dozens of attributes of products they already use and know well, so you must focus on a few key qualities. When polled, consumers don't describe the experience of shopping in a favorite store with endless florid paragraphs. They say they liked it or not and give only brief descriptions of why.

Some marketing professionals sum up what consumers want in the Five Fs:

1. **Function.** What does the product or service do to meet consumer needs?
2. **Finances.** How does a purchase impact the consumer's finances? These attributes include price, cost savings, and payment plans.
3. **Freedom.** Does the product or service save time for its customers?
4. **Feelings.** How does the product or service affect the customer's self image or sense of well-being?
5. **Future.** Because of your product's reliability, service, or new technology, will the consumer look back on this purchase positively?

A 30-second commercial has about 50 words. After stating your company's name, address, location, and hours of operation, you have about 25 words left to deliver your central message. Draft several sample 25-word messages, see if they reflect your marketing approach, and try them out on some potential customers to make sure they understand them and react positively.

Use advertising effectively. The main tool of promotion is advertising. Television, billboards, radio, newspapers, magazines, the Internet, and even blimps comprise some of the many options for paid advertising. Follow the 4 Ps to make your advertising campaign specific, the results measurable, and the expenditures accountable. Paid advertising can deliver highly quantified measurements of how many people will see or hear your ad.

Advertising is measured in *reach*, which is the number of different people who will see or hear your ad, and *frequency*, which is the average number of times each of those people will see or hear your ad. Reach multiplied by frequency gives you the total number of *impressions* your advertising will make. We are all exposed to dozens, even hundreds of advertising messages daily. Most, quite literally, go in one ear and out the other. So you need to deliver the same message to the same people multiple times—and often in multiple ways—to ensure that your message is received.

Successful advertising requires careful planning and execution. In designing your advertising, these are the steps to follow: Research the competition's advertising, talk with advertising representatives, and develop a focused, accountable campaign.

You probably have noticed every competitor's ads already, much more than their own customers have. Create a table that lists your competitors, where and how they advertise, and what their main messages are, such as price, sales, or features.

Advertising representatives from radio stations, magazines, and other media outlets are a great source of information about your competitors' advertising and your own options. Meet with them, tell them you're developing a media plan and see what the advertising reps suggest. Most will give you specific information about what kinds of advertising have worked best in your industry and how you can develop your own effective advertising strategy.

Take all this information and distill it into the best method of reaching your most important target markets. Your media campaign should include the reach and frequency data that the advertising representatives give you, as well as detailed cost estimates. Describe what you expect to achieve in terms of foot traffic into your store, or calls from potential customers, or name recognition within target markets. Finally, develop your system for tracking results and holding these expenditures accountable.

Develop a Marketing Campaign that Is Financially Sensible and Operationally Reasonable

Some businesspeople view marketing as a luxury and try to keep these expenditures as low as possible. Their businesses are failing to connect with their markets and, as a result, often fail. Other entrepreneurs have such confidence in their product or service that they are sure that all their marketing expenses will create returns many times over. These companies often spend beyond their financial capacity and discover they were overly optimistic about the market's reaction. They, too, are likely to fail in short order.

The entrepreneur must create a marketing campaign that:

- Considers all the relevant information including overall strategic and financial issues.
- Establishes goals that are operationally and financially feasible. Companies can literally grow themselves out of business if they let marketing get ahead of operational or financial capacity to deliver their product to meet the demand their marketing has produced.
- Embodies the best method of reaching your most important target markets.
- Creates specific objectives such as foot traffic into your store, calls from potential customers, or name recognition in target markets.
- Implements a system for tracking results and holding these expenditures accountable such as tallying foot traffic, volume, Web site hits, and sales.

Target Your Market Like a Bull's-Eye

The more tightly defined your target market, the more likely your plan will attract funding sources. Accurately identifying prospective purchasers of your product or service will produce the greatest return on your marketing expenditures.

Suppose your business is Howie's House of Hubcaps, specializing in replacement hubcaps for 1955 to 1960 Chevys. On one hand, you could advertise during the Superbowl, but that would bankrupt you and waste the vast majority of your advertising budget to reach people who don't own 1955 to 1960 Chevys. On the other hand, if your research revealed vintage Chevy clubs that sell ads in their newsletters or would sell you their lists, restorers who specialize in these cars, or annual gatherings of owners of vintage Chevys, you could build an effective marketing program very cheaply. This would make the financials look better and impress your potential investors.

If your plan is to open Bobbie's Sox, a store selling a wide variety of socks, your research might give you information about the age, income, professions, and gender of people who tend to spend the most money on socks. Then you can target your location, store design, inventory choices, and advertising to this segment of the market that purchases the most socks.

Understanding the motivations of your potential customers will help you target customer groups for your marketing strategy. Examples of customer motivation include:

- Low price
- Status
- Quality
- Speed of delivery
- Service
- Design

For example, if you have a glassware manufacturing business, you need to find out what influences your customers. Do they tend to buy your product when they purchase a second home, or rent a new apartment following a divorce? Is it an item that young couples list on their wedding registries? Or do customers view your glassware as a basic product they buy any time because of function, design, and price? Answers to these questions can help you identify the appropriate target market and incorporate its description into your plan. IKEA's research revealed that two of their best markets consisted of people buying country homes outside big cities, and divorcing couples setting up new homes fast. This knowledge helped IKEA to organize its stores, price its products, and plan one of its most memorable and successful promotions: "Starting up or starting over."

A recent Chinese immigrant took note of how often she was sought out by parents in her Brooklyn neighborhood who were raising adopted babies from China. They wanted her advice about how to keep their children connected to their Chinese heritage. She thought there might be a business selling Chinese children's books, language lessons, clothing, and other products to this highly targeted market. Within a short time, she had researched the size and characteristics of the market, talked to many parents in her neighborhood, and communicated with friends in China to estimate the costs of purchasing products for children. Her business became profitable within a few months, which is more than most dot.com business founders can say. Today `www.chinasprout.com` continues to thrive by applying strategies that helped it grow from the initial 100 products sold to its small, original market, to providing over 3,000 products to a much broader market, including retailers, educators and wholesalers.

The Entrepreneur's Toolkit: Ways to Define and Segment Your Market

Dividing your potential customers into groups that can be targeted separately is called *market segmentation.* Market segmentation is a powerful tool for companies and should be a key element in business plans because it:

1. Reduces costs by eliminating marketing expenditures to those customers who are unlikely to purchase.
2. Increases sales by making each dollar of marketing expenditures as productive as possible.
3. Enables the marketing campaign to be tailored to each market segment by focusing on the needs and issues of those particular customers.
4. Targets products and services so they have the greatest appeal to each market segment.

Market segmentation can only be successful when the effectiveness of reaching the targeted group can be measured and the results tracked for profitability. This requires keeping records of sales, store traffic, Web site hits, or phone inquires by day or even hour and comparing these numbers to your advertising and promotional activities.

The many ways to segment markets include:

- Age
- Gender
- Ethnicity
- Income
- Education
- Geographic location
- Profession
- Product usage rates
- Media habits
- Religion
- Political orientation
- Family status
- Sexual orientation
- Self-concept

- Purchasing patterns by time, such as holidays or family events
- Past product purchasing patterns
- Attitudes and values on issues, such as the environment, savings, or consumption
- Personality characteristics, such as sociability, adaptability, or aggressiveness

When market segments are defined so that the targeted groups become quite small, they are referred to as *niches*. The following example defines a niche market:

Korean women wear traditional dresses for special occasions. A business in Los Angeles that sells traditional Korean dresses would have the following target market: women between the ages of 25 and 49, born in Korea or in the United States of Korean ancestry, who live in Los Angeles, are married with children, and whose families have annual incomes of over $50,000, and own minivans. Why define the market this way?

The answer is because women over 49 probably already own one or more traditional dresses, while younger women are still buying them. The dresses are expensive, so women from families with higher-than-average incomes are more apt to buy them. Married women with children are more oriented toward family events and, therefore, are more likely to have a need for traditional dresses. People who own minivans are probably more family and community oriented.

Utilize Free Media

Business owners love the idea of attracting all kinds of attention to their products or services without having to spend a penny. A good example of this occurred in 2002 when inventor Dean Kamen unveiled his riding device, Segway, The Human Transporter. It attracted huge amounts of attention on the evening news and in newspapers. Companies, such as Amazon.com and Yahoo!, were competing to give one away in exchange for publicizing it. However, the fundamental fact is that free media *ain't* free.

It's not that NBC was paid to put the story on the evening news. It's that an enormous amount of thought, effort, time, and expense went into creating this story.

For years, Kamen's company had been building interest in its upcoming product by spreading the word that he was working on a revolutionary invention. Keeping it a mystery helped raise interest and expectations, so hype was built far in advance of the product's unveiling.

When the Segway was finally revealed, the company had already produced professional-quality video clips, still photographs, and news releases. Its paid staff members contacted the media and arranged for interviews, demonstrations, and test drives. And, of course, millions were spent to produce this innovative machine.

The company continues to generate free media coverage by alerting local newspapers and television stations whenever a city buys Segways for their police force or a major business purchases them for navigating their gigantic warehouses, but this, too, is the result of the efforts of paid professional promoters. Five years after its introduction, the Segway continues to be an innovative product that is garnering large amounts of attention. But the Segway has yet to be financially successful.

However you can develop the free media element of your bankable business plan if you can create stories that attract attention while enhancing your business. Here are some guidelines for attracting free media:

Create specific stories to attract attention. Maybe you are a former IBM executive who is starting a software company, or a retired beloved ballerina who is opening a dance school. Perhaps your recycling business will be the first to use a new technology. Write the stories and place them in the appendix of your plan.

Make certain that the stories will enhance your business. There have been several instances of former convicts who started security businesses. This creates an interesting story, but is this actually good for business? Or attractive to potential investors? Doubtful.

Plan for the long term. You can't control whether the media will like your idea, when they will use it, or how much attention they will give it. The most successful free media efforts create a steady stream of potential stories. Some get picked up, others don't.

Focus on Research: The Tools for Effectively Influencing Others

Entrepreneurs perform many tasks that can be described as influencing other people. They must encourage backers to support their ventures, convince customers to buy their products or services, and inspire their employees to work hard. Professor Robert B. Cialdini of Arizona State University has researched the process of influencing others through extensive laboratory and workplace studies[4, 5].

Cialdini concludes that there are six principles which guide the process of influencing others:

1. **People are predisposed to comply more readily with requests from those who have already provided them with something.** If you have given potential customers free samples or shared helpful industry information, recommendations, gifts, or favors with suppliers, you will find them more willing to do business with your company.

2. **It is easier to influence people to take an action that is seen as consistent with other actions they have taken in the past.** Consumers who have recently joined health clubs are more likely to purchase low-calorie foods. Parents who have sent their children to supplementary education programs are more likely to purchase books for their children.

3. **People are more easily influenced by experts and authority figures.** Most people are more likely to take medical advice from a physician than from a colleague at work. The higher up in the organizational structure people are, the more easily they can influence others.

4. **People follow others.** Asking people to perform a task they regard as usual, such as writing a letter of recommendation, is much easier

than asking them to do something they consider more out of the ordinary, such as telephoning a prospective employer to offer a recommendation. People also respond to trends. The bigger and faster-growing the trend, the more likely they are to follow it. This is why trends generally build slowly at first and then grow more rapidly as they become more widespread.

5. **Scarcity creates attraction.** Marketers use many tools to convey scarcity: "limited time offer," "going out-of-business sale," "last one left in inventory," "only 100 will ever be sold" all send a message of scarcity. Products with waiting lists, such as popular cars, or with a limited supply, such as waterfront property or diamonds, create a psychology of attraction that motivates buyers to act quickly and pay higher prices.

6. **People prefer to do business with people they like.** This does not mean that salespeople and entrepreneurs need to be best buddies with everyone they contact, but they should recognize that if they are likeable, people will find it easier to buy their products or do business with them.

Because bankable business plans are built on the capacity to influence others, you should include some of Cialdini's principles. For example, marketing strategies that provide free samples, employ an expert as a spokesperson, show how popular a product is, or emphasize the limited nature of an offer, are much more likely to be effective.

Cialdini's principles can be similarly applied to your future sales efforts by acknowledging those salespeople whom your clients tend to like, by using experts to share their opinions with customers, and by showing how similar companies have successfully used your product or service. Once you become a manager of employees, you can apply these same principles by establishing company ethical values, by being generous with favors, perks, and pay, and by making major decisions yourself, rather than delegating them to lower levels of your organization.

CASE ON POINT

MARGO SWITCHES COASTS

For 17 years Margo Williams owned a jewelry store called Margo's Diamond Mine near the naval base in San Diego. The large majority of her customers were sailors and their families and her most successful items were wedding rings, inexpensive necklaces, and low-priced brand-name watches. Because her customers were often stretching their finances to make what they felt was a major purchase, Margo's store provided lay-away plans that allowed her clients to pay for items over time.

Margo's mother, who lived in Ft. Lauderdale, recently became ill, so Margo decided it was time to close the store in San Diego and relocate both her home and business to Florida. She found a vacant store at a reasonable price in a small upscale strip mall in which the other businesses included an expensive dress shop, a gourmet food store, and a craft outlet. The surrounding area consisted mostly of high-end condominium developments which catered to retirees and people who spent about half the year in Florida.

Margo knows the jewelry business, including how to value items she takes on trade-ins, which suppliers are best to work with, and how to design and manage a store. Although she doesn't know her new Florida market very well, some issues are clear:

- The new market is older, wealthier, and includes many retired people.
- People appear to wear much more expensive items.
- The existing competition consists of two well-known chain jewelry stores that aim their products at middle-income markets.

- Advertising and promotion tend to be concentrated in newspapers and pennysavers.

Margo was not sure she wanted to use the Margo's Diamond Mine name in this new market and she really did not know how to go about designing a marketing and promotion plan for the Florida market. To get started, Margo focused on two issues. First, she wanted a preliminary plan that would address—as best she could—the new marketing challenge she faces. Second, she wanted to research background information so she could refine her preliminary marketing plan.

CASE EXERCISE:

You are Margo. What are the new marketing challenges you face? Based on the material covered in this chapter, use the 4 Ps of marketing to create a preliminary marketing plan.

End of Chapter Questions

1. What are the 4 Ps of Marketing? Choose a product and identify the remaining 3 Ps for that product.
2. What product characteristics do you think are most important in building a strong competitive advantage?
3. Study the advertising patterns for at least three local companies within the same category, such as car dealers, sports teams, or health clubs. How do these businesses generally advertise and promote? How are they different from each other in their advertising and promotion strategies?
4. What "free" media options are available to many companies?

NOTES

1. Robert F. Hartley. *Marketing Mistakes and Successes,* 9th Edition, (New York: John Wiley and Sons, 2004), pp. 108–121.
2. "Thunder Road," *Forbes*, July 18, 1983, p. 32.
3. Robert L. Rose, "Vrooming Back," *The Wall Street Journal*, August 31, 1990, p. 1.
4. Robert B. Cialdini. *Influence: Science and Practice,* 3rd Edition, (New York: Harper Collins, 1993).
5. Robert B. Cialdini, "Of Tricks and Tumors: Some Little Recognized Costs of Dishonest Use of Effective Social Influence," *Psychology & Marketing*, Vol. 16, No. 2, (March 1999), pp. 91–98.

CHAPTER 6

ISSUE 6: BUILD A SALES EFFORT

What Were They Thinking? The Poor Sales Ethics of MCI WorldCom

In the mid 1990s, a sales consultant named Neal Irish (a real person, but not his real name), was hired to train salespeople at MCI. He was thrilled because if the company liked him they would give him enormous amounts of work. He was sent to an office in New Jersey to learn the MCI system, observe their salespeople during sales calls, and do research on their major competitors.

Two weeks later Neal quit.

After seeing the MCI sales staff at close range, Neal noticed many flaws. Salespeople never put together proposals for clients; in fact, they never put anything in writing for prospective customers. But they made a lot of promises. MCI's salespeople offered to beat any proposal from any other company. If the competitor's proposal was exceptionally strong, they sometimes brought in the District Sales Manager to make the promise—only verbally, of course. Some promises were even too big for the District Sales Manager to make, so they brought in the Regional Sales Manager.

But none of these promises were kept. The company relied upon the fact that most people don't check their phone bills in detail and many who do can't figure out the intentionally confusing charges. If customers did realize that they were not given what was promised, there was no written document to reference. A small number of customers took their business elsewhere, but by then a new flock of pigeons had been issued verbal contracts. Neal quit because he believed in written proposals, clear statements of competitive advantages, and building long-term relationships with clients through service and honesty.

As revelations came out beginning in 2002, Neal was proved right. The lies got bigger in proportion to how high up in the organization one went. External investigations carried out in 2003 documented a culture of fraud that riddled the organization as it struggled to deliver promised financial results to Wall Street. But it did so only by overstating profits by $7 billion. The company's $150 billion bankruptcy, which was filed on July 21, 2002, weighed in as the biggest in history, more than twice as large as Enron's. The bankruptcy court eliminated $36 billion in debt. The collapse of its stock price eliminated $150 billion in shareholder wealth, much of it among employees who owned company stock, and more than 23,000 employees lost their jobs. CEO Bernie Ebber's conviction on fraud charges in 2005 showed that ethical problems went all the way to the top.

Underlying this corporate disaster were the numerous failings of MCI's sales approach which Neal Irish had noticed:

- MCI focused on reaching short-term sales goals at the expense of building long-term, mutually beneficial business relationships with their customers.
- MCI didn't provide their customers with a system of accountability to demonstrate the value that MCI promised.
- MCI's sales approach focused exclusively on price as their competitive advantage, ignoring issues such as service, reliability, flexibility and special features.
- MCI failed to value their own credibility with customers, undermining their customers' trust, and sacrificing their management's personal reputations.

Companies are built on the foundation of their relationships with their customers, and in many organizations that relationship is handled primarily by the sales department. Without a quality sales effort, MCI's failure was inevitable.

Demonstrate Your Commitment to Sales

Your potential investors and bankers want to know that you are highly sales oriented. They have all seen entrepreneurs with great ideas go down in flames because they didn't build a strong enough sales effort. First you must be clear about how sales is different from marketing. Marketing is the overall way you position and promote your product or service. Its covers areas such as advertising, marketing research, distribution, and packaging. Sales is the interaction with the customers that produces orders. Sales is a specific process that takes place just prior to the order being written up or the cash register ringing. The word "sales" covers all the issues about contacting your actual customers once you have established how to reach them through your marketing campaign.

Your bankable business plan must establish that you are committed to an effective sales campaign by embracing one or more of the following approaches:

- The best time to start is yesterday
- Make sales a priority for everyone
- Never delegate yourself out of sales
- Identify key salespeople
- Create the right ethical environment
- Be highly organized
- Build a system of accountability for your clients
- Compensate based on performance and for the long term
- Build your sales force into a strong competitive advantage

The Best Time to Start Is Yesterday

The most bankable business plan shows that you already have commitments for orders. In fact, some very successful ventures were started with an order for a product even before there was a means to sell it. In 1975, a young entrepreneur discovered that IBM needed an operating system for the new personal computers they were eager to market in competition with an upstart company called Apple. The entrepreneur knew where he could obtain the right program and he made a deal with IBM before he even had the product in hand. His name was Bill Gates and he named the company he founded on that first sale Microsoft[1].

The same principle applies to you and can be projected in your plan. Identify key potential customers, talk with them, and obtain commitments to buy when you are ready to sell. Nothing will make your plan more bankable.

One way to present this in your plan is to provide a list or table that shows who you expect your initial clients to be, what contact you have made with them, how much they currently spend on your product or service category, and the status of your discussions with them. Table 6.1 shows this information for Fast Eddie's Luxury Limousine Service:

TABLE 6.1
MAJOR POTENTIAL CLIENTS FOR FAST EDDIE'S LUXURY LIMOUSINE SERVICE

Potential Client	Type of Business	Limousine Annual Budget	Date of Last Contact	Status of Discussions	Notes
Sports Arena	10,000 seat arena with 200 events per year	$200,000	May 10	Promised to try us	Need to contact specific event managers as well
Mega Publishing	Rich, global publishing giant with 500 employees in local office	$50,000	April 12	Need price lower than what they currently pay	Use limousines to transport visiting authors
Romance Wedding Planners	Wedding planner that runs 30 large weddings per year	$20,000	June 1	Promised to try us for a few weddings	Focused on providing luxury to their clients
Carefree Travel Agency	Travel planner and agency that often books limousines for its clients	$35,000	May 20	Interested, said to call back when we are in operation	Need drivers who are familiar with airport
The Smart Family	Rich family that uses lots of limousines	$15,000	June 15	Have one regular full-time driver, but will try us when he is not available	Want high status experience with professional drivers and excellent vehicles

MAKE SALES A PRIORITY FOR EVERYONE

Your plan should emphasize that you are making sales a central function for virtually every employee in every department within your company. You need to assure potential investors and lenders that you will employ a team-selling concept to address any possible questions from prospective customers. For example, if you're starting a software, consulting, or manufacturing company, you should take your technical people, not just your sales staff, to see prospective clients.

A good restaurant business plan, for example, might mention that the chef will leave the kitchen once a night to meet customers and ask for their feedback on the food. A plan for a business in which clients often deal with receptionists and assistants could make reference to the fact that these particular employees will be trained and supervised to ensure that they will be the best. Making sales a priority works in the plan and it works in the business because it communicates that attracting customers and keeping them happy is a top priority.

Never Delegate Yourself out of Sales

Although most entrepreneurs recognize that they must be sales oriented, many don't actually enjoy selling. They may have started their ventures because they preferred to run their own shows, but not sell the tickets, or they were excited about inventing a new computer application, not convincing people to try it. Some entrepreneurs want the financial rewards of business ownership, but expect their products to virtually sell themselves and structure their firms so they are far from the front lines of selling. This is not just an organizational mistake, it is a costly management error which can displease potential investors.

Many clients prefer to deal with the founder and head of the business because it boosts their egos to have that level of attention. Others believe they will get the best price and service only from top management. To attract and satisfy these potential customers, your business plan must assure investors that you will not delegate all sales responsibility to others. Moreover, to demonstrate throughout your organization—even if you employ only a few people—that sales is a major priority, you must have regular contact with customers yourself.

Identify Key Salespeople

Most readers of your plan will know how important personal contacts can be to an effective sales process. In addition to enumerating major clients that you are developing, you can also identify key salespeople who may come on board once your company gets started. Because these potential salespeople will likely have current positions, you may only be able to describe them in general and anonymously. Discussing their experience, qualifications, and the primary accounts you plan to assign them will make your sales strategy stronger. Here are some sample descriptions of potential salespeople:

- Bob W. has 12 years of experience as a salesperson in our industry. He currently bills $15,000 per month for his employer. He doesn't have a contract that will prevent him from taking a job with us and he expects that six of his clients who spend on average $4,500 per month will come with him when he joins our company.
- Sally M. is a former salesperson and manager for Ace Industries. Sally left Ace four years ago when her daughter was born. She is now interested in working 20 hours per week. She has strong contacts with ten potential clients and her part-time work schedule fits our first-year budget.

Focus on Research: Are Selling and Entrepreneurship Similar?

Although entrepreneurs come in too great a variety to be reduced to one stereotype, some research into the entrepreneurial personality is useful for new entrepreneurs planning ventures. In 1990, professors Michael H. Morris, Ramon Avila, and Eugene Teeple tested the thesis that sales and entrepreneurship activities require similar personal traits.[2] The authors defined entrepreneurial characteristics as being proactive, innovative and having a willingness to take risks. They hypothesized that within larger organizations these qualities are most likely to be found among sales managers and their staff since they are not under constant supervision and have ample opportunity to show initiative. Simply choosing this profession indicates a willingness to take risks because most salespeople and sales managers earn a substantial portion of their compensation from commissions. To be successful in the competitive, constantly changing sales arena may require that a person also be entrepreneurial.

The data that Morris, Avila and Teeple collected from 114 firms with over 100 employees supported this conclusion. Specifically, the sales managers and their staff members believed that:

- Being entrepreneurial is a major determinant of success in sales.

- Sales is the most entrepreneurial function within their company.
- Entrepreneurial thinking greatly helps firms develop successful strategies.
- The leading obstacle to entrepreneurship within sales is excessive control by top management.

If, as this study suggests, selling and entrepreneurship are closely related, then entrepreneurs should have an affinity for sales. Since sales is so important to the success of entrepreneurial ventures, this natural connection between the two may give many entrepreneurs a sizable head start in building their companies.

Create the Right Ethical Environment

Selling is not about fooling someone into buying something they don't need. Selling is about finding a long-term way to work together for the mutual benefit of both your business and your customers. If your approach to selling hinges on manipulation or being less than truthful, then your plan and your business will be built on shaky ground.

During the 1990's there were many telecommunications companies, including Winstar, Global Crossing, and XO Communications, that grew because they positioned themselves as low price providers in a rapidly growing market. This approach promised prospective clients the moon for the price of a balloon. But when growth started to trend down, the pressure for increased sales from investors and top management did not. They tried to raise prices, but clients were expecting low prices and could easily switch to other providers. Unable to raise prices to levels at which they could make a profit, and rapidly running out of cash reserves, these companies failed. Their fundamental mistake was to promise more than they could deliver.

Your plan should stress that you are committed to developing and maintaining strong relationships with your customers by delivering what you promise and ensuring that everyone within your organization shares these ethical values. This can be accomplished through the example you yourself set, by building your relationships with clients on the bedrock of honesty, and by developing a strong competitive advantage based on product quality, good pricing, and unequaled service.

Be Highly Organized

By its nature, sales requires keeping track of multiple interactions with many current and potential clients. There are a number of software sales tracking programs such as Salesforce.com, Goldmine, or ACT!, as well as database systems, such as Access, that can help your staff maintain account lists and client interactions. In many cases, keeping a detailed notebook or a card file is sufficient. Whatever system you use, the key is to be highly organized so you can provide the proper follow up and don't lose track of your customers and their requirements.

Some systems give management a huge amount of data including the number of sales calls made and the size of the average order. This can be useful information to some extent, but entrepreneurs should not be fooled into believing that these statistics are as important as building long-term, mutually beneficial relationships achieved by personally meeting with clients and focusing on their needs. Establishing a few dependable and satisfied customers is almost always better than convincing many clients to buy your product or service only once.

If your business plan has a significant sales component—and most do—it's important to describe your sales system and objectives fully.

Build a System of Accountability for Your Clients

Your company and your salespeople need to prove that they are client oriented, credible, and can deliver what is promised. One of the best ways to accomplish this is to establish a system of accountability to help clients track the results they expect from the product or service that you are selling. Your plan should include a discussion of the system you will establish. Items that are often important to clients and can be tracked include:

- Meeting schedules.
- Responding in a timely manner to service issues.
- Maintaining product performance and reliability.
- Working within budgets.

Your system of accountability should be built with the client and followed by regular reports from your company to show how well you have met the goals. What happens when you haven't met the goals? You work with the client to figure out how to improve your accountability.

Entrepreneur's Toolkit: Sales Tracking Systems

One of the most important tools in the entrepreneur's toolkit is a system for tracking accounts and sales. Presenting these in your business plan is an excellent way to demonstrate your focus on building and managing a strong sales effort. An effective sales tracking system will:

- **Keep a database** of all current and potential accounts including contact names, addresses, e-mail addresses, and phone numbers.
- **Track all contacts** that the business has with every account, including when calls were made, by whom, what transpired, and the outcome of the calls.
- **Track all orders** for every account including what and how much was sold, the price paid, and a probable reorder date.
- **Produce reports** that summarize sales activity by salesperson, industry, geography, business size, and any other characteristic that could reveal more about the selling process and lead to the most effective approaches to future sales.
- **Take very little time from the salespeople** and managers, and be easy to use.

This data can be kept on the simplest file card system or in the latest Web-based sales management system. Custom-designed systems can be created using any of several currently available software packages. The right system for your business depends on the size of your company, the number of accounts and salespeople you maintain, and the way the data will be compiled and analyzed by your management team.

The following charts, Tables 6.2 and 6.3, show some sample sales management reports. For companies that are selling multiple products or product lines, the reports can also be created for each product or line.

Compensate Based on Performance and for the Long Term

Salespeople should earn financial rewards based on performance, but performance should be defined effectively. A commission based solely on sales, may, in fact, encourage staff to over-promise, pressure clients into buying, or even write up phony orders. Some organizations believe they are giving their salespeople the right incentives, but in reality they are encouraging their staff to concentrate on hard-sell, short-term, unethical techniques that eventually erode customer trust and satisfaction, as well as future sales. You can assure potential investors and lenders that you understand these problems and can avoid them by stating in your business plan that you will:

- Pay commissions based on collections, not orders.
- Set long-term goals and give financial incentives for reaching them, instead of relying only on weekly or monthly goals.
- Give salespeople a fixed financial base, so they're not under tremendous financial pressure to meet short-term quotas and commissions.
- Communicate your goal of building strong relationships with long-term clients.
- Recruit salespeople who are interested in working collaboratively with clients to help them meet mutually beneficial goals.
- Train your salespeople to deliver better service based on their understanding of your client's needs and goals.

TABLE 6.2
SALESPERSON PERFORMANCE REPORT

	Salesperson Current Month	Staff Average Current Month	Salesperson Previous 3 Months	Staff Avg. Previous 3 Months	Salesperson Previous 12 Months	Staff Average Previous 12 Months
Number of Accounts						
Number of Accounts Added						
Number of Accounts Removed						
Total Sales						
Cost of Goods Sold						
Salesperson Compensation						
Profit on Sales						
Number of Sales Calls						
Cost per Sales Call: Sales Costs/ Number of Calls						
Number of Orders						
Average Order Size						
Average Profit per Order						
Number of Orders to New Accounts						
Sales Goal						
Percent of Sales Goal Attained						
Market Share of Clients' Expenditures						
Manager's Assessment of Performance (A through F Scale)						

TABLE 6.3
ACCOUNT INFORMATION REPORT

	Current Month	Previous 3 Months	Previous 12 Months
Salesperson			
Number of Sales Calls Made			
Number of Orders			
Total Sales			
Average Order Size			
Cost of Goods Sold			
Salesperson Compensation			
Profit on Sales			
Cost per Sales Call: Sales Costs/ Number of Calls			
Average Profit per Order			
Sales Goal for this Account			
Percent of Sales Goal Attained			
Amount Spent with Competitors			
Our Market Share of Client's Expenditures			

BUILD YOUR SALES FORCE INTO A STRONG COMPETITIVE ADVANTAGE

Managing your sales force effectively will provide a major competitive advantage for your company—and it will make your business plan more compelling. Many entrepreneurs view their sales staff as an expensive and hard-to-manage, but necessary evil. If your sales staff is more client oriented, more knowledgeable about your product, and delivers better service than your competitors, you can build and maintain strong customer relationships. A well-designed sales effort can help bring in larger market shares than your competitors can achieve and it will keep business steady even during economic downturns. You can bank on it! And your plan should say so.

CASE ON POINT
SELLING WEB SITE SERVICES

Judy Reiser and Elyse Larsen are college friends who followed the dot.com boom together into a Web site services company that hired them right after they graduated in 1995. In 1998, the company imploded—it ran out of cash, failed to meet the needs of their customers, and lost key employees faster than they could be replaced. By 1999, the company closed and Judy and Elyse were thinking about graduate school, in part because job opportunities in technology industries were so few.

Three months after they lost their jobs, Judy and Elyse were having dinner at an inexpensive local restaurant. They shared news about former colleagues, other dot. com businesses that had closed, and talked about graduate school options. Elyse mentioned that she had run into one of her former clients, the owner of a custom-made furniture business, who complained that he was having trouble finding someone to host and update his Web site. He had asked Elyse if she was doing any work independently. Judy had a similar experience when her aunt, the manager of a medical practice, asked if Judy knew any people who could create a Web site. Judy knew of two people who could, but she didn't admire their work enough to recommend them to her aunt.

At this point, Elyse had an epiphany: Their old company had failed because it spent too much money and was badly managed, not because the demand for Web site services was small. In fact, demand was growing faster than ever, as virtually every business realized it needed a Web site. Judy agreed and within 15 minutes, the two friends had consented to start their own company. They even had a name for it: Finesse Systems. The two friends knew the technology, where to rent inexpensive offices with high-speed connections, and who to hire as demand for their services grew. The only thing they didn't know how to do was sign up clients.

The next week, Judy and Elyse met with several people who worked in sales and sales management to learn more about the selling process. After these meetings, they didn't have the answers but they did have some specific questions.

CASE QUESTIONS:

- Which one of them should focus her efforts on sales?
- How could they create a list of potential customers?
- How should they communicate with these potential customers?
- What kind of client tracking system did they need?
- When they could finally afford to hire salespeople, what qualifications should they have?
- What kind of sales compensation system would work best for them and their business?
- When should they start reaching out to potential customers?

End of Chapter Questions

1. How should an entrepreneur manage the sales function?
2. What ways can an entrepreneur stay directly involved in selling?
3. What are some systems of accountability that can be built into sales?
4. How can a sales department be a competitive advantage?

NOTES

1. Stephen Manes and Paul Andrews. *Gates: How Microsoft's Mogul Reinvented an Industry–and Made Himself the Richest Man in America*, (New York: Touchstone, 1994).
2. Michael H. Morris, Ramon Avila, and Eugene Teeple, "Sales Management as an Entrepreneurial Activity," *Journal of Personal Selling and Sales Management*, Vol. 10, No. 2, (Spring 1990), pp. 1–15

CHAPTER 7

ISSUE 7: ORGANIZE THE COMPANY

What They Did Right: How David Neeleman Built JetBlue

In 1982 David Neeleman entered the travel business by opening a travel agency and running charter flights from his home town of Salt Lake City. In 1984 he founded a discount airline, Utah Air, which was modeled on Southwest Airlines and based in Salt Lake City. Eight years later, he sold Utah Air to Southwest for $129 million and joined Southwest's management team.

This gave Neeleman the detailed knowledge and experience to understand Southwest's success, which was based on profit sharing plans that kept unionization at bay and included such policies as having their pilots load bags in order to keep their planes running on time. Neeleman eventually left Southwest to become an entrepreneur again and toyed with various ideas, including a chain of family dental clinics[1] .

Neeleman passed on the dental clinics and other concepts and returned to the airline industry with a plan to imitate Southwest's overall approach, but with his own marketing concepts. Neeleman's plan for his new airline, which he named JetBlue, called for a low-cost strategy that would allow JetBlue to underprice the competition while also being profitable. For this strategy to be successful, operations, finance, marketing, and human resources needed coordinated approaches.

To help keep costs low, Neeleman decided to fly only new, efficient AirBus A320s while providing a first-class feel with leather seats and individual televisions. His main targets were the high-volume, high-priced routes from New York to Florida and California[2]. Neeleman also decided to use airports at which JetBlue could get gates inexpensively such as Long Beach outside of Los Angeles, or Kennedy Airport in New York. While often less convenient for many flyers, the location of these airports mattered less to price-sensitive travelers. Also, on such high-volume routes, JetBlue would only need to garner a tiny market share to fill its planes.

Neeleman believes that JetBlue's greatest competitive advantage is its people, so he adopted a human resource strategy similar to Southwest Airlines: hire self-motivated people who don't need constant supervision, have a strong customer-service orientation, and possess personalities that make them compatible with co-workers and customers. To attract these people, JetBlue pays well, gives extensive training, has a profit sharing plan, and works to encourage these values throughout the company. These strategies allow JetBlue to have a people-friendly style that many describe as "warm and fuzzy," and which is crafted to suit a top company business goal of having highly motivated and friendly workers who pitch in to keep operations efficient and costs down.[3]

Profitability, rapid growth, admiration in the industry, and appreciation from customers positioned JetBlue firmly with investors. First, the company attracted money from private investment funds and later went public, raising the company's value to over $2 billion. This strong initial strategy has been supported by all departments of the company and has produced a high-flying airline.[4]

By this point you have defined your venture, its initial needs, your targeted markets, and the most appropriate strategy for achieving your goals. You have also considered your marketing and sales efforts. Now it is time to design the organization structure that will support your concept and bring your business plan into reality. Among the issues covered in this chapter are legal forms of organization, hiring and managing employees, and organization structures. You may hope to run your company as one big happy family—and it may work out that way—but organizations require formal structure.

The primary goal of this chapter is to help you design an organization that will be capable of utilizing the strategies you have chosen. The effective implementation of your business plan may be the single greatest determinant of business success. No matter how strong your business plan is, a weak execution will doom your venture. Investors and lenders know this and will look for a strong management component in your plan.

Imagine that you own a tuba manufacturing plant and plan to purchase a competitor's operation. You have been running your grandfather's tuba plant since his death, but the operation is still small and old fashioned. Buying the new plant will enable you to bring your manufacturing methods up-to-date and expand your customer base. Investors will want to know if you're capable of running the show by yourself after you take over the plant. Do you need to bring in experienced managers right away? Will you keep some of the existing employees or hire all new people? And where do you find these potential employees?

Funding sources will also want to know if any of your partners expect to work alongside you, or if their obligations are only financial. How will you make changes at the new tuba plant while maintaining the trust and cooperation of the employees you retain from your previous plant and the staff at the newly acquired plant? And how will you reassure both plants' customers that your new tubas will be as good as, if not better than, the tubas that used to roll off the old assembly lines?

Your plan will need to specify the key management jobs and roles. Positions such as president, vice presidents, chief financial officer, and department managers should be defined along with stating who reports to whom. Running a manufacturing plant will require you to deal with dozens if not hundreds of employees, but what if you're someone who wants to build a better mousetrap? You will have some of the same issues, such as handling partners who may want to work side-by-side with you on your venture or convincing investors of your qualifications, but you may be the sole full-time employee for quite some time. How will you find the right consultants to advise you or the best vendors to supply your materials? Will you collect a salary? When will you know you need to hire a staff? What skills must they have? How do you recruit them? How will you structure your company so that the chain of command and quality control are maintained if the company grows dramatically?

And as soon as you have employees, you need to consider how you will handle their salaries and wages, their insurance and retirement benefits, as well as analyzing the extent of your knowledge of tax-related issues. As you think about hiring personnel and organizing your workforce, you must also confront your desire and ability to be a good boss. If you haven't contemplated this aspect of your commitment to owning your own company, now is the time to give it serious consideration.

Options for Organization Structures

You might want to review the basic strategic options covered in Chapter 3 because they will be important in choosing the best structure for your company. For example, if you are planning to take over your uncle's tuba factory and combine operations with another tuba manufacturer, you have several organizational options. You can set up each factory autonomously, have each one specialize in different parts of the manufacturing process, or focus each plant on different kinds of tubas serving different markets. Each of these options requires a different structure with different jobs, reporting systems, and varying management responsibilities.

A graphic representation of these structural relationships is presented through *organization charts.* Organization charts have two dimensions. The north/south dimension or vertical axis shows power relationships. The higher up (more to the north) on the chart a position is, the more power that position has. Generally, a person's boss is shown above him or her on an organization chart. The east/west dimension or horizontal axis shows how tasks are divided. Questions such as "Who covers Borneo?" or "Which department manages cuddlefish farms?" can be answered by looking horizontally, east to west, on the organization chart.

Organizations are defined by how the first level below the top is structured. Although you can mix and match structures in infinite varieties, there are five basic organizational types: Functional, product, geographical, matrix, and hybrid.

Functional Structure. The first level below the CEO is broken out by functions such as finance, sales, and manufacturing. Smaller organizations in stable businesses, with limited product lines and routine technology, are typically organized functionally. A functional structure enables companies to grow while benefiting from economies of scale and maintaining skill development within the departments. For example, a real estate management company will probably be organized functionally, having departments such as accounting, marketing, maintenance, and human resources. Because this structure tends to have centralized decision making, it can burden a staff that is not innovative and is slow to make decisions.

Product Structure. The first level is organized by products or product lines. Food companies generally organize this way, with each product having its own management team to oversee advertising, distribution, packaging, and promotions. When companies have many products, each of which may be competing in a rapidly changing environment, then product structure may be the most appropriate choice because decision making can be placed at the product manager level.

Geographic Structure. As the name implies, organizing by location such as states, counties, or neighborhoods produces a geographic structure. Businesses such as real estate brokerages, fast-food companies, and many professional firms organize by geography because their products do not vary from location to location and this is an efficient way to manage customer relationships.

Matrix Structure. Some organizations are structured into teams of specialists according to the task at hand. These matrix structures are generally established in high technology companies where specialized, technical groups are built to work on specific problems. Matrix organizations usually have team leaders, with specialists reporting upwards to each leader. Companies that create complex products such as computers or airplanes usually organize this way so a manager can be assigned to develop a specific component or solve a particular problem and then pull the needed specialists onto the team.

Hybrid Structure. These organizations combine elements of both functional and product structures. Part of the company is functionally structured, such as the finance and distribution departments, while other portions are product organized, such as the ice cream and the potato chip divisions. A hybrid structure allows for the responsiveness of a product organization and the specialization and efficiency of a functional organization.

If your company requires about a dozen or more people, it is wise to provide a full organization chart with your business plan, although it could go in the appendix.

FIGURES 7.1 — 7.5

Functional Structure

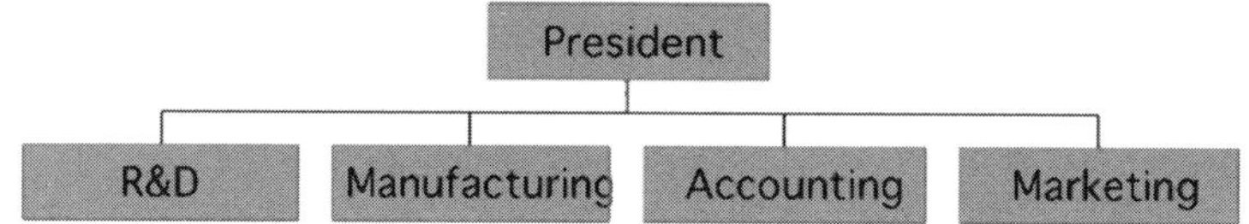

Product Structure

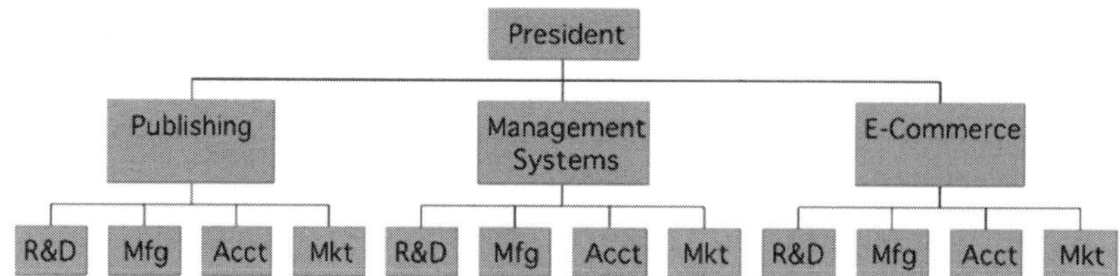

Geographical Structure

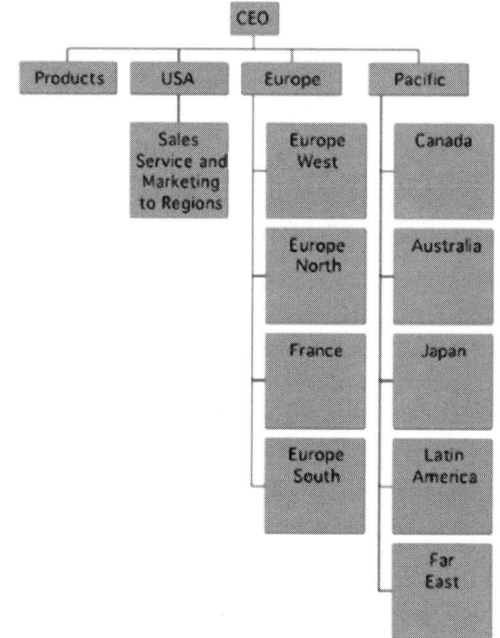

Matrix Structure

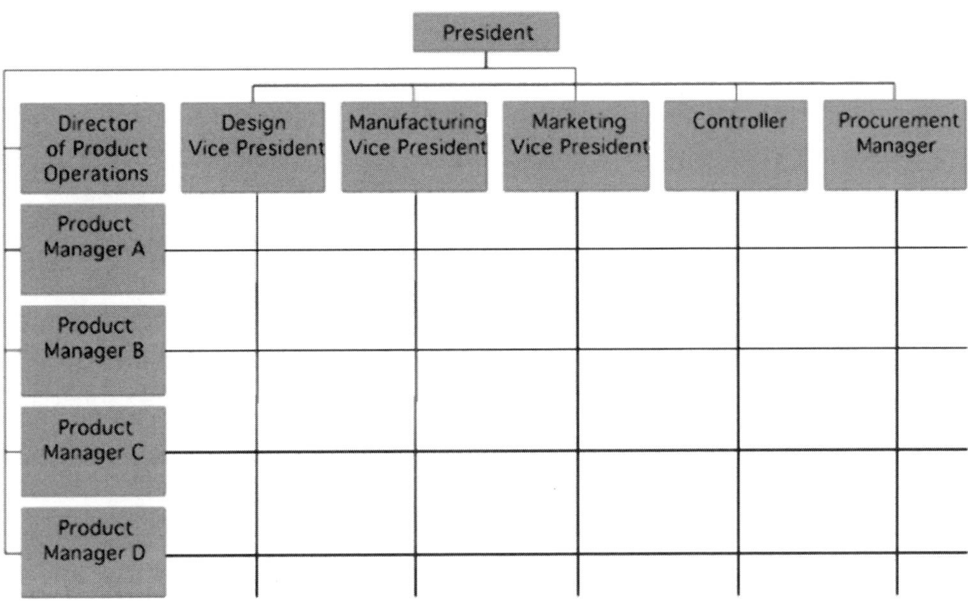

Hybrid Structure

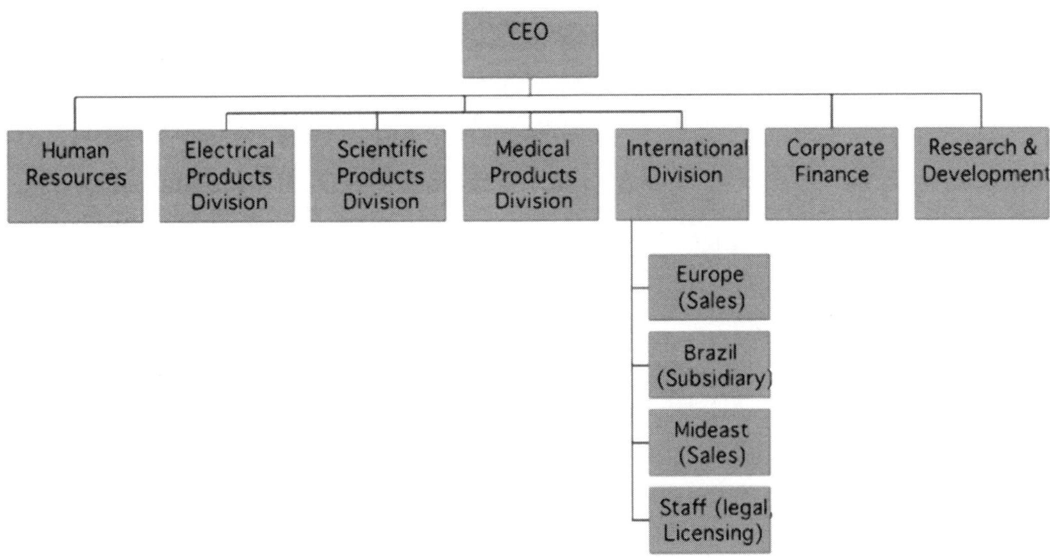

Managing Your Organization

If your plan calls for a sizeable organization, you must demonstrate that you will have the means to control it with an appropriate structure. Here are several basic issues you should consider specifying in your plan:

- **Span of control** is the number of people who report to one boss. This should be stated for organizations with large sales forces, manufacturing operations, or sizeable support departments, such as accounting.
- **Reporting tools** are ways of keeping management informed of staff activities, through weekly staff meetings, memos, or sales reporting systems. In manufacturing and other departments, where cost and efficiency are always important, systems that track each employee's production may be needed.
- **Organizational culture** is the atmosphere of morale and company spirit that exists among the staff. Creating the appropriate organizational culture is an important part of the success of many businesses. All organizations develop a culture that reflects their underlying values and creates an atmosphere of morale and company spirit among the staff. Both employees and customers are sensitive to an organization's culture and can describe it accurately in terms of honesty, service, innovation, profitability, and growth. This is also true for negative values including cheating, mustering minimal effort, treating customers poorly, and preventing other employees from being successful. Tools that create and reinforce positive values include the recognition of people who have demonstrated exceptional qualities, the use of printed material, and slogans such as Ford's use of "Quality is Job #1" and Avis's "We Try Harder."

  Organizational culture evolves from the top down. If the CEO and other top managers demonstrate poor values, as was the case with both MCI and Enron, it is only a matter of time until they infest the rest of the company. Since good values will also flow from the top, it is important for your plan to define the organizational culture you desire for your business and state how you will reinforce these values.

Management Styles

Management theorists Tom Burns and G.M. Stalker have identified two management styles which they believe work best in certain business environments. Companies in stable environments, Burns and Stalker believe, should maintain a clear management hierarchy and use a formal, rather rigid style, which they call *mechanistic.* Organizations that function in rapidly changing and unpredictable environments should use a more flexible, less structured management style which the researchers call *organic.* Organic managers delegate more, adjust structures and tasks to adapt quickly, and stress communication among all organization members.

This simple dichotomy between management styles has broad applications for entrepreneurs and should be addressed in your business plan:

- The rate and degree of change of the business environment should be identified and the appropriate management style selected.
- The appropriate style, along with a specific list of the major management tools, should be discussed.
- If the venture's success is related to creating new products, or to applying technology in new ways to improve products, processes, and customer service, the plan should identify the specific "organic" management approaches that will be used.

The plan should also allow for the use of both styles within the same organization. For example, administrative and manufacturing functions are generally managed mechanistically. On the other hand, professionals such as lawyers, scientists, and members of creative teams should be managed organically. The use of organic and mechanistic styles within the same organization is call "ambidextrous management[5]."

Entrepreneurship Is a Team Sport

Perhaps entrepreneurs are best described as business people who undertake ventures without regard to the resources under their direct control. Limiting yourself to a venture you could do solely with your own resources—both human and financial—would probably result in a pretty small business. Your human resources would be confined to your own muscle and brain power during waking hours only, and your financial resources would be limited to your investments, retirement accounts, the value of your home, your credit card maximums, the cash you have in the bank and those few treasured items, such as the original set of Batman comics that your uncle gave you when you were a kid.

Even if you are enormously wealthy, you probably won't want to risk it all—especially the Batman comics—on your business idea. Moreover, you need to be realistic and recognize the possibility that your business could fail and take all your assets with it.

So let's start with the assumption that on the financial side, you are probably going to need help, either through loans from family, friends, a bank, or a credit card company, or through investments from family, friends, business partners, or an investment group. Lenders let you borrow their money for a set period of time and are paid interest along with their loan amount, called principal, paid back in full. Investors buy equity or ownership shares in your company and receive a share of your profits from operations or an eventual sale of your company.

As for the human resource side, do you really think you can operate a business completely alone? Very few companies work that way. Consultants, free-lancers, and individual investors may qualify as true one-man bands, but even for them, success (and sometimes failure) may spoil their solitude and require them to bring in employees and partners. And don't forget suppliers. The most solo operation still requires basic office supplies, such as paper and pencils. And absolutely no business operates without those important people, clients and customers.

No doubt about it, entrepreneurship is a team sport, requiring the contribution of others with different backgrounds, skills, and needs in order for you to build a successful venture.

Human Resource Management

If hiring and retaining the right employees is fundamental to your company's success, you should state your approach to human resource management in your business plan. Here are some of the issues you need to consider:

Identify Key Employees. Since business is a team sport, choosing your teammates may be the most important decision you make. It is useful to fill out the following grid for every key position in the organization. A summary of the information can go in the main plan and the full details can be placed in an appendix.

TABLE 7.1
KEY INFORMATION REQUIRED FOR MAJOR POSITIONS

Title of the position.
Job description.
Required degrees, training, and experience for someone who will fill the position.
Compensation including salary, bonus, stock ownership and stock incentives.
Is the position currently filled? If yes, provide the employee's resume.
Do you have someone in mind for the position? If yes, provide the resume.
Do you need to run a search for the position? If yes, state how you will conduct the search.

Design a Board of Directors or a Board of Advisors. People who are not full-time employees but who offer their expertise, experience, and contacts to help your company can be integral to your success. A Board of Directors is a formal entity with ultimate legal control over the company and with potential personal liability for its actions. A Board of Advisors is an informal group working to help the company, but without legal authority over the company or any potential personal liability for its actions. Directors and Advisors with industry experience, financial backgrounds, and technical understanding can help your organization. Showing potential investors or lenders that you have recruited a high-powered, capable, and contributing group of Directors and Advisors will make your plan much stronger. For each proposed Board member or member of your Board of Advisors, you should complete the same template as you would for key employees.

Employee Compensation and Benefit Plans. Your approach to compensation and benefits should fit your overall strategy. For example, if you are opening a fast food franchise, then most of your employees will be young people who don't see their jobs with your company as a career, but rather a way to make as much money in the short run to pay for school or buy a car. For these employees, a compensation plan that maximizes their paychecks at the expense of long-term benefits such as pension plans is probably best. On the other hand, if you are developing a consulting firm and want to keep your employees for the long run because they will build strong, ongoing relationships with your clients, a plan that stresses long-term benefits such as health insurance, stock ownership or pensions, is probably best.

Employee benefits is a very complex, highly regulated, rapidly changing area. You should consult with a benefits company or a financial planner and receive actual proposals for employee benefits to include in your business plan. Place a summary in the body of the plan and attach the proposal as an appendix.

Principal Suppliers and Contractors. Henry Ford's first automobile plant functioned by funneling coal, iron ore, and other raw materials in one door and rolling finished Model T's off the assembly line and out the other door. When Ford began his business, there were no suppliers of car parts, so his factory had to do it all. In today's world, most companies subcontract out large portions of their essential processes. Dell assembles computers from components it purchases from hundreds of different suppliers. In certain cases, Toyota requires its suppliers to locate their facilities adjacent to the Toyota plants so parts can be ordered and delivered within a few hours.

Chances are that your business plan will describe a venture more like Dell or Toyota than Henry Ford's original factory and you will need to identify major suppliers. Here are questions about suppliers that should be addressed in your plan:

- What materials will they actually be supplying?
- How long have they been in business?
- What are their credentials and track records?
- Why have you selected them? Price? Quality? Ability to supply the adequate quantity on time?
- Have they made a binding offer to supply certain products or services at a definite price?
- What is your backup plan if they don't do what they promised?

Suppliers with strong track records and excellent reputations will not only contribute quality materials to your business, they will also give your plan a powerful endorsement. If Intel has agreed to supply semiconductors for your product, investors and bankers will definitely take notice.

Because so many products follow a supply chain moving from process to process, company to company, and even country to country, the competitiveness of your final product may largely depend on your ability to manage this movement along the supply chain. If this applies to your company, then discussing it in your business plan will be important to readers who are familiar with your industry operations. Supply chain management requires choosing the right supplier, integrating operations, and sharing information with your supplier, all of which is increasingly accomplished through Web-based applications. The software tracks inventory levels and anticipates future needs and follows the supplier's inventory levels and, given normal shipping times, projects when shipments will have to be ready.

The purpose of this system is to reduce inventory levels generally. Keeping unneeded inventory is a waste of precious financing, it requires storage facilities, and runs the risk of damage or theft, or of never being needed. Careful supply chain management reduces these risks and can create a significant competitive advantage.

Family Business Issues

Family businesses have been described as "the institution hidden in plain sight" because one in every ten U.S. households owns a business. Estimates indicate that family-owned companies generate nearly half the business revenue in the U.S.[6] Although some family businesses have grown into huge, successful empires such as Ford, Johnson & Johnson, and McGraw-Hill, many people immediately assume that the goal of a family-owned company is to remain small. If you are designing a family-owned company and smallness is not your intention, your business plan must make it very clear that growth is one of your major objectives.

Other questions about a family business that must be addressed in your plan include:

- **Will family issues be a distraction to building your company?** You might want to emphasize that you will keep your own work hours to a fixed schedule and that you will maintain a separate, private space for your company. You must also reassure potential funders that your family members accept these specific conditions and are fully committed to supporting your business in every way.
- **Will business funds be intermingled with family funds?** Investors may fear that business funds will be used to pay for family expenses simply because of your family's involvement in your venture. Your plan must stress that professional record keeping will be used in all phases of the company.

- **How will family members contribute to the business?** One of the pluses of family businesses is the commitment and availability family members bring to the venture, including additional human and financial resources in peak times, or providing particular areas of expertise. If your family members will be able to offer these strengths, you should emphasize this benefit in your plan.
- **Will business goals be subordinate to family goals?** Investors, employees, partners, and suppliers want to know that your venture will be run like a business with profit making as the primary goal. They may fear that earning revenue will be secondary to providing opportunities for unqualified family members or even supporting family members who will do little work. Your plan must state explicitly that family members will work to support the company—and not the other way around.

Service Firms

Service firms in areas such as healthcare, education, and the food industry constitute an increasing share of the U.S. economy. Service businesses have several characteristics that create special demands on management:

- **Simultaneous production and consumption of the service they provide.** Service firms cannot "warehouse" tennis lessons, medical check-ups, or computer repairs.
- **Customized output.** Service firms almost always customize what they provide to match the customer's preferences.
- **Large amount of customer interaction.** Many service firms provide their services directly to the customer, or they require a direct interaction through pick-up, delivery, or personalized order taking.
- **Intangible products.** Teaching, entertainment, and counseling are intangible products. But even restaurants that provide a tangible product, do so in the context of a service delivery system that

may be as important as the food itself in determining customer satisfaction.

- **Labor intensity.** Virtually all service firms require a large human resources component. Certain technologies, such as Web site ordering, word processing, or voice mail, may replace human hours, but service companies are almost entirely dependent on people to deliver a quality service.

This means that an entrepreneur must develop strategies for recruiting, training and managing quality employees so that the actual service matches the concept in the business plan. When the reality does not match the plan, companies such as restaurants, medical practices, spas, beauty parlors, and airlines, disappoint and alienate their customers and eventually fail.

Your plan for a service firm should deal specifically with how you will recruit and train your staff, and make the service you provide satisfy the needs of your customers.

Using Outside Advisors and Professionals

No business has all the human resources it needs within its own organization. Companies use outside experts, professionals, and advisors to help the business without having to employ them full-time. The "Entrepreneur's Toolkit" section of this Chapter supplies an exercise to build a list of people who would be valuable on a Board of Advisors. Once individuals have agreed to serve in this capacity, you should include their resumes and skills in your plan.

Key outside roles include:

- Advisors who volunteer to give their opinions and connect with industry contacts to help your venture.
- Experts such as engineers, market research specialists, and consultants, who will work either for an hourly rate or in exchange for a small share of the company.
- Professionals such as lawyers and accountants who will work on an hourly or per job rate.

A strong and impressive list of outside advisors, experts, and professionals will send the message to potential investors and lenders that your business has the support of people whose knowledge about the industry and contacts will help make your business successful.

THE ENTREPRENEUR'S TOOLKIT: BUILD A BOARD OF ADVISORS

A Board of Advisors is an informal group of people who want to help your business by providing their expertise and access to their network of contacts. Boards of Directors are legally sanctioned to run the business in the best interest of the shareholders and are paid to do so. A position on a Board of Directors has clear responsibilities and exposure to liabilities if the Board does something wrong. But a Board of Advisors has no legal responsibilities, usually carries no compensation, and conveys primarily a moral obligation to help the business.

Most entrepreneurs tend to ask people they like to be on their Board of Advisors and run meetings like pot-luck suppers, but this can miss the great opportunities provided by a properly created and managed Board of Advisors. The following chart (Table 7.2) provides a model in building your Board of Advisors.

Table 7.2
Worksheet for Building a Board of Advisors

Step 1. Fill in the following table to identify the expertise and connections that would be valuable to your business.

Categories of Positives that Members of the Board of Advisors Could Deliver	Specifics of Each Category	Particular People Who Could Bring These to Your Board
Specialized knowledge such as particular skills, languages, degrees, and certifications that would be useful in your business.		
Membership in organizations such as professional societies, local business groups, country clubs and fraternal associations that would bring you access to people who could be customers, investors, or providers of any other resource your business could use.		
Connections to particular people such as potential major customers, investors, possible purchasers of your business (or sellers of companies you would like to buy), or major suppliers that would help your business accomplish its goals more quickly.		
Experience with companies or industries that could be applied to your business and would help you make the best decisions and avoid mistakes.		
Personality types such as people who are very cautious, aggressive, upbeat, or known as motivators who would help your Board of Advisors and company run more effectively.		

Step 2. Rank the people listed in the third column in order of who will offer the most to the business right now.

Step 3. Develop a plan for contacting the potential board members. You may know some people personally and others through friends or colleagues. If you have no personal connection to the person, write a letter, send an e-mail, or call. The great majority of people will be flattered by your interest in them, will probably want to help, and may even say yes. For those who are less gracious, resolve never to treat others this way should you be in their situation, and move on to the next person on your list.

Step 4. Keep in touch with Board of Advisors members often through e-mail, telephone calls, and meetings. Hold full meetings between two and four times per year at convenient times and places. Make each meeting a productive working session by establishing an agenda, placing questions you are pondering on the table for Board comment, and identifying specific company needs with a discussion of who can help you fill them.

Options for Legal Structures

Many entrepreneurs find choosing a legal structure for their companies a daunting prospect and immediately hire a lawyer. A lawyer may be necessary at some point in establishing your venture, but legal services are not an expense you have to assume while preparing your business plan. Whether you hire a lawyer immediately or not, understanding the choices of legal structures is a good idea and, in fact, may not be as complicated as you think.

There are three considerations in choosing a legal structure for your venture:

- **Tax considerations**. Some types of structures, such as Limited Partnerships, don't pay taxes directly, but pass profits and losses directly to their owners. The owners then pay taxes based on their own tax situations.
- **Liability considerations**. Other legal entities, such as Corporations, protect their owners from liability arising from actions of the company or its employees through what is known as the "corporate veil." This protection is not perfect, and in cases of fraud or illegal activity, the corporate veil can be pierced.
- **Investor considerations**. The type, number, and wealth of investors that you anticipate having for your venture is important because some structures, such as S Corporations, limit the number of possible investors. Others, such as General Partnerships, have only one class of investors, while C Corporations allow for many. The option of having more than one class of investors means you can give varying voting or economic power to different

groups of investors. The government reporting requirements are also different for companies that only raise money from professional investment groups and wealthy individuals.

Once you analyze these considerations, you can match your needs with the types of legal entities available and make the best choice. Table 7.3 below shows how you can match the three considerations above with the legal form that is best for your company:

TABLE 7.3
CHOICES FOR LEGAL STRUCTURES

Form	One or Many Shareholders/Partners	Personal Liability	Taxed at Company or on Owners' Taxes
Sole Proprietorship	1	Yes	Owner's
General Partnership	Many	Yes	Owners'
Limited Partnership	Many	No	Owners'
S Corporation	Up to 75	No	Owners'
C Corporation	Many	No	Company
Limited Liability Company	Many	No	Owners'
Limited Liability Partnership	Many	No	Owners'
Professional Corporation	1	Yes	Owner's

- **Sole Proprietorships** have one owner who manages the business and contributes to the investment. There is no liability protection and profits and losses are passed through directly to the owner's tax return.
- **General Partnerships** can have as many partners as desired, all of whom are collectively responsible for managing the business, contributing to the investment and sharing in the profits. There is no liability protection, and profits and losses pass through directly to the partners' individual tax returns.

- **Limited Partnerships** have two classes of partners. The General Partners are responsible for the management of the business, while the Limited Partners are investors (General Partners can also invest as Limited Partners). Based on the profit-sharing agreement between the classes of partners, profits and losses pass through to both the General and Limited Partners' individual tax returns. The General Partners have no personal liability protection, but the Limited Partners do.
- **S Corporations** are taxed like partnerships but provide the liability protection of a corporation. This allows profits and losses to pass through to the shareholders. There are some restrictions, including that the number of shareholders must be 75 or fewer, that there can be only one class of stock, and that all shares must be owned by only certain types of shareholders, such as individuals, trusts, or estates.
- **C Corporations** are usually the structure of choice for large companies. They can have an unlimited number of shareholders and an unlimited number of classes of stock. The shareholders have no personal liability and the company is managed by a Board of Directors which can be held liable for the company's actions in certain cases. The corporation pays taxes on its profits. The profits then pass through to the shareholders in the form of dividends, which are then taxed again on the individual shareholder's tax return.
- **Limited Liability Companies** allow for an unlimited number of investors, called members. The owners can elect to let profits and losses pass through to the members' individual tax returns or be taxed at the corporate level. The members cannot be held liable for actions of the company.
- **Limited Liability Partnerships and Professional Corporations** are state-sanctioned organizational forms that are designed for licensed professionals such as lawyers, accountants, doctors, and dentists. If you are doing a plan for such a profession, you should ask your attorney about the advantages of using one of these forms.

Matching the Legal Structure with Your Investors

The number and characteristics of your investors may influence your choice of legal structure. Raising capital from private sources, such as family members, venture capital funds, or individuals is referred to as *private placements*, and will require a lawyer who is a specialist. The key concept here is called the *accredited investor*, which is an institution, such as an insurance company, a pension fund, or an investment firm. An accredited investor may also be an individual with a net worth in excess of $1 million, or an individual income of $200,000, or a joint income of $300,000 or more. When working with accredited investors to raise money for your business, you have much more flexibility than dealing with less wealthy and, therefore (according to the law), less sophisticated investors.

If you're aiming at this market of institutional or wealthy and sophisticated accredited investors, you must produce a private placement memorandum and file it with the Securities and Exchange Commission (SEC), a process which requires the services of a securities lawyer. To raise money from the broader public, called an *initial public offering*, or IPO, requires a much more expensive and time-consuming process of filing a prospectus with the Securities and Exchange Commission. You will require an experienced lawyer, if not a law firm, and an investment bank, or a consortium of investment banks, to sell the shares through the public market. Although many entrepreneurs dream of the day their IPO takes place, this is a very rare event. In any given year only a few dozen companies file for IPOs.

By analyzing the available legal structures, you will be able to choose the most appropriate method of organizing your potential business. This will help convince investors and lenders that you have researched the options, even if you haven't made a final decision or hired a lawyer. In fact, once you have established that you have considered this issue in your business plan, lenders and investors may offer helpful suggestions on choosing a legal structure.

The Franchise Option

Some entrepreneurs believe that buying a franchise eliminates the need to prepare a business plan. The decision to buy a franchise certainly dictates many of the issues that your business plan must include, but it does not remove the necessity of creating a plan. The most important issue in a franchise business plan is proving that the location you have chosen will be profitable.

Franchisors should provide potential franchisees with the basic business model for the franchise, including detailed cost estimates, average revenue for existing franchises, and typical financing structures. The plan for your specific franchise should cover the following:

- **A detailed analysis of local competition** from other franchises for the same company as well as for other competitive businesses.
- **A line-by-line comparison of the expenses** that the franchisor projects with the local costs for your franchise. For example, if the franchisor gives you projections that indicate rent at $50 per square foot, you will need to demonstrate that you can obtain space at or below that amount.
- **An analysis of the franchise agreement** that shows you have sufficient protections to ensure that no other franchises will be sold directly in your vicinity. Also, you should show that the franchisor is capable of fulfilling all promises, such as national advertising, or new product development, to keep your business viable.
- **Interviews with existing franchisees** (who were *not* suggested by the franchisor) to substantiate the claims made by the franchisor and to further demonstrate business viability.
- **Legal advice from a franchise expert** is a necessity. There is a surfeit of laws governing franchises, including many local regulations. You need to have a lawyer who is highly experienced in this area, and who can contribute advice, as well as help you negotiate the terms of various agreements, including the franchise contract and leases. Mention the lawyer with details on her credentials prominently in your plan.

The Key Questions about Franchises

The key question to ask yourself about purchasing a franchise is "Do I need to buy a franchise to be in this business?" Many people buy franchises because they like the idea of having a proven model for a business that comes with a template for operation. Others believe that a franchise has a greater chance of success than a non-franchised business. In one of the few objective studies about franchises, Professor Timothy Bates of Wayne State University found the opposite to be true[7].

Between 1984 and 1991, Bates studied a sample of 20,000 newly established small companies from the Census Bureau's survey and compared the business survival rates between franchise and non-franchised firms. One startling conclusion is that franchise businesses fail more often than non-franchised businesses. Among companies that survived for at least four years, franchises failed 45.1% of the time compared to 29.9% for the non-franchised ventures. Bates's study also found that those franchise businesses which do survive, earn less than the non-franchised businesses.

There are two categories of costs related to franchises. First, there is the cost of purchasing the franchise, and second, the cost of ongoing fees calculated from revenues and paid to the franchisor. It is not unusual for a franchise to pay 10% or more of its revenue to the franchisor in fees and mandated contributions to collective advertising. Think about how much of your profit is represented by these fees. The price of a great name brand franchise may make these costs a bargain, but your plan still needs to address what you're getting from being a franchise relative to what you are paying for the honor.

It may be better to be a franchisor than a franchisee. Franchisors can experience significant growth by selling many franchises. Although there are substantial up-front regulatory, legal, and planning costs, once a franchisee becomes profitable, it rarely requires additional investment and sends a steady stream of franchise fees back to the franchisor. Also, when you have mastered the franchising system, you have an expertise that can be applied to a number of different industries. In fact, many companies own multiple franchise systems. Cendant Corporation, for example, is the franchisor of AmeriHost Inn, Super 8 Motels, and Howard Johnson Motor Lodges, among others. Allied Domecq franchises Dunkin' Donuts, Baskin Robbins, and Togo's Eateries.

Focus on Research: Does Success Impede Long-Term Innovation and Flexibility?

Robert Burgelman, the Edmund W. Littlefield Professor of Management at Stanford University, has studied the top management and strategic choices of Intel Corporation[8] since the 1980s. Founded in 1968, Intel has been one of the most successful technology companies in history. By 1987, Intel's annual revenues had grown to $1.9 billion and ballooned to over $30 billion by 2003.

Burgelman divides Intel's history into three epochs: The first, from 1968 to 1985 under Gordon Moore, was focused on computer memory products. The second epoch, from 1985–1998 with Andy Grove at the helm, concentrated on microprocessors. During the third epoch, from 1998 on, led by Craig Barrett, Intel has been dedicated to Internet enabling technology, such as Ethernet, and wireless connectivity products.

Intel's great success hinged on two major events: their invention of the microprocessor in 1970 and the fact that IBM chose Intel's design for microprocessors as the PC standard shortly thereafter. While Intel grew steadily under Gordon Moore's leadership, the Andy Grove era saw the company's revenue escalate at the explosive rate of nearly 30% per year and profits at nearly 40% per year, which Burgelman ascribes to Grove's recognition of the microprocessor opportunity. However, Burgelman believes that Grove's tremendous success may have also planted the seeds for future problems.

Because Intel's business and research were focused on this single, albeit hugely successful family of products, there was barely any management support for research and development in other areas. Grove enforced his focus on the microprocessor business by centralizing the organization structure rather than by maintaining the matrix structure which characterized Intel's operations under Gordon Moore. By 1998, 80% of Intel's revenue and virtually all its profits came from microprocessors.

With this single-minded microprocessor orientation, Intel began to lose the knowledge, expertise, and experience to succeed in other segments of the market. The company suffered a series of failures during the 1990s with products such as video conferencing, networking and the merging of personal computer and television systems.

During the period when Intel was effectively "locked into" high-performance microprocessors, the company had a difficult time doing anything else. Its long-time competitor, Advanced Micro Devices (AMD), began to vie with Intel in lower-cost chips, and by 2004, had surpassed Intel in market share for microprocessors[9].

The entrepreneurial lesson from Intel's experience is clear: No matter how successful your company is in certain areas, it must maintain the flexibility to adjust to changes in the market and the competition. Stating this as a management goal along with explaining how this will be achieved is a must for a truly bankable business plan.

LOU KIM CONSIDERS AN AUTO REPAIR FRANCHISE

Lou Kim has always been interested in cars. When he was in high school, he rebuilt a broken down Ford Falcon his father bought for $200 into a spiffy hot rod, a feat he accomplished for less than $500 by scavenging parts from auto wreckers and doing all the work himself.

When Lou graduated from high school, he got a job as a helper in the repair shop of a car dealer, attended college at night for six years to earn his Bachelor's in Business Administration, and participated in every training program the car dealer offered. He has now worked at the same local Tucson dealership for nearly 20 years, the last eight of which he has served as shop manager, at a current salary of $80,000. Lou believes that he has gone as far as he can at this or any other car dealership. The owner of the dealership has spoken with Lou about moving him over to the sales side of the business, which would put him on a career track towards being a sales manager, followed by dealership manager, but Lou likes the service and repair aspects of the business best.

Lou is now thinking about starting his own auto service business and believes there are a number of options, such as an auto body repair shop, a general purpose repair shop, or a speed shop that would build and repair high-performance cars and trucks. He is also considering the purchase of a franchise for one of the many car repair chains that specialize in transmissions, brakes, mufflers, lubrication, or tires. Since he has never owned a business before, Lou thinks a franchise might be a good option since the franchisor has created and tested the business concept and provided an operating guide.

As part of examining the franchise option, Lou has received about a dozen Uniform Franchise Offering Circulars from various companies that detail the financial, operating, and management issues, along with the average performances of their franchisees. Based on these materials, Lou has created a list of pluses and minuses for buying a franchise and an average estimate of what the financial performance of his own franchise would be.

On the plus side, Lou believes that the franchises often have well-known names, proven operating models, established business systems, extensive training to franchise owners and their employees, and could be sold more easily than an independent operation. On the minus side, a franchise cannot deviate from the franchise business model, it must pay significant fees to the franchisor, and it could be subjected to the competition of additional franchises in his local area. Some auto repair franchise companies have received negative publicity about their selling unnecessary services to customers. Lou also wonders if a franchise with all its operating rules is the way to benefit from his knowledge and experience.

Lou created a financial projection of start-up investment and operating results for the franchises he liked the most. He projects the start-up costs as an initial franchising fee of $25,000, renovations and equipment of $300,000—assuming a rented location—and an additional $400,000 if he wants to buy the building and land. Of this total required investment of $325,000 to $725,000, Lou believes he could borrow about half if he rented the location and about 70% if he bought the building. This would make his investment about $160,000 if he rents a location and $220,000 if he purchases a location. Lou could afford to make either of these investments, but all of the loans would require the collateral of his house.

Lou created a table to summarize the likely financial results for a franchise:

TABLE 7.4
LOU KIM'S FRANCHISE DECISION: COMPARISON OF OPTIONS

Category	Average Franchise Performance in Rental Location	Estimated Performance for Lou's Shop if Rented Location	Average Franchise Performance in Owned Location	Estimated Performance for Lou's Shop if Location Is Purchased
Revenue	100%	$500,000	100%	$500,000
Fees to Franchisor for royalties and group advertising	13%	$65,000	13%	$65,000
Cost of goods sold	30%	$145,000	30%	$145,000
Mechanics' wages	23%	$115,000	23%	$115,000
Rent	7%	$35,000	---	---
Fixed overhead such as receptionist, legal, accounting, phone, computer, etc.	15%	$75,000	15%	$75,000
Advertising for Lou's Shop	3%	$15,000	3%	$15,000
Interest on $220,000 loan at 7% annually	---	---	3% (1)	$15,400
Profit(2)	**10%**	**$50,000**	**14%**	**$69,600**

(1) Principal payments on the loan would begin in the third year and would be $30,000 annually.

(2) Any salary to Lou would be paid out of the profits.

CASE QUESTIONS:

1. Lou now faces some major decisions. Should he leave his current position to pursue owning his own business?
2. If he does leave, should he purchase a franchise or start an independent business?
3. And if he does purchase a franchise, should he buy or rent the location?

End of Chapter Questions:

1. What are major types of organization structures and what are the pluses and minuses of each?
2. Who do you think are the key employees within entrepreneurial ventures? Why?
3. How do you think an entrepreneurial venture impacts the family of the entrepreneur?
4. What type of culture would you like to see in a business that you own? How will you create that culture?

NOTES

1. Arlyn Tobias Gahilan, "The Amazing JetBlue," *Fortune Small Business*, May 1, 2003. Vol. 13, 4.
2. Caroline Daniel, "Start of a Longer Haul into the JetBlue Yonder," *Financial Times*, August 26, 2002, p. 8.
3. Robert C. Ford, "David Neeleman, CEO of JetBlue Airways, on people + strategy = growth," *Academy of Management Executive*, Vol. 18, No. 2, (Spring, 2004), pp. 139–143.
4. Nick Pachetti, "JetBlue Skies: The Upstart Discount Airline is Cruising in an Otherwise Turbulent Industry. Will Fierce Head Winds Throw It off Course?" *Money*, Vol. 32, No. 4, (April, 2003), p. 56
5. Robert B. Duncan, "The Ambidextrous Organization: Designing Dual Structures for Innovation," in Ralph H. Killman, Louis R. Pondy, and Dennis Slevin, eds., *The Management of Organizations,* Vol. 1 (New York: North-Holland, New York), pp. 167–188.
6. Ramona K. Z. Heck, and Kay Stafford, (2001). Ibid.
7. Timothy Bates, "Analysis of Survival Rates Among Franchise and Independent Startups," *Journal of Small Business Management*, Vol, 33, No. 2, (April 1995), pp. 26–36.
8. Robert A. Burgelman, "Strategy as Vector and the Inertia of Coevolutionary Lock-In," *Administrative Science Quarterly*, Vol. 47. No. 2, (Spring 2002) p. 325.
9. John Markoff, "Intel's Big Shift after Hitting Technical Wall," *The New York Times,* May 17, 2004, p. C1.

CHAPTER 8

ISSUE 8: IDENTIFY POTENTIAL FUNDING SOURCES

As your business concept takes shape, you should focus on the most likely financing sources. Issues such as the size of your business, the industry it is in, whether you are starting a new business or buying an existing one, and whether you can provide collateral to a lender must be considered in creating a target list of funding sources. Banks and other funding sources don't lend money because people with interesting business ideas are nice. They follow specific guidelines which are designed to insure that they will make money by investing in or lending to your venture.

For the vast majority of entrepreneurs, well known, high-profile means of raising money, such as through venture capital firms or by going public, are not viable options. Your own credit history, credit score, and business history are key factors in obtaining financing for your company through Small Business Administration (SBA) guaranteed loans and other bank credit options. Your ability to tap into your personal network of friends, family, and professional contacts is crucial to raising money beyond what your own personal funds or credit can provide. In all these cases, there are important considerations, including the potential impact on relationships when family and friends become investors.

When you have completed this process of identifying the best potential funding sources for your business, you will be able to write a bankable business plan that addresses their issues and answers their questions, even before they ask them! Remember that a strong plan must meet the needs of financial supporters, whether they are bankers interested in prompt loan payments, investors who are looking for long-term profits, or family members who simply want you to have the chance to pursue your dream.

There are two main types of funding:

Debt. Debt is an agreement to borrow money and pay it back with interest and to pay the amount of the loan, called principal, back on a fixed schedule. Types of debt include loans, mortgages, lines of credit, and leases. Banks, credit companies, or individuals lending the money want to reduce the risk of not being paid back, so they often require collateral—specific assets that they can confiscate and sell to pay the loan in case the borrower does not. Collateral can be equipment, company stocks, or real estate, including a person's home. Debt with collateral is called secured debt and is often required for new ventures.

Debt is ranked by the order in which it is paid in the event of a default, liquidation, or bankruptcy. Senior debt is reimbursed first. Junior debt, also called subordinated debt, is paid only after senior debt has been fully discharged. As a borrower develops a track record for being a successful businessperson and making loan payments on time, lenders become more comfortable increasing the size of loans and reducing the amount of collateral. Most banks, however, are reluctant to give up collateral they already have, which can force some borrowers to change banks in order to reduce collateral.

There are also types of short term debt that can help companies manage variable cash needs, which include borrowing against receivables, obtaining a line of credit, or factoring, a type of financing for businesses with seasonal needs, such as the fashion industry.

Equity. Equity is ownership in a business. It can take the form of stock in a corporation or shares in a partnership. When investors buy equity, the entrepreneur is promising to give them a share of the profits from business operations or from an eventual sale of the company. Some equity investors require control of the companies they invest in and may want at least 51% of the stock, while others are content to be minority shareholders without control. In either case, stock sales in private companies usually involve a contract specifying the precise terms of the investment and the rights of the shareholders. These rights can vary greatly but often include an option to buy more shares or force the company to buy the stock back within a certain time at a preset price. Creating a shareholders' agreement requires an experienced lawyer who specializes in this area.

Deciding on the Balance between Debt and Equity

Whether debt or equity is preferable for your company or how much of each should be used is based on how much of each your venture can obtain. Because debt requires interest and principle payments on a fixed schedule, your company needs to generate enough cash to make those payments. These mandated payments reduce a company's financial flexibility, but because debt is generally the least expensive form of financing, usually below 10% annual interest, most businesses try to arrange as much debt as possible.

Equity investment does not require fixed, scheduled payments, which gives the company the greatest financial flexibility, but it does come at a cost. Because equity investors do not receive any financial returns until the debt is paid, they assume greater risk and uncertainty and expect much higher returns in the long run, often at levels two or three times the interest rate on debt. Equity investors usually receive significant control of the company through their ownership of shares—often a majority of the shares.

The availability of debt and equity also depends on the track record of the entrepreneur, including business and personal collateral. Investors are swayed by the attractiveness of the industry and the presence of a clear exit strategy, such as a sale of the company that will pay off the debt and provide them with profits.

One important question is "How much should the entrepreneur invest?" There is no right answer, but the tradeoff, like most financial questions, is one between risk and reward. You may want to invest as little as possible to reduce your financial risk or because you don't have enough money to invest, but this will reduce your share of any eventual profits. On the other hand, you may feel so positive about your company's prospects that you want to invest the most money possible. The next section about sources of financing, demonstrates that the answer involves both a financial and a personal decision.

Potential Funding Sources

Here's an overview of potential funding sources:

THE ENTREPRENEUR

About 90% of businesses start with the financial support of the entrepreneur[1]. Most entrepreneurs invest in their ventures by providing collateral, using their credit cards, or taking out personal loans. But this is a step you should consider very carefully. Personally signing on loans will require you to pay them back if your business cannot. No matter how much confidence you have in the likelihood of success for your bald men's head waxing salon, the reality is that most new businesses fail. You have to decide objectively whether you are prepared to sell your house, give up your retirement account, or even file for personal bankruptcy if the worst happens.

Many entrepreneurs see their venture as just one part of their financial situation. They may start the business on a part-time basis, have other businesses going at the same time, or plan on opening other new ventures in the future. They may also be focused on a relatively short-term strategy for their businesses including building it and selling it within a few years. Many of these entrepreneurs adopt the "O.P.M" strategy—Other People's Money. They prefer risking as little of their own money as possible while maintaining the flexibility to undertake other ventures. Others see their ventures as a long-term undertaking that they want to control completely. For them, focusing on the financing they can provide is the best strategy.

Family and Friends

Relatives and close friends are a common source of financing for entrepreneurial ventures because their agendas are more personal than business oriented—they want to help you succeed. Some would like to share in your success, and they may see investing in your business as an opportunity to get in on the ground floor, but these goals are usually secondary. Family and friends make good investors because they are accessible and you can use your personal relationship to encourage their investment. The negative is that if the business fails, you will have to deal with the "Thanksgiving Factor," meaning that you'll still be seeing them often!

One entrepreneur who started a moving company with investments from family members, including his parents and his father-in-law, saw his business fail despite his good efforts when the city in which he had established his company experienced a sudden downturn in the economy. His parents treated the investment as a gift to their son. They told him they thought he did the best job possible, and they said they would invest again if he wanted to start another business in the future. His father-in-law, however, could never come to terms with his financial loss and raises it every time he sees his son-in-law.

There are several important lessons here. First, be selective about whom you ask for money, avoiding friends or relatives whose relationship with you might suffer too much if your business fails. Second, be sure to warn your investors of the real financial risk they are taking and give them every opportunity to say "no." Third, be prepared for the long-term negative consequences from some individuals, no matter how thoroughly they were warned, if your business does fail.

All these caveats not withstanding, family and friends represent strong potential funding sources for most entrepreneurs.

Focus on Research: Do You Need Personal Financial Resources to Be an Entrepreneur?

Most people would answer an unqualified "yes" when asked if people who are rich are more likely to be entrepreneurs, and more likely to be successful entrepreneurs. It's true that many studies have shown that being well-educated, male, married, a member of certain ethnic groups, especially Asians and whites, *and* rich does correlate with high levels of entrepreneurship. However, in 2004, Erik Hurst of the University of Chicago, and Annamaria Lusardi of Dartmouth College[2], published research on the relationship between wealth and entrepreneurship that made some startling conclusions, including the fact that wealth does *not* matter for the vast majority of people when they become entrepreneurs.

Because measuring wealth is complicated and personal data can be difficult to obtain, Hurst and Lusardi used two "proxies" for wealth: recent increases in home values and inheritances received. Since many people use equity in their homes to finance new ventures and inheritances can give people the immediate means to realize their entrepreneurial dreams, these are useful determinants of wealth.

Hurst and Lusardi concluded that only for the richest 5% of people did wealth actually correlate with higher rates of entrepreneurship. In addition, the amount of people's wealth did not correspond to the size of the companies they founded, perhaps because most entrepreneurs start ventures with less than $35,000. Nor did inheritance have an effect on the likelihood of starting a business, except for the wealthiest 5%. Certainly one of the key findings is that wealth does not appear to be a major factor in determining whether someone becomes an entrepreneur.

Why is this so? More research needs to be done, but perhaps people in the lower income brackets start businesses for reasons having little to do with how much money they have. They may be immigrants and see entrepreneurship as a fast track to success in America. Perhaps they need to replace lost jobs or supplement their regular incomes. On the other hand, those wealthiest 5% may find that additional money changes the amount of risk they are willing to take and encourages them to turn a dream into reality.

Angels

Angels are wealthy individuals who invest directly in businesses. Although there are numerous Web-based matching services linking entrepreneurs and potential angels, you are more likely to find an angel investor through an established personal or business relationship with an accountant, perhaps, or a lawyer who handles your business dealings. Angel investors tend to focus on industries they know through their direct experience or previous success. Most angels know exactly how much risk they are taking by investing in a start-up or a relatively new business, so they expect to earn high returns on their stake if the business becomes successful. Some will ask for a seat on your Board of Directors or for an option to purchase enough stock to control the company.

Making a deal with an angel is a bit like getting married and requires careful thought before the actual commitment is made. Angel investors who are experienced in your industry will have strong ideas about how your business should be run. Unless these ideas closely match your own, you may be in for a struggle. Many angel investors are also very tough, experienced negotiators when it comes to making deals. They know how important obtaining financing is for you because many have been in the same position, so be prepared for potentially long and complex negotiations.

Venture Capital

Venture capital firms are generally large, professionally managed funds. Many are organized as Small Business Investment Corporations (SBICs) which enables them to obtain Small Business Administration (SBA) guarantees on part of the investments they make in ventures. The capital that venture capital firms have usually comes from pension funds, large corporations, and wealthy individuals. Many entrepreneurs think that venture capital is a serious option for them, but in reality, venture capital is a relatively small and highly specialized source of funding. Even in peak years, the venture capital industry makes fewer than 10,000 investments.

In most cases, venture capital firms are looking for large private companies with a strong probability of growth in which they can invest several million dollars or more. They prefer to invest in businesses that will result in a clear and profitable exit within a few years when they are sold, go public, or merge with another company. Despite having invested in start-ups during the dot-com boom, venture capital firms rarely invest in new businesses.

Venture capital firms generally prefer to control the companies in which they invest. This gives them the control to determine when a business is sold, what other financing it obtains, or even if the founding entrepreneur is retained to operate the business. When the entrepreneur and the venture capital firm share the same financial agenda, things generally work well. When their goals are different, conflict usually follows. The entrepreneur may feel that the venture capitalists don't have confidence in the long-run prospects of the company, and the venture capitalists may think that making money is not the entrepreneur's main objective.

Corporations

Occasionally, corporations will make direct investments in outside ventures. This is most often seen in technology industries, when a large company, such as Intel, invests in a small company that is developing a product Intel would eventually like to own. This type of investment is rare, and almost always carries an agreement to sell the company to the corporate investor at some point in the future if the investor wants to buy your product. It makes sense to look for this type of investor if you have personal contacts at a specific company, know your product would be very useful to them, and you feel comfortable becoming a division of the corporation in the future if you are successful.

Banks

Although banks make loans to companies, they usually focus on the financial record and strength of the individual entrepreneur. They look at the entrepreneur's business record, reputation in the industry, and credit scoring, which is discussed later in this chapter in the section called "How Banks and Other Leaders Make Loans." Banks almost always want the owner of the company to stand behind the loans by signing a personal guarantee or using assets, including a home, as collateral to pay the loan if the business fails. If the company has a very strong record of profitability (and, therefore, the ability to pay both interest and principal), or if the business assets are more than enough to secure the loan, this personal risk can sometimes be avoided.

Banks tend to be "formula" lenders, meaning that they have established guidelines for whether or how much they are willing to lend in any particular situation. This formula might be a percentage of business assets, a multiple of cash balances the company maintains in the bank, a multiple of profits, or a multiple of revenue.

Leasing is a way of financing assets such as equipment and vehicles. With leasing, the financing firm, which may be a bank or a commercial credit company, maintains ownership of the equipment until the lease is fully paid. If the lease falls into arrears, they reclaim the equipment, which is what makes it easier to obtain approval of a lease than of a business loan.

Many entrepreneurs are frustrated by banks and their rather rigid lending guidelines because they feel banks don't recognize the unique opportunities of their ventures. Trying to change a bank's guidelines is usually impossible because they are set by senior bank officers to whom the prospective borrower doesn't have access. Banks do negotiate the specific details of any loan and different banks have different lending guidelines. Therefore, the best strategy for entrepreneurs is to "shop" at as many banks as possible and take the best deal offered.

Table 8.1 below summarizes some of the important characteristics and differences among various funding sources.

TABLE 8.1
CHARACTERISTICS OF VARIOUS FUNDING SOURCES

Financing Source	Requires Current Payments?	Requires Share of Profits?	Wants Operating Control?	Cost of Capital
Entrepreneur	No	Yes	Yes	High
Family and Friends	Probably Not	Probably Yes	No	Low
Angel Investors	No	Yes	Input on operations but probably not control	High
Venture Capital	No	Yes	Yes	High
Corporations	Probably Not	No	Eventually, through buyout	High
Banks	Yes	No	No	Low
Public Investors after company goes public	No	Yes	No	Low

Going Public

For most businesses, going public is the equivalent of winning the lottery. Just look at the numbers. There are more than 10 million businesses in the United States, but only about 17,000 public companies. Of these, 2,800 are traded on the New York Stock Exchange and 3,300 are traded on the NASDAQ exchange. It is true that during the dot.com boom, many companies with little more than a cute logo were sold to the public, but that period was an aberration and is now as faint a memory as much of the money that was invested. To be a candidate for a public offering, a company usually needs to have at least $20 million in annual revenue and be in an industry that Wall Street feels positive about.

Being a public company is very different from being a private company. Public companies have their performance held up to the bright light of Wall Street scrutiny every quarter, are subject to extensive reporting and regulatory requirements, and are generally quite visible to their industry and their competitors. Many entrepreneurs have a difficult time making the transition from running a private company to running a public company and often view going public as a personal exit strategy that will put a high value on their stock and give them a means to sell these shares easily.

What They Did Right: Jeff Bezos Writes the Plan for Amazon.com

Most entrepreneurs whose businesses have grown through multiple rounds of financings usually end up holding less than 10% of their company stock. Growing companies require new capital to finance expansion, marketing efforts, acquisitions, receivables, and operating losses. Each new round of investment dilutes the value of existing shareholders' equity because new investors are buying newly issued shares of stock. This increases the total number of outstanding shares and leaves the existing shareholders with the same number of shares, but a lower overall percentage of the company. Since virtually all investors expect to receive high returns, they want to acquire a significant share of the company.

But Jeff Bezos, who founded Amazon.com in his garage in 1994, and built it into the Internet's preeminent retailer with $7 billion in annual sales only ten years later, still owned over 25% of Amazon.com stock in 2004, even after selling more than 2 million shares annually for several years. At a price of $50 per share, Bezos's stock was worth $5 billion in 2004. How did Bezos manage this? His strategy is a guide for entrepreneurs who want to keep as much of their companies as possible:

- Bezos started the company with $84,000 of his own money, providing him with 100% of the initial stock.
- Early in Amazon.com's growth, he sold stock to family members who were motivated to help him as much as they were to make money. This enabled Bezos to keep more of the company than deals with investment angels or venture capital firms would have allowed.
- Amazon.com grew so rapidly and Internet stocks became so prized that the valuation of the company grew enormously. In 1995, Amazon.com was valued at $4 million. A year later its value was $60 million.[3]
- In 1997, when the company went public with a valuation of $500 million,[4] Bezos and his family were able to keep 52% of the stock and still raise more than $50 million by selling less than 10% of the company.
- Later valuations grew even more rapidly. By 1999, Amazon.com was worth over $36 billion, allowing Bezos to raise even greater amounts of capital by selling even smaller amounts of stock[5].
- Amazon.com raised a significant amount of capital by issuing debt that required little or no equity dilution. By 2000, the company had raised more than $2 billion by issuing debt.
- Bezos kept his eye on cash. Despite having to raise capital to finance its rapid growth, after going public, Amazon.com never had less than $1 billion of cash. This prevented the company from ever becoming desperate for new capital and having to sell shares at unattractive prices, a strategy which allowed it to weather the bursting bubble of most other Internet stock valuations.
- Bezos always kept great customer service as a priority. By maintaining its reputation and service standards, Amazon.com never risked being viewed by investors as a company that was losing its edge.

While some might think that Bezos's success was based on being in the right industry, remember that the vast majority of Internet firms failed. Bezos and Amazon.com have prospered because of superior financial planning that accompanied a well-executed business plan.

Estimating Company Value

Many people will ask you "What is your business worth?" or "How much will it be worth?" These are central questions for any business, but they are not easy to answer. Many experienced entrepreneurs know that the best answer to the question of a company's value is "What someone will pay for it." But business valuations are based on certain approaches and theories that are selected to fit the goals of the purchaser, not the seller. Your business plan should include estimates of your company's worth for every year of financial projections you provide. Investors and lenders want to know where they stand if the company is sold or has to be closed at any given point. Calculating the company's value depends a great deal on the industry. You need to research your specific industry with owners, investors, and lenders to learn how businesses in your industry are valued.

Typical financial methods of calculating a company's value include:

Discounted Cash Flow: This approach relies upon estimating profits for the next ten or fifteen years and then calculating the current cash equivalent of this stream of cash inflows (profits) and outflows (investment and losses).

Asset Based: This method focuses on the value of the assets whether they are physical assets, such as real estate and equipment, or non-material assets, such as patents, customer lists and relationships, brand names, and contracts. Lenders will often ask businesses to calculate their Book Value, which is a company's total assets less total liabilities—two numbers that can be found in the financial statements on the Balance Sheet. Since assets are likely to have changed in their actual value since they were first recorded on the company's Balance Sheet, sometimes an Adjusted Book Value is created that is based on the current market value of the company's assets.

Replacement Value: Sometimes businesses are valued on what it would cost to duplicate them. An entrepreneur may have confidence that she *could* duplicate an existing business, but it might be easier to purchase an existing business. The replacement value approach might apply to companies such as a research firm with a strong team of scientists and unique technical systems or a restaurant with a well-known name, a good location and a long-term lease.

Liquidation Value: Liquidation value is what a company would produce if sold quickly. Liquidation value might include the value of accounts, databases, inventory, physical assets, contracts, leases, or what another company or a competitor might pay to purchase the entire business. The calculation of liquidation value should also account for the costs related to these sales, such as commissions, legal fees, moving expenses, and penalties on leases or contracts.

Revenue or Profit-Based: Some industries, such as real estate, retail businesses, or the media industry, have relatively well-accepted guidelines for estimating value based on revenue or profits. It is not unusual for retail businesses to sell for one or two times annual revenue, or for real estate to sell for ten to twenty times profits. Public companies are generally valued at a multiple of their earnings, called the Price/Earnings Ratio. Public companies' shares generally sell in the range of 10 to 30 times the earnings per share.

Cash Flow (EBITDA) Based: Private companies are more often valued at a multiple of Cash Flow, which is Earnings Before Interest, Taxes, Depreciation, and Amortization (EBITDA.) This measure is useful for private companies because it tells a prospective purchaser how much cash the company is producing from its operations. A new owner is not likely to assume the loans that the company currently has, so interest and principal payments (amortization) are likely to change after the sale. Depreciation is not a cash item, so it will reduce profitability on the bottom line of the accounting statements but not have an impact on the amount of cash a company is generating. Taxes are similarly very specific to the ownership situation and the amount of interest a company is paying. Using EBITDA is a good way to value a private company because it allows for the prospective owner to decide on the amount and type of financing to obtain and to calculate what the new tax situation will be. Private companies generally sell in the range of 3 to 10 times Cash Flow or EBITDA.

How Banks and Other Lenders Decide on Loans

Every time lenders such as banks, equipment leasing companies, commercial credit companies, or credit card companies make a loan, they assume the risk that they might not be paid back. They manage this gamble several ways: by lending to low-risk people, whom they call "creditworthy," by lending less than the customer is requesting, by exacting a guarantee from a third party whom they judge to be creditworthy, by charging higher interest rates and fees to compensate for accepting the risk, by obtaining collateral to seize and sell if the loan is not paid back, and, most often, by not lending at all. Loan decisions are made by looking at such personal factors as the entrepreneur's:

Credit History. In this electronic age, lending sources can instantly evaluate how quickly and thoroughly you have paid your bills and obligations to banks and other financial companies. Information about late payments, delinquent loans, bankruptcies, and how much credit you have been extended by banks, credit card companies, department stores, and credit bureaus is readily available to potential financial sources at the touch of a few computer keys.

Character. The loan decision often comes down to a personal evaluation made by one or more loan officers. Sometimes financing may be denied to people with stellar credit histories because the loan officer's sixth sense was triggered. Other times, albeit rarely, loans are granted to entrepreneurs with very low credit scores or even bankruptcies in their past. A loan made to someone without enough credit worthiness is called a *character loan*. A bank might make such a character loan to meet its internal guidelines for lending within certain geographic areas or because the bank is truly impressed with the entrepreneur.

Collateral. Nothing makes a lender happier than collateral to back up a loan. Mortgages are collateralized by the houses they finance. Leases are collateralized by the equipment that is being leased. Having collateral is a way for a bank to be paid if the loan payments are in arrears or the business defaults on the loan. Most lending sources require existing collateral such as an entrepreneur's house, securities, or other assets, before they will grant a small business loan.

Personal Guarantee. Lending sources want to make entrepreneurs generally liable for the loan, not just the business they're starting. A personal guarantee provides this assurance without necessarily specifying the particular collateral. If you have few assets, a personal guarantee may not mean much, but if you have a home with significant equity value, or a large savings or investment account, giving the bank a personal guarantee will make the officers very happy, just as it should make you very nervous.

Government Loan Guarantees. Federal agencies, such as the Small Business Administration, and various state programs help banks say "yes" to loans by agreeing to guarantee repayment of some portion of the loan, ranging between 50% to 90%. While these government loan guarantees carry a paperwork burden for both the entrepreneur and the lender, they encourage lenders to feel more comfortable approving loans. Making loans on which they can receive an SBA guarantee is excellent business for banks for several reasons:

- Banks often obtain government guarantees on loans they would have made without the guarantee. This increases the safety of the loan without reducing its profitability.
- Banks can "bundle" and sell the guaranteed portion of these loans to larger financing companies or on the public bond market, thus earning an immediate profit.
- Banks receive credit with bank regulators for making SBA guaranteed loans, helping the bank stay in good standing with the government regulators.

The presence of a government guarantee rarely stops a lender from asking for—and usually receiving—other collateral or personal guarantees for the loan. This gives bankers more than 100% in collateral and guarantees and is rather like wearing both a belt and suspenders—unnecessary and unattractive, but it certainly keeps your pants up.

Credit Scoring. Some credit research firms, most notably Fair, Isaac and Company, calculate a single figure into what they call a *credit score*. Factors such as your payment history, the amount of borrowing relative to your credit lines, recent inquiries by other financial institutions, and the types of credit you use, are put into a computer model that produces a single number, which is scored on a scale from a low of 400, representing poor credit, to a high of 900, representing strong credit. Although there is no single credit score number that banks require, most prefer a credit score of 680 or higher to make a business loan to an entrepreneur.

A ***credit report*** lists the history of all your financial activity and is different from a credit score which pulls all this information together and calculates a single number. Credit reports and scores are produced by three main credit-ratings companies: Transamerica, Equifax, and Experian. You can check your credit report with the credit-ratings companies directly, or go to www.myfico.com and purchase your credit reports and the scores from all three credit-ratings companies for about $45. There is also a nationwide system in the U.S., currently being rolled out state by state, that will enable individuals to obtain their credit scores from the credit-ratings companies at no charge once per year.

The best loan for any banker is one in which the business generates enough money to make the interest payments comfortably and eventually return the entire amount of the bank's money. Government guarantees, personal guarantees, and collateral are just fall back positions in case the business fails and the entrepreneur defaults on the loan. Collecting from a guarantor or taking and selling collateral generates a huge amount of work and aggravation for the bank and invariably marks the end of its business relationship with the borrower. When a company performs as anticipated, meets its obligations, and even grows to the point that its credit needs increase, the bank, the loan officers, and the entrepreneur have a win-win situation on which they can build a long-term, mutually beneficial business relationship.

This long-range, productive business relationship must start with financial projections the bankers find credible, which then *prove* to be credible. Of course, you want to have a strong credit score, show yourself to be of good character, and be able to offer as much in collateral or guarantees as are needed so the bank makes the loan, but credibility followed by a strong financial performance are what make a business truly bankable.

The Entrepreneur's Tool Kit: Creating Financial Models

Because your projections represent the heart of your business plan, it is critical that you have a superb financial model that combines all the financial aspects of your venture. Financial models are usually produced with a spreadsheet program to allow the numbers to be linked, so that a change in one automatically translates into related changes on all of the projected statements and analyses.

Creating a model from scratch is an excellent exercise because it forces you to consider all the financial assumptions in your business plan and it will teach you how the model works before you make changes in future versions. In addition to the financial projections on the sample business plans in the Appendix, there are several other readily available spreadsheet tools that can help you:

- `www.bankablebusinessplans.com` has many resources related to the book including sample spreadsheets that you can review and download.
- One of the best spreadsheet models is Active Money produced by the Columbus Enterprise Development Corporation. It is comprehensive, all the tables are linked, and it is free. It is available at: `www.cedcorp.com`.

- One of the easiest financial projections model is available on the Missouri SBDC Web site: www.missouribusiness.net/library/finance.asp. Produced by Aldis Jakubovskis, this model is not overwhelmingly detailed, but clearly shows which assumptions have to be entered, and produces completed projected statements based on the assumptions.
- Commerce Clearing House (CCH) has a very useful site for entrepreneurs at www.toolkit.cch.com. It has model spreadsheets, as well as useful and up-to-date tax planning tools.
- Find a plan with a financial model for a business in your industry. Many quality plans are available on Web sites for business plan competitions such as the MOOT Corp. competition at the University of Texas, at www.businessplan.org.Because of the large number of quality plans on such Web sites, you have a good chance of finding one for a business in your industry.
- Excel templates are available with the CD that accompanies the *MBA's Guide to Microsoft Excel 2002* by Stephen L. Nelson, published by Redmond Technology Press.

If you build your financial model from scratch or modify an existing one, there are several guidelines that you should follow:

- Examine your finished model *in detail.* It is not sufficient to review the model to see if it "looks" correct. You must test it by proofreading it carefully and checking all the spreadsheet cell references and formulas.
- Test the model by making changes to assumptions and checking to see if the changes flow through the rest of the model.
- Compare the model to others for similar companies to ensure that it uses standard industry categories.
- Have some of your advisors who are accountants, financial professionals, or people with industry experience, review the model.

CASE ON POINT

THE DIM BULB COMPANY

Alvin Einstein is what is often called a “serial entrepreneur.” In the past 17 years he has owned nine businesses including a commercial laundry, two restaurants, a paving company, and a lumber yard. Alvin has done quite well, turning a $1.5 million trust fund that he received when he celebrated his 25th birthday into nearly $13 million. He recently came across a new business that appeals to him: The Dim Bulb Company.

The Dim Bulb Company is a lighting equipment firm that specializes in manufacturing specialty items such as low-light and cool operating bulbs, and novelty Christmas tree lights in various shapes, including cows and horses. The company has existed for 23 years and has always been owned by the Light brothers, Hyman and Gray, who were generally referred to as High Beam and Low Beam. The Light brothers were ready to retire and wanted to sell their business.

The company had revenues of $30 million and Operating Cash Flow of $6 million. The Light brothers felt the business was worth $30 million and were unwilling to give a buyer terms so that part of the purchase price could be paid over time. Alvin is ready to commit half his fortune, or about $7 million, to the purchase and now needs a financial plan to raise the other $23 million. He realizes he has several options:

- Alvin’s family is quite wealthy and probably would finance $10 million. Unlike many family investors, they only want to do the deal on competitive business terms that any private angel investor or private company would accept.
- The Dim Bulb Company owns a building and land at their Florida factory that is worth $5 million. Alvin’s bank has said they would lend him $4 million against the building and another $15 million based on the company’s profitability.

- Dim Bulb recently began subcontracting manufacturing to several foreign companies and Alvin thinks that one or more of the subcontractors might be interested in investing in Dim Bulb.
- A venture capital group with several large investments in the lighting industry is interested in buying 80% of the equity and allowing Alvin to purchase the other 20%, but they want to put as much debt on the company as possible before layering in the equity investment.

The Light brothers want a proposal within two weeks and Alvin promised them one. Now he has to develop a financial plan.

Case Questions:

1. What are Alvin's financing options?
2. From Alvin's point of view, what are the pluses and minuses of each option?
3. How does the option of foreign outsourcing change Alvin's options?
4. Which option would you recommend to Alvin and why?

End of Chapter Questions:

1. List the major sources of funding for entrepreneurial ventures and explain what each hopes to achieve through its investment.
2. What is the most appropriate way for you to value the company you are designing for your business plan? Why?
3. How do banks decide upon loans for relatively new entrepreneurial ventures?

NOTES

1. Ramona K.Z. Heck and Kay Stafford, Ibid.
2. Erik Hurst and Annamaria Lusardi, "Liquidity Constraints, Household Wealth, and Entrepreneurship," The Journal of Political Economy, Vol. 112, No. 2, (April 2004), pp. 319–347.
3. Lawrence E. Katz and William A. Sahlman, "Amazon.com—Going Public," Harvard Business School case, 1998.
4. Lynda Applegate, "Amazon.com Valuation Exercise," Harvard Business School case, 2000.
5. Lynda Applegate, Ibid.

CHAPTER 9

ISSUE 9: PRODUCE FINANCIAL PROJECTIONS

The accuracy of your financial figures and projections is absolutely critical in convincing investors, loan sources, and partners that your business concept is worthy of support. The data must also be scrupulously honest, extremely clear, and compare well to other companies in your industry. The actual number-crunching portion of your business plan is not the place to talk about your pie-in-the-sky hopes for opening a tuba plant in every country around the globe, or for convincing the U.S. Army that squid-flavored pancakes should become standard fare in all military mess halls. It *is* the place to discuss how and why you need certain equipment, time, or talent; how much these items will cost; when you expect to turn a profit; and how much return and other benefits your investors will receive.

More new businesses fail bccause they simply run out of cash reserves than for any other reason. When projections are not met, investors lose confidence in the entrepreneur and the company, and become reluctant to invest more. Had the projections been less optimistic and the investors asked to invest more in the beginning, they probably would have done so. In most cases, proper planning and more accurate projections could have prevented this problem completely.

Start analyzing your financial information by going back to your list of the tangibles and intangibles required to start your company and the costs you have estimated. Your business plan should clearly state the financing you need, how soon you require it, and how long before you start repaying investors. You should also explain what type of financing you hope to acquire, either *equity* (such as the sale of ownership shares in your company) or *debt* (such as loans to the company), and if you require capital expenditures to buy an automated pancake maker or working capital to pay for mousetrap design and market research. If you're planning to buy an existing business, or already own a business you would like to improve or expand, you should provide a detailed historical financial summary of how well—or poorly—the business has done in the past.

By the time you've pulled together all the important financial data, you'll have a clearer picture of how much of your own funds you'll be able to commit, the amount of money you'll need to borrow, and the number of investors you'll have to secure. This is also a good time to take a crash course in accounting principles or learn how to create spread sheets on a computer program. No matter what business you intend to start, you will need to know how to analyze not only projected profits and losses, but actual profits and losses as soon as your first customer walks through your pancake house door or buys a bottle of your bubble gum-scented bubble bath.

The Essential Financial Statements

Bankable business plans present clear, convincing numbers in several financial statements. The following are essential:

Income Statements are summaries of an existing company's performance over a period of time. Income Statements are usually prepared using the accrual system, which recognizes revenues when products or services are sold and expenses at the time goods or services are consumed—not when the revenue is received or the expenses are paid. Income Statements that cover past periods of time are called Historical Income Statements. Those which estimate a company's performance in future years are called Projected or Pro Forma Income Statements. Historical Income Statements, if available, and Projected Income Statements are absolute requirements for any bankable business plan.

Balance Sheets are statements that present the financial status of an existing or projected business at a particular point in time. An overview of a company's capital position, such as how much debt it owes and the value of its assets, is located on the Balance Sheet.

Cash Flow Statements are income statements revised to show the actual inflows and outflows of money. A company's Cash Flow can differ significantly from what the Income Statement shows. Because keeping adequate cash reserves is necessary for the company to continue to operate, the projected Cash Flow Statements are essential. Cash Flow Statements differ from Income Statements in the following ways:

- Revenue shows up on the Cash Flow Statements when payment is received, which for most businesses is between 30 and 90 days after bills are sent out. On an Income Statement, revenue is recorded when the product or service is sold.

- Expenses are recorded on Cash Flow Statements when they are actually paid, which is usually 30 or 60 days after the bill is received. Income Statements show expenses when the obligation to pay for them is incurred.
- Depreciation, which is recorded as an expense on the Income Statement but is not a cash item, is not included on the Cash Flow Statement.
- Principal payments on loans or purchases of stock from shareholders are included as a use of cash on the Cash Flow Statement, but do not appear on the Income Statement.

Operating Cash Flow is the actual cash that results from the *operations* of the business measured at the time the money is spent or received. Operating Cash Flow does not include the effects of sales or purchases of assets, depreciation, interest or principal paid on loans, and taxes.

Statements of Sources and Uses show all the ways a business receives and spends money. Information from the Income Statement and Balance Sheet are combined to produce the Statement of Sources and Uses. Sources of funds typically include investment, increases in loans, and profits. Uses include items such as investment in equipment, loan repayments, dividends, and operating losses.

Debt Management Schedules are projections that indicate your company's ability to pay interest and principal in accordance with your loan agreements. It is absolutely critical that the projections show that your company's obligations to its lenders will be met. Failure to pay interest and principal on time will result in the company's credit being reduced and can eventually lead to foreclosure and bankruptcy. An essential financial projection is a separate statement or table that shows the interest payment and principal repayment schedule and the company's ability to pay them. Since payments are made from cash flow, the Cash Flow Statements must show what percentage of cash flow is going to make payments and how much cash the company still has after paying its debt obligations.

Returns Analysis is a statement that shows the projected financial returns on the investment in your company. Potential investors need to see how much their investment will earn for them through current payments, such as dividends, or by distributions from the sale of stock or the company as a whole. Whatever your particular strategy for producing returns for your investors, your plan must explain this strategy and calculate what the returns will be. The returns analysis combines profit distributions (such as dividends) with the value of the company when it is sold, and compares that total with the initial investment. Thus, $1 million invested in year one, earns 50% annually if it is worth $2 million in year three (two years later). If you plan to sell the business in a few years, the returns will largely be a function of the value of the company at the time it is sold. If you plan to own the business for a long period of time, the returns will largely be a function of profit distributions to the owners (including yourself) over time.

Schedules of Investment and Capital Expenditures are lists of the amounts of money that need to be spent on items with long usable lives. The initial startup of your business—either by purchasing an existing company or founding a new one entirely from scratch—requires investment. A schedule that details this initial investment, including items such as legal expenses, equipment, banking fees, and rent deposits, is essential. Every year will likely require further capital expenditures for new equipment, buildings, or product development. This should also be presented in the Schedules of Investments and Capital Expenditures, the total of which is then carried over to the Cash Flow Statement.

The Six Critical Financial Assumptions

You need to be careful about all of your financial estimates. Mistakes undermine the confidence of anyone who reads your plan and will probably doom your efforts. The key to passing this test is taking the time to explain your assumptions fully. Here are six critical financial assumptions that will help provide a strong basis for your financial projections. The test of your projected financial statements is whether someone can read them and understand them without having to ask you questions.

1. Up-Front Costs. No matter how successful you expect your business to be, if you overpay to start it, it just won't work. Daimler-Benz's purchase of Chrysler and Hewlett-Packard's purchase of Compaq provide examples of this on a large scale. On a smaller scale, the famous Russian Tea Room next to Carnegie Hall in New York City flourished for decades through good and bad economic times. In 1996 new owners purchased the restaurant for $6.5 million and spent $36 million on a lavish renovation. Within two years, The Russian Tea Room shut its doors and filed for bankruptcy. This New York icon reopened in November in 2006, hopefully under the stewardship of more fiscally conservative owners.

There are two steps that must be followed to avoid making so large an up-front investment that the business cannot meet its financial goals. First, you must thoroughly research all costs carefully. "Guesstimates" are not part of a bankable business plan. Second, your major assumptions must be conservative. Daimler-Benz and Hewlett-Packard significantly overestimated both the cost savings and revenue growth they would realize from the acquisitions they made.

The components of up-front costs include:

- Acquisition costs of buying an existing business.
- Capital Investment in land, building, renovations, and equipment prior to starting operations.
- Operating Losses during the start-up phase, which usually arise from operations prior to achieving sales goals and heavy, initial marketing expenses.

2. Sales and Revenue. Many entrepreneurs believe that their biggest problem will be handling the volume their businesses will generate, with customers beating a path to their doors. Reality is often quite different. As most experienced entrepreneurs will attest, sales and revenue projections are difficult to estimate—especially for new, start-up companies. Generating first-time orders is one of the toughest assignments in business and expanding a list of customers is a close second. Because of this, many entrepreneurs pull their projections out of thin air, which doesn't work. The solution is twofold:

- **Anchor revenue projections to reality** by supplying lists of potential customers, pre-testing your products or services through surveys or focus groups, comparing your product's features and price to the existing competition, and by comparing your revenue projections to industry averages or to particular businesses that you know.
- **Be conservative in the extreme.** After you have created projections that you are certain approximate reality, cut them mercilessly. When revenue projections seem ludicrously low to the entrepreneur, they are usually approaching reality!

3. Costs. Estimating costs requires a tremendous amount of work, but they are easier to estimate if you detail them. To make certain you have covered each item, use the following as a checklist:

- **Estimate every item** from fixed costs, such as rent, utilities, advertising, employees, and employees' benefits, to variable costs, such as raw materials, shipping of your products, and commissions to your salespeople. These are used in the Break-Even Analysis which is discussed later in this Chapter.
- **Estimate your costs** using as many detailed categories as you can and provide an explanation of how you determined the estimate, so if people question your numbers they can follow your process. Providing this back-up to your numbers helps establish you as a thorough manager who will inspire investors to have confidence in you.
- **Build in contingencies** for issues such as additional advertising, legal expenses, travel to meet with customers, and terminating employees who don't work out. After making these provisions, add a general contingency number of at least 5% to your total estimated expenses.

4. Debt. Estimating how much debt your business will be able to obtain also requires research. You should speak with lenders about their particular guidelines for loaning money to your specific type of business. Entrepreneurs often make the great mistake of assuming that they will get a bank to lend them more than it usually does. Banks have precise guidelines and rarely deviate from them. By speaking with bankers, experienced entrepreneurs, and accountants you can uncover these guidelines and adjust your projections accordingly. Remember, your financial projections must show that your company will be able to make its interest and principal payments comfortably.

5. Equity Investment. The amount of investment you are seeking in the form of stock or partnership shares requires that you project credible returns to investors. Because equity investors earn money from company profits and from the increase in the company's value, these figures must be calculated on how much investors will put in and how much they will get back. If the return on their investment looks like a number you might earn from a savings account in a bank, you need to rethink the deal.

Table 9.1 shows what an investor in Doc Willard's School of Painless Dental Techniques can expect to earn. The investor will receive 50% of the equity for a $1 million investment and will earn money both from yearly profits and a 50% share of the sale proceeds after the debt is repaid. This translates into $862,000 from yearly profits and $1,500,000 from the sale projected to take place at the end of the fifth year, when the company will be sold for eight times profit. This equals a 22% annual rate of return for the investor. See the Entrepreneur's Toolkit in this Chapter for an explanation of returns calculations.

TABLE 9.1
DOC WILLARD'S SCHOOL OF PAINLESS DENTAL TECHNIQUES
PROJECTED RETURNS ANALYSIS FOR EQUITY INVESTORS

Assumption: $1 million investment for 50% of the shares of the company
Company borrows debt of $1 million
This type of business is worth 8 times profits

	Company Profits	Share of Profits to Investor
Year 1	$150,000	$75,000
Year 2	$250,000	$125,000
Year 3	$400,000	$200,000
Year 4	$425,000	$212,500
Year 5	$500,000	$250,000
Total Yearly Profits to Investor		$862,500
Sale of Company at End of Year 5		
8 Times Profits		$4,000,000
Less Debt Repaid		$1,000,000
Sale Proceeds to be Distributed		$3,000,000
Investor's Share of Sale Proceeds		$1,500,000
Total Payments to Investor over 5 years		$2,362,500
Annual Rate of Return		22.0%

6. The Company's Value. Tracking your company's estimated worth should appear throughout the entire period of your projections. Investors and lenders want to know where they stand, and you will need to know where you stand if the company is sold or has to be closed at any given point. As discussed in greater detail in Chapter 8, Identify Potential Sources of Financing, there are many ways to establish the value of Identify Potential Sources of Financing, there are many ways to establish the value of a business. Calculating the company's value depends a great deal on the industry. Some businesses, such as restaurants, sell for the value of their real estate, leases, and fixed assets. Technology companies, such as manufacturers of high tech medical products, will sell as a multiple of their revenue, while media companies, such as magazines, will sell for a multiple of annual cash flow. Of course, some ventures, such as a one-person consulting firm, will sell for little because there is no assurance that clients will move to the new owner. Lenders will often ask companies to calculate *Book Value*, which is assets less liabilities.

Typical financial methods of calculating a company's value include estimating profits for the next five or ten years (or the projected length of the investment) and then calculating the current cash equivalent, called *Net Present Value*, of this stream of payments. In the table for Doc Willard's School, the *Annual Rate of Return* is calculated and answers the question "how much is my investment earning?" You need to do the research in your industry to come up with the appropriate business valuation method to use for your financial projections.

Of course, there can be complications. For example the Rate of Return may not be the same in all years. How much and when an investment is made may vary and take place over a number of years, and the value of the investment at the end may be complicated by multiple payments over time. These variables can make calculating the numbers by hand very complicated, but a spreadsheet program or a financial calculator can produce these figures easily.

Another complication is choosing the *Annual Growth Rate* when calculating Net Present Value and Net Future Value. The estimated Annual Growth Rate is chosen to reflect how much investors hope to earn on their investments or what the typical investment of this type is estimated to earn. When referring to the rate of returns for similar investments, it is generally called a Discount Rate.

What They Did Right: How Community Capital Bank Represents a New Trend in Banking—Old-Fashioned Banking

Most banks design the process of being considered for a loan as a series of hurdles. Miss even one hurdle and your loan application will probably be rejected. These hurdles usually include:

- Having a high credit score (generally 680 or above).
- Never having been through a bankruptcy.
- Never having been late on past loan payments.
- Being in an industry that the bank considers its specialty, which is often a loan portfolio it hopes to expand.

However, at Community Capital Bank in Brooklyn, New York, a loan application that fails to clear one, or even all of these standard hurdles, is still seriously considered. In fact, Community Capital doesn't even obtain the credit scores for potential applicants. John Tear, the bank's Senior Vice President in charge of reviewing all loan applications, says that some of his greatest successes were applicants which other banks had rejected. Community Capital's mission is to be financially successful by supporting businesses that are in economically challenged areas other banks generally avoid, or by financing entrepreneurs who have been passed over by more traditional banks.

Not only is Community Capital successful as a business in its own right, but it has regularly performed better than large traditional banks. Tear's branch is in an industrial section of Brooklyn and occupies a building that Chase Bank, one of the largest in the world, abandoned because it never became profitable. Three years after opening in this site, Tear's Community Capital branch became profitable and remains so. It now handles more business than Chase ever did in the same building.

There are several reasons for this success. Community Capital is one of over 500 federally-designated Community Development Financial Institutions (CDFI) that include banks, credit unions, loan funds, and venture capital funds. This designation allows Community Capital to receive investment from other banks, invest in economically disadvantaged areas, and then pass the credit for these loans back to the banks that provided the funds. CDFIs are also eligible for modest federal grants and have attracted the attention of socially responsible investment funds[1].

While these advantages can help start banks like Community Capital, their long-term success—like any business—still comes from being profitable. For banks this means they must approve loans to ventures that will make their interest payments regularly and pay back their principal on schedule. Good loans enable banks to raise additional capital and grow.

While Community Capital has received funds from other banks that want the regulatory credits and from investment funds that want to support its social mission, the long-term success of Community Capital rests on making smart loans and providing great service to its customers. In a throw back to small-town banking, most customers at Tear's branch are greeted by name and are encouraged to use the short lines for the well-trained tellers rather than just visit the ATM machines. Tear and his team visit their clients before making a loan and regularly, thereafter. Customers who want to meet the bank's President, Charlie Koehler, are encouraged to do so. Has this worked? Community Capital has a lower than average turnover of clients and a higher than average loan portfolio performance. One of the largest purchasers of the bank's stock is its own customers.

Operating like this does have its costs. Banks that look at every loan application with the attitude of "let's see if we can find a way to do this," need highly experienced and savvy loan officers who spend more time reviewing loan applications than they would if they just made their decisions "by the numbers" alone. Tear had a successful career with a more traditional bank before deciding that the flexibility and challenge of this environment was irresistible. His customers run the gamut from a tugboat operator to a dog kennel owner to an airplane parts manufacturer—a range that would be impossible at a large bank where loan officers specialize by industry.

This strategy creates many winners:

- Companies that wouldn't be considered for loans at other banks are able to obtain loans and grow.
- The communities in which these businesses exist receive an economic boost.
- The bank's customers, both for borrowing and retail banking, have a very positive experience.
- The bank's employees have challenging jobs that produce social benefits they are proud of.
- The bank's investors and partners benefit from excellent financial performance.

Tear sums up the difference this way: "A traditional bank exists to make a profit. Community Capital exists to make a difference and make a profit."[2]

The Entrepreneur's Toolkit: Calculating Returns to Investors

The three most important measures of financial success that entrepreneurs must use to demonstrate profitability to their investors are *Net Present Value, Net Future Value* and *Internal Rate of Return.* Theses measures are basically different sides of the same equation and can be easily calculated on a financial calculator or a spreadsheet program.

The process of investing and earning returns consists of three steps:

1. Money is invested.
2. Over time it grows (or shrinks) at an annual rate.
3. The investment ends and the initial investment along with any earnings are returned.

If you know any two of these three numbers, you can solve for the third. Which two you know determines which measure of returns you are solving for. The following Table summarizes this process.

Table 9.2
Comparison of Measures of Financial Return

What You Know	What You Are Solving For	What It Is Called
Annual Rate of Return and Value of Investment when the investment ends	How much money is invested at the beginning	Net Present Value
Initial Investment and Annual Growth Rate	Value of investment when the investment ends	Net Future Value
Initial Investment and Value of Investment when investment ends	Annual rate of growth	Internal Rate of Return

Of course, there can be complications. For example, the *Rate of Return* may not be the same in all years. How much and when an investment is made may vary and take place over a number of years, and the value of the investment at the end may be complicated by multiple payments over time. These variables can make calculating the numbers by hand very complicated, but a spreadsheet program or a financial calculator can produce these figures easily.

Another complication is choosing the *Annual Growth Rate* when calculating Net Present Value and Net Future Value. The estimated Annual Growth Rate is chosen to reflect how much investors hope to earn on their investments or what the typical investment of this type is estimated to earn. When referring to the rate of returns for similar investments, it is generally called a Discount Rate.

Prepare a Break-Even Analysis

A *Break-Even Analysis* answers several key questions including how much revenue your company will need to earn back the money invested, what your fixed costs are, and how much the company will earn on every dollar of sales after breaking even. These figures will be useful for your own understanding of your business, but potential lenders and investors will expect to be provided with this information.

The key to preparing a Break-Even Analysis is separating your costs into fixed costs and variable costs. Fixed costs remain the same regardless of your revenue. These include items such as salaries, rent, interest payments, and insurance. Variable costs go up with greater revenue and include items such as the costs of raw materials, royalties, shipping, and handling returns. Here is the process of calculating the Break-Even Point (BEP):

Step 1. Estimate Fixed and Variable costs. Fixed costs are those that remain the same regardless of volume sold. Variable costs are those that change with each additional unit sold. The Variable Costs should be expressed as a per unit value.

Step 2. Estimate Revenue per Unit which is the price the company expects to receive for each unit sold.

Step 3. Subtract the Variable Costs per Unit from the Revenue per Unit to arrive at a Contribution to Fixed Costs per Unit.

Step 4. Divide the Fixed Costs by Contribution to Fixed Costs per Unit. The result is the Break-Even Point or number of units that have to be sold for the company to break even.

EXAMPLE

Bill's Reconditioned Racquets buys used tennis racquets, refurbishes them, and then sells them to schools and tennis centers. Racquets cost $5 to buy and $10 to recondition, including pay for the hourly workers who do the reconditioning. Racquets are sold for $75 each. Bill's has a fixed cost of rent, salaries, advertising, and professional fees of $120,000 annually.

The calculations looks like this:

Fixed Costs: $120,000

Variable Costs per Racquet: $15

Revenue per Racquet: $75

Contribution to Fixed Cost per Racquet: $60

Fixed Costs of $120,000 divided by
Contribution to Fixed Cost per Racquet of $60 equals 2000.

Bill's Break-Even Point is 2000 racquets sold per year.

FIGURE 9.1
BREAK-EVEN ANALYSIS AND GRAPH

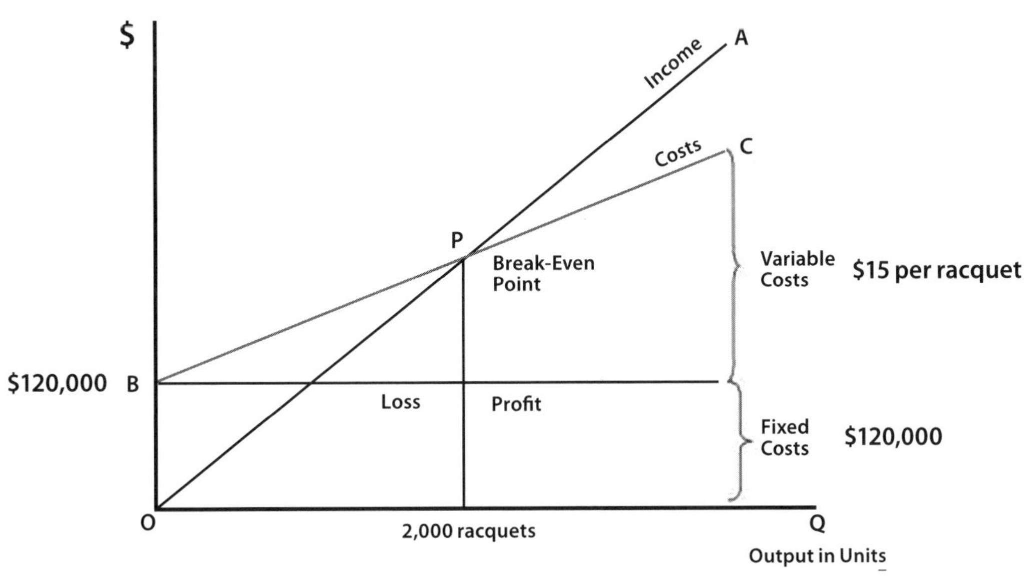

How to Create Statements

Many people are intimidated by the prospect of producing financial projections. However, if you manage the process by breaking it down into its components, such as doing what you can do best, finding resources to make other parts easier, and bringing in outside people to help with the remaining pieces, you can learn a great deal about the financial aspects of your business. If you have gone through the previous chapters carefully, you are well prepared to produce professional-quality financial statements because you can base your projections on information you have already gathered. Here are four basic steps to follow:

Step 1: Research (which you have already done)

Research, research, and more research will be your key to writing a bankable business plan. Thorough research helps you understand your industry, your competitors, the price of raw materials, the costs and availability of financing, and many other aspects that are relevant to your business.

Step 2: Build the Structure of Your Statements

Obtain copies of financial statements from companies in your industry through your lawyer, accountant, industry trade group, or books about your industry. If you have not been able to obtain such statements, use standard accounting statement forms or examples within this Chapter or from the www.bankablebusinessplans.com Web site.

Step 3: Start Filling in the Blanks

Now, do the best you can by filling in the blanks. Most people are able to do very well creating projected Start-Up Costs, Income Statements, Cash Flow Statements, and Debt Management Schedules. The key technical accounting issues are the differences in the timing of expenses and revenue between the Income Statement and the Cash Flow Statement. The Income Statement recognizes income based on an accrual system, which is when the income is earned or expenses are incurred, and the Cash Flow Statement recognizes income when it is received and expenses when they are paid.

Statements of Sources and Uses and Balance Sheets have more technical accounting issues to manage. If you cannot complete the statements yourself, then take advantage of the resources later in the book or below in Step 4.

Step 4: Use Some Outside Help

If you are not experienced enough to prepare statements yourself, consider one of the following strategies:

- Use a template similar to those available on the Web site for the book, www.bankablebusinessplans.com or from those other resources provided in Chapter 8. Quicken and Quickbooks also offer statement templates.
- Obtain technical assistance from a Small Business Development Center or other type of Entrepreneurship Center. Once you have researched solid estimates and produced statements as well as you can, the rest is not a big job for someone experienced at producing financial statements.
- Ask your accountant for help. Finishing the statements is not a daunting task for a professional accountant, but you probably want to keep the expenses down, so do this as a last resort. Do as much as you can yourself and get a fixed price from the accountant to finish the statements before you agree to use her services.

Tables 9.3 through 9.7 represent the sample financial statements for the fictional company, Lightning Larry's, Inc.

TABLE 9.3
LIGHTNING LARRY'S, INC.
INCOME STATEMENT

	Year 1
Revenue	1,200,000
Minus: Cost of Goods Sold	180,000
Estimated Gross Profit	**1,020,000**
Expenses	
Employees	220,000
Owner's Salary	60,000
Payroll Taxes	32,400
Supplies	5,200
Insurance	22,500
Rent	16,000
Promotion	9,000
Advertising	6,000
Telephone & Utilities	11,250
Professional Fees	4,500
Miscellaneous	11,300
Operating Expenses	398,150
Interest	78,175
Depreciation	45,000
Taxes	78,175
Total Expenses	599,500
Profit	420,500

Table 9.4
Lightning Larry's, Inc.
Cash Flow Statement

	Year 1
Cash Receipts	900,000
Minus: Cost of Goods Sold	180,000
Estimated Gross Profit	**720,000**
Expenses	
Employees	190,000
Owner's Salary	50,000
Payroll Taxes	28,000
Supplies	3,700
Insurance	22,500
Rent	12,000
Promotion	7,500
Advertising	4,000
Telephone and Utilities	9,650
Professional Fees	3,200
Miscellaneous	9,000
Operating Expenses	339,550
Cash Flow (EBITDA)	380,450
Depreciation	45,000
Amortization of Loan	49,561
Cash Flow (EBIT)	285,889

TABLE 9.5
LIGHTNING LARRY'S, INC.
STATEMENT OF SOURCES AND USES OF FUNDS
YEAR 1 (INCLUDES PURCHASE AND 1 YEAR OF OPERATION)

	Uses			**Sources**
Purchase of Assets	1,500,000		Bank Loan	450,000
Legal Expenses for Purchase	25,000		Owner's Investment	800,000
Name Change Expenses	7,500		Seller Note	500,000
Capital Expenditures	15,000		Cash Flow – EBITDA	380,450
Working Capital	65,000		Decrease in Working Capital	10,225
Interest Payments	78,175			
Total Uses	1,690,675		**Total Sources**	1,690,675

TABLE 9.6
LIGHTNING LARRY'S, INC.
YEAR 1 BALANCE SHEET

Assets	Year 1
Current assets:	
Cash & Cash Equivalents	54,775
Accounts Receivable	300,000
Other Short-Term Assets	
Total Current Assets	*354,775*
Fixed assets:	
Furniture & Equipment, Cost	315,000
Goodwill	1,532,264
Equipment	22,500
Less Accumulative Depreciation	45,000
Total Fixed Assets	*1,824,764*
OtherAssets:	0
Total Other Assets	*0*
TOTAL ASSETS	**2,179,539**
Liabilities & Stockholders' Equity	
Current Liabilities:	
Accounts Payable	58,600
Short -Term Bank Borrowing	0
Other Short Term Liabilities	0
Total Current Liabilities	*58,600*
Non Current Liabilities:	
Seller Note	500,000
Long Term Bank Debt	400,439
Total Non Current Liabilities	900,439
Stockholders' Equity:	
Common Stock	800,000
Retained Earning	0
Income	420,500
Total Stockholders' Equity	*1,220,500*
TOTAL LIABILITIES & STOCKHOLDERS' EQUITY	**2,179,539**

TABLE 9.7
LIGHTNING LARRY'S, INC.
PROJECTION OF RETURNS ANALYSIS

Purchase Price	1,500,000	
Owner's Equity	800,000	
Company Value at End of Year 1		
EBITDA	380,450	
Sale Multiple	5	
Company Value	1,902,250	
Less:		
Bank Debt	450,000	
Seller Note	500,000	
Net Proceeds	952,250	
Change in Owner's Investment		152,250
Rate of Return		19.03%

Check Your Projections Against the Answer Key

Now that you've learned how to create a credible, thoughtful, detailed, conservative, and properly presented bankable business plan, you're prepared to apply the advantage of the Risk Management Association (RMA) database. Most potential lenders and investors will compare your projections to the data supplied by the RMA, an association of over 3,100 banks and other financial institutions which pool their business clients' financial information. The RMA's purpose is to help members limit risk by avoiding loans to companies whose numbers are inaccurate or unrealistic. The RMA database serves as an answer key against which bankers can double check the financial projections of any business plan in any industry. If you compare your figures to the RMA database *before* you submit your business plan to potential lenders or investors, you will improve your chances of achieving the financial support you need to start your venture.

No matter how high your credit score, or how many government guarantees you can produce, or how much collateral you can offer, there is no replacement for credible, accurate projections. Some bankers will simply pass on making a business loan if the projections are not convincing. Others will decline to make a business loan, but will offer to make a personal loan if your collateral or guarantees are strong enough. Neither of these options is as attractive to you and your company as obtaining a business loan, which reduces your personal risk and builds your company's credit.

While virtually all banks and many other funding sources use the RMA data, few entrepreneurs take advantage of this significant resource. But you can, and should. The RMA data may seem intimidating at first because their publication, *Annual Statement Studies*, looks like the Manhattan telephone directory, but it's actually quite straightforward and easy to decipher. Most libraries with some focus on business and most Small Business Development Centers have the RMA's *Annual Statement Studies* book. Since you will need copies of only a few pages, it is not difficult to obtain the data through them. The RMA also sells their data through their Web site for $110 for each business category at `www.rmahq.com`. Most people, however, find the books easier to use than the Web site.

The following four steps will help guide you through the process of finding the right data for your business plan and using it to your advantage:

Step 1: Locate the page that pertains to your business. While the RMA book is a huge volume filled with minuscule numbers, there are only a few pages that pertain to you and your company. For example, suppose you're planning to open a gas station. You find those pages by looking through the Table of Contents to locate the section on retail businesses and then read down the list until you find gas stations. The RMA book is organized by government codes for business types, called NAICS (North American Industrial Classification System) codes, so you can find the NAICS code from the SBA Web site, `www.sba.gov`, first. But it is simpler just to look down the list. NAICS codes recently replaced an older classification system dating to the 1930s called SIC (Standard Industrial Classification).

Step 2: Find the column that matches your business size. There are two pages for gas stations. One page sorts their sample of gas stations by the amount of assets reported on the gas stations' financial Balance Sheets. But ignore that page for now because it is easier to look at the next page which sorts the gas stations based on their annual revenues. Find the column that most closely matches the sales you project. This column of numbers is all you will need for your comparison.

Step 3: Place your numbers next to the RMA numbers. The earlier section of this chapter called "The Six Critical Financial Assumptions" outlines which pieces of financial information are most important to a banker or an investor. These figures have been organized so they match the items in the RMA data. Now your projections and the RMA data can be easily compared.

Step 4: Explain the differences or adjust your projections. If your projections closely match or are more conservative than the RMA data, you have nothing more to do—other than to point this out proudly to your potential funders. If your projections are more optimistic than the RMA data, you need to explain this discrepancy in the text of your plan or revise your projections.

The Primary RMA Data

Although the RMA's *Annual Statement Studies* is thick, there is only one column of numbers that will be of importance to you. This is the column that contains 81 numbers gleaned from companies of similar size to yours on the page that presents your industry. Of these 81 numbers you probably need to compare only the 16 outlined here to see whether or not your projections will pass the bankers' test. You'll find these 16 numbers referenced on the sample RMA pages that are provided in Figures 9.2 and 9.3.

There are two RMA pages for each industry. One presents the data sorted by the amount of sales and the other by the amount of assets the business has. Two considerations should guide your decision on which one to use for your comparison. First, some companies, such as consulting firms or real estate agencies, have few physical assets, so using data sorted by sales is best. However, a manufacturing plant with lots of valuable physical assets is best compared to companies that are sorted by asset size. The second consideration is that you should use data from larger samples. The first line in each column tells you how many businesses make up the group sampled. If the relevant sample sorted by sales is only 15, but the group sorted by assets is 90, use the latter.

Here are the most significant financial figures to compare to yours. The numbers at the beginning of each paragraph correspond to the highlighted numbers on the sample RMA pages, which follow on pages 219 and 220.

1. **Trade Receivables (net)** are how much your company is owed by its customers, with a reasonable allowance for accounts that will never pay. Some industries, such as fast food restaurants, have almost no receivables, while other industries, such as contractors who sell to government agencies, have huge receivables. If your assumption

is more optimistic than the industry norm, you may find yourself running short of cash. And running short of cash closes more businesses than anything else.

2. Notes Payable–Short-Term and 3. Long-Term Debt together represent how much money your company owes. Notes Payable (Short-Term debt) generally have a term of one year or less. Long-Term Debt has a term longer than one year. Since a bank's loans are usually made in the form of Long-Term debt, a banker will be very attentive to your projections here.

THE GROUP OF NUMBERS LABELED "INCOME DATA" INCLUDES:

4. Net Sales are Gross Sales less Returns and Discounts.

5. Gross Profit is Net Sales minus the cost of the items or services you sold.

6. Operating Profit is Gross Profit minus the Operating Expenses. Operating Expenses includes all selling, administrative, and depreciation costs (but not interest expense). The category "All Other Expenses" covers interest and miscellaneous expenses not included in Operating Expenses.

7. Profit Before Taxes is the company's profit after all expenses, including interest, are subtracted (but not taxes!).

Ratios are calculations used to evaluate business performance. The RMA data presents three numbers for each ratio: the average of the top quartile of companies, the median ratio for the entire sample, and the average for the bottom quartile. Presenting the numbers this way gives you a sense of the average (median) and the range for each ratio. All ratios are used as indicators of potential problems. When a ratio seems too far from the norm, it usually signals the need for further analysis.

THE KEY RATIOS ARE:

8. Current Ratio is Current Assets (generally the company's cash, receivables, inventory) divided by Current Liabilities (generally short-term loans and upcoming loan payments, payables, and taxes currently owed) and is a rough indication of a company's ability to pay its current obligations. The higher the ratio, the stronger the company.

9. Quick Ratio, or **Acid Test**, is Cash and Equivalents (such as money market accounts the company may have) plus Receivables minus allowances for non-paying accounts divided by Current Liabilities. This is a similar, but stricter, measure of a company's ability to pay its bills.

10. Sales Divided by Receivables calculates invoices that your company has sent out but which have not yet been paid. This gives a measure of turnover or how many days on average it takes your customers to pay. The higher this number, the fewer days on average for your customers to pay.

11. **Cost of Sales Divided by Inventory** (items waiting to be sold) measures how often your inventory turns over in a year. A fruit store turns over its inventory every week or less. An antique store turns over its inventory a few times a year. A high ratio can mean efficient use of inventory or it might mean that a company starved for cash has cut its inventory to the bone.

12. **Cost of Sales Divided by Payables** (bills received but not paid) shows how quickly a company pays its bills. A high ratio means that bills are being paid promptly. A low ratio may indicate a company that is experiencing a cash shortage and is paying its suppliers too slowly.

13. **EBIT (Earnings Before Interest and Taxes) Divided by Interest** shows the ability to pay interest. It is unusual to see this ratio below 2 for small businesses.

14. **Net Profit Plus Depreciation and Amortization Divided by the Current Portion of Long-Term Debt** shows an ability to pay similar to EBIT, but for scheduled principal repayments. Depreciation is a non-cash item that is usually calculated by your accountant to reflect how your company's long-term assets are used over time. Amortization is the payment of the principal of your company's loans.

15. **Fixed/Worth** (Net Fixed Assets divided by Tangible Net Worth) shows what percentage of the long-term assets, such as a manufacturing plant and equipment, has been paid for by the owners' investment. The lower the ratio, the more it appears that the owners have invested in their company for the long term.

16. **Debt/Worth** (Total Liabilities divided by Tangible Net Worth) shows the relationship between the owners' and the lenders' capital. The higher the ratio, the less the owners have put into the company relative to the lenders.

Most libraries with some focus on business and virtually all Small Business Development Centers have the RMA book. Since you will only need a copy of a few pages, it is not difficult or expensive to obtain the data you need this way.

When you produce a meticulous set of financial projections and compare them to the RMA data, along with either explaining or reducing the differences, a banker or investor is likely to say "your numbers look good." This is the best possible reaction.

FIGURE 9.2
SAMPLE RMA PAGE

RETAIL—GASOLINE SERVICE STATIONS SIC# 5541 (NAICS 44711, 44719) **847**

Comparative Historical Data				Current Data Sorted By Sales					
			Type of Statement						
99	96	88	Unqualified		3	2	3	14	66
120	108	101	Reviewed	1	8	7	12	31	42
234	245	186	Compiled	19	60	23	30	34	20
99	145	128	Tax Returns	17	70	19	13	5	4
191	249	212	Other	16	54	31	26	33	52
4/1/97-3/31/98	4/1/98-3/31/99	4/1/99-3/31/00			168 (4/1-9/30/99)		547 (10/1/99-3/31/00)		
ALL	ALL	ALL		0-1MM	1-3MM	3-5MM	5-10MM	10-25MM	25MM & OVER
743	843	715	NUMBER OF STATEMENTS	53	195	82	84	117	184
%	%	%	**ASSETS**	%	%	%	%	%	%
10.2	10.9	9.8	Cash & Equivalents	7.7	9.8	9.4	11.3	10.7	9.4
9.8	8.6	8.6	(1) Trade Receivables - (net)	8.8	6.8	7.5	9.7	9.7	9.8
15.0	14.6	15.6	Inventory	20.6	18.4	17.1	15.1	14.1	11.6
1.5	2.3	2.4	All Other Current	1.3	2.4	1.9	1.5	3.8	2.4
36.5	36.3	36.4	Total Current	38.4	37.4	36.0	37.5	38.3	33.2
52.4	51.7	52.6	Fixed Assets (net)	55.4	50.2	53.3	50.6	50.5	56.3
4.5	5.0	4.9	Intangibles (net)	2.9	7.9	4.4	4.2	4.2	3.2
6.6	7.0	6.2	All Other Non-Current	3.2	4.5	6.3	7.7	7.1	7.4
100.0	100.0	100.0	Total	100.0	100.0	100.0	100.0	100.0	100.0
			LIABILITIES						
4.1	4.2	5.0	(2) Notes Payable-Short Term	7.1	6.4	4.4	5.2	4.6	3.2
4.7	4.0	4.3	Cur. Mat.-L/T/D	3.1	5.8	4.0	4.6	3.3	3.8
15.1	14.4	16.4	Trade Payables	13.7	15.6	13.3	17.8	17.7	17.9
.2	.3	.2	Income Taxes Payable	.2	.1	.1	.1	.3	.2
8.8	8.5	9.5	All Other Current	9.6	8.6	16.0	7.9	8.7	8.7
32.9	31.5	35.3	Total Current	33.8	36.5	37.8	35.7	34.7	33.8
32.2	35.8	35.9	(3) Long Term Debt	37.4	44.2	40.4	30.8	31.7	29.9
.5	.4	.4	Deferred Taxes	.1	.0	.0	.2	.4	1.0
4.2	7.2	6.4	All Other Non-Current	6.0	8.2	14.9	6.6	3.2	2.7
30.1	25.2	22.0	Net Worth	22.7	11.1	6.9	26.7	29.9	32.7
100.0	100.0	100.0	Total Liabilities & Net Worth	100.0	100.0	100.0	100.0	100.0	100.0
			INCOME DATA						
100.0	100.0	100.0	(4) Net Sales	100.0	100.0	100.0	100.0	100.0	100.0
18.8	20.8	19.9	Gross Profit (5)	29.5	20.3	19.4	20.4	17.7	18.1
17.1	19.1	19.4	Operating Expenses	27.6	22.4	17.9	18.9	16.5	16.6
1.8	1.7	.5	(6) Operating Profit	1.9	-2.1	1.5	1.5	1.2	1.5
.3	.3	-.8	All Other Expenses (net)	.3	-2.5	.1	-.5	-.1	-.1
1.4	1.4	1.3	Profit Before Taxes (7)	1.6	.4	1.4	2.1	1.4	1.6
			RATIOS						
1.7	1.9	1.7		2.5	2.1	2.5	1.9	1.6	1.3
1.1	1.1	1.1	(8) Current	1.3	1.2	1.3	1.0	1.1	.9
.7	.7	.7		.7	.7	.7	.8	.8	.7
1.0	1.1	1.0		1.0	1.0	1.4	1.0	1.0	.8
(740) .5	(837) .6	(713) .5	(9) Quick	.5	(194) .5	(81) .7	.6	.5	.5
.3	.3	.3		.1	.2	.3	.3	.3	.3
1 295.7	1 351.4	1 391.0		0 UND	0 999.8	1 528.9	1 620.4	2 237.6	3 134.5
4 90.1	3 111.0	4 101.5	(10) Sales/Receivables	3 109.4	2 214.3	3 139.2	3 119.1	5 78.1	6 62.1
9 40.0	9 42.9	9 39.6		10 35.2	6 65.9	6 63.0	10 38.4	10 36.1	12 31.7
7 55.7	7 53.7	8 47.4		13 28.6	7 48.9	7 55.3	8 47.9	8 48.3	8 43.4
10 35.5	10 35.0	11 32.6	(11) Cost of Sales/Inventory	20 17.8	12 31.3	9 39.7	10 35.6	11 34.7	11 32.1
15 24.2	15 23.6	17 21.8		39 9.2	20 18.6	14 26.6	15 24.0	15 24.4	16 23.5
5 72.6	5 73.9	6 62.1		2 179.0	3 143.5	2 173.3	6 63.2	10 36.4	14 26.9
12 31.1	12 31.6	14 26.9	(12) Cost of Sales/Payables	11 34.2	8 44.9	7 51.8	14 26.7	15 24.2	19 19.3
18 20.7	19 19.7	21 17.1		23 15.8	16 23.1	16 22.2	20 18.5	21 17.7	24 15.2
35.2	29.8	35.5		14.8	34.2	26.9	39.7	45.0	48.9
246.3	186.3	225.6	Sales/Working Capital	60.7	109.3	108.4	476.7	191.4	-231.3
-54.6	-56.6	-46.4		-37.3	-43.4	-61.6	-58.8	-59.8	-39.8
4.3	4.8	4.0		6.5	2.7	4.1	4.8	4.1	4.5
(671) 2.1	(737) 2.1	(626) 1.9	(13) EBIT/Interest	(39) 1.6	(166) 1.2	(71) 1.6	(76) 1.7	(100) 2.1	(174) 2.7
1.1	1.0	.9		.7	.1	.8	.7	1.3	1.4
3.9	4.5	4.5			6.4		4.3	3.3	5.1
(187) 2.0	(173) 2.2	(141) 2.4	(14) Net Profit + Depr., Dep., Amort./Cur. Mat. L/T/D		(11) 2.7		(16) 2.0	(35) 2.2	(72) 2.5
1.4	1.3	1.2			1.2		1.3	.9	1.6
1.1	.9	1.1		1.0	.9	1.2	1.0	1.0	1.2
2.1	2.4	2.5	(15) Fixed/Worth	2.4	6.5	4.4	2.3	2.1	2.2
6.0	12.4	18.5		-6.5	-3.8	-14.7	4.7	6.9	3.4
1.2	1.1	1.3		.8	1.4	1.5	1.4	1.2	1.4
2.8	3.3	3.6	(16) Debt/Worth	3.3	10.7	5.1	3.3	2.9	2.5
9.3	20.2	34.2		-8.4	-7.2	-23.3	12.4	9.9	4.9
37.8	42.9	37.9		53.9	47.9	47.3	34.3	34.3	30.0
(629) 16.9	(674) 19.6	(555) 16.5	% Profit Before Taxes/Tangible Net Worth	(37) 22.0	(116) 14.6	(59) 16.5	(68) 14.2	(103) 15.3	(172) 16.9
4.6	5.4	2.2		.2	-2.1	-1.8	.5	3.5	8.2
10.1	11.4	9.7		18.1	10.4	13.3	8.6	7.8	8.8
4.4	4.9	4.0	% Profit Before Taxes/Total Assets	4.5	2.2	3.6	3.3	3.5	4.8
.5	.2	-.5		-1.9	-5.0	-1.5	-.3	.9	1.6
22.7	23.8	19.0		15.0	33.3	28.3	24.8	19.3	12.0
9.1	8.5	8.2	Sales/Net Fixed Assets	5.7	9.4	8.8	9.3	10.4	6.1
4.7	3.9	4.0		2.4	3.8	3.7	3.9	4.6	4.4
7.9	7.3	7.1		5.2	9.5	8.6	7.7	7.2	5.6
4.7	4.4	4.1	Sales/Total Assets	2.9	4.5	4.6	4.5	4.5	3.7
3.1	2.7	2.6		1.8	2.6	2.5	2.7	2.7	2.8
.9	1.0	1.1		1.4	.7	.9	1.1	1.0	1.2
(674) 1.5	(749) 1.6	(642) 1.8	% Depr., Dep., Amort./Sales	(41) 2.1	(169) 1.8	(68) 1.8	(78) 1.8	(112) 1.4	(174) 1.8
2.2	2.5	2.6		3.6	2.9	2.7	2.6	2.4	2.4
.8	.8	.8		1.8	1.3	1.1	.9	.6	.3
(303) 1.6	(363) 1.6	(271) 1.5	% Officers', Directors', Owners' Comp/Sales	(18) 4.3	(93) 2.0	(37) 1.9	(31) 1.6	(52) 1.1	(40) .6
3.1	3.2	3.1		6.4	3.4	2.8	3.6	2.2	1.3
26114455M	27124271M	21175985M	Net Sales ($)	37414M	372569M	322097M	579465M	1933430M	17931010M
6394229M	7978306M	6357405M	Total Assets ($)	16859M	104620M	89363M	171160M	525408M	5449995M

M = $ thousand MM = $ million

See Pages 11 through 20 for Explanation of Ratios and Data

Figure 9.3
Sample RMA Page

846 **RETAIL—GASOLINE SERVICE STATIONS** SIC# 5541 (NAICS 44711, 44719)

	Current Data Sorted By Assets						Comparative Historical Data	
Type of Statement								
Unqualified	1	7	18	48	10	4	100	89
Reviewed	1	23	55	22			102	117
Compiled	65	65	43	12	1		194	230
Tax Returns	73	43	11	1			63	78
Other	51	67	56	26	6	6	175	210
		168 (4/1-9/30/99)		547 (10/1/99-3/31/00)			4/1/95-3/31/96	4/1/96-3/31/97
	0-500M	500M-2MM	2-10MM	10-50MM	50-100MM	100-250MM	ALL	ALL
NUMBER OF STATEMENTS	191	205	183	109	17	10	634	724
ASSETS	%	%	%	%	%	%	%	%
Cash & Equivalents	11.4	8.9	10.2	9.0	6.1	7.1	11.7	10.6
(1) Trade Receivables - (net)	7.9	8.7	9.8	8.0	8.1	4.3	9.7	10.2
Inventory	26.6	12.8	12.0	8.7	10.8	8.5	15.9	16.3
All Other Current	2.7	2.0	2.6	2.3	1.0	2.3	2.2	1.7
Total Current	48.7	32.4	34.7	28.0	25.9	22.2	39.4	38.8
Fixed Assets (net)	39.6	56.7	55.5	59.2	66.0	68.7	49.9	49.3
Intangibles (net)	7.2	4.9	3.2	3.9	2.6	3.2	3.2	4.2
All Other Non-Current	4.5	6.0	6.6	8.8	5.4	5.9	7.5	7.7
Total	100.0	100.0	100.0	100.0	100.0	100.0	100.0	100.0
LIABILITIES								
(2) Notes Payable-Short Term	6.2	6.1	3.5	3.2	2.5	7.2	5.5	4.6
Cur. Mat.-L/T/D	3.9	5.2	4.3	3.8	3.6	2.3	4.3	4.1
Trade Payables	21.9	12.2	17.4	13.9	13.1	10.9	15.4	16.2
Income Taxes Payable	.2	.2	.2	.2	.2	.0	.3	.2
All Other Current	15.0	7.5	7.7	7.4	5.9	7.5	9.5	8.9
Total Current	47.2	31.1	33.1	28.5	25.3	27.8	34.9	34.1
(3) Long Term Debt	33.9	41.5	33.4	34.0	36.2	28.4	28.5	29.8
Deferred Taxes	.0	.2	.4	.9	1.4	2.3	.5	.5
All Other Non-Current	11.4	7.2	2.9	2.8	3.5	1.5	3.8	4.4
Net Worth	7.4	20.0	30.3	33.7	33.6	40.0	32.3	31.3
Total Liabilities & Net Worth	100.0	100.0	100.0	100.0	100.0	100.0	100.0	100.0
INCOME DATA								
(4) Net Sales	100.0	100.0	100.0	100.0	100.0	100.0	100.0	100.0
Gross Profit (5)	21.9	20.1	18.2	18.6	20.1	20.7	19.8	18.9
Operating Expenses	24.1	19.2	16.7	16.6	17.7	16.7	17.8	17.1
(6) Operating Profit	-2.1	1.0	1.5	2.0	2.4	4.0	2.0	1.8
All Other Expenses (net)	-3.1	.5	-.3	-.3	.9	.5	.4	.3
Profit Before Taxes (7)	.9	.4	1.8	2.3	1.6	3.5	1.6	1.4
RATIOS								
(8) Current	2.4	2.0	1.5	1.3	1.2	1.4	1.8	1.8
	1.3	1.1	1.1	.9	1.1	.9	1.1	1.1
	.7	.7	.7	.7	.8	.5	.7	.8
(9) Quick	1.0	1.0	.9	.9	.7	.7	1.0	1.0
	(189) .5	.5	.6	.5	.6	.4	(631) .6	(720) .6
	.2	.3	.3	.3	.3	.2	.3	.3
(10) Sales/Receivables	0 999.8	1 573.8	2 206.0	3 144.8	4 90.8	2 160.7	1 260.9	1 283.9
	2 220.5	3 119.9	5 71.8	5 80.1	10 35.3	7 50.9	4 92.0	4 88.0
	5 67.4	9 42.2	11 32.8	11 33.8	16 23.5	19 18.7	9 38.9	10 37.8
(11) Cost of Sales/Inventory	8 48.5	7 49.0	8 47.8	8 43.0	11 32.2	9 38.5	7 48.8	7 51.7
	11 31.9	10 35.3	11 32.6	11 32.3	15 24.3	15 24.8	11 32.8	11 34.4
	20 18.3	17 21.4	16 23.2	14 25.5	25 14.9	21 17.3	16 23.4	15 24.7
(12) Cost of Sales/Payables	3 112.4	4 97.8	10 35.5	13 28.6	15 24.5	19 19.3	6 62.5	5 72.3
	9 42.6	10 37.3	16 22.2	19 19.0	19 19.3	23 15.9	13 29.0	12 30.2
	16 22.5	17 21.6	24 15.1	24 15.5	23 15.9	30 12.3	19 19.1	19 19.6
Sales/Working Capital	36.9	28.4	31.8	40.8	45.9	29.6	29.8	33.9
	86.5	218.5	275.9	-143.8	128.3	-522.7	202.4	270.7
	-65.2	-46.7	-48.7	-37.3	-59.7	-15.9	-51.0	-56.6
(13) EBIT/Interest	4.8	3.2	4.1	4.3	3.3		5.4	4.7
	(143) 2.0	(183) 1.4	(173) 1.8	(102) 2.7	(16) 2.7		(560) 2.5	(630) 2.2
	-.2	.5	.9	1.5	1.2		1.4	1.1
(14) Net Profit + Depr., Dep., Amort./Cur. Mat. L/T/D	10.2	3.6	4.3	4.4	3.7		4.2	5.6
	(10) 4.1	(22) 1.8	(52) 2.2	(44) 2.4	(10) 2.6		(178) 2.2	(189) 2.1
	.6	1.2	1.1	1.5	1.4		1.5	1.4
(15) Fixed/Worth	.7	1.3	1.1	1.4	1.7	1.3	.9	.9
	3.0	4.0	2.2	2.3	2.4	2.4	1.9	2.0
	-4.2	-8.9	4.8	4.4	3.2	2.9	5.2	5.3
(16) Debt/Worth	1.0	1.5	1.4	1.3	1.6	.9	1.1	1.1
	6.6	5.5	2.9	2.5	2.6	2.3	2.4	2.6
	-5.7	-14.4	6.6	5.1	3.8	2.8	7.8	8.4
% Profit Before Taxes/Tangible Net Worth	63.2	43.2	30.6	29.0	22.8		38.3	35.0
	(120) 22.4	(143) 14.8	(168) 12.0	(99) 17.7	(16) 18.1		(551) 19.2	(616) 16.2
	.0	.0	1.6	9.6	14.4		7.4	2.9
% Profit Before Taxes/Total Assets	17.1	7.9	7.8	8.5	8.1	7.4	12.2	10.5
	5.3	2.3	2.8	5.3	6.1	4.7	5.5	4.4
	-5.0	-2.0	-.1	2.3	1.6	3.9	1.9	.4
Sales/Net Fixed Assets	93.4	15.1	13.0	8.2	5.5	5.6	21.9	29.7
	24.1	7.5	6.9	5.2	3.9	3.6	9.6	10.1
	8.4	3.2	3.8	3.9	3.3	1.9	5.2	5.1
Sales/Total Assets	15.2	6.5	6.0	4.4	3.6	4.0	7.4	8.6
	7.9	3.8	3.8	3.3	2.9	2.0	4.9	5.1
	4.5	2.3	2.4	2.4	2.4	1.3	3.2	3.3
% Depr., Dep., Amort./Sales	.5	1.2	1.2	1.4	2.0		.8	.8
	(154) 1.3	(184) 2.0	(175) 1.7	(106) 1.9	(16) 2.4		(583) 1.5	(642) 1.4
	2.0	2.9	2.4	2.6	3.1		2.2	2.1
% Officers', Directors', Owners' Comp/Sales	1.4	.9	.5	.3			1.0	.8
	(98) 2.0	(84) 1.6	(65) .9	(24) .7			(247) 1.8	(298) 1.6
	3.5	3.2	1.9	1.3			3.4	3.0
Net Sales ($)	393588M	1066027M	3931811M	8957946M	3313130M	3513483M	24996429M	26726477M
Total Assets ($)	45533M	219183M	902983M	2580470M	1123260M	1485976M	5669565M	6067154M

M = $ thousand MM = $ million

See Pages 11 through 20 for Explanation of Ratios and Data

SIMPLE AS PIE BREAK-EVEN ANALYSIS

Rob and Joan Russell started baking pies from their home eight years ago. Their business idea was simple: There were no top-quality pies sold commercially in their mid-sized New England town. They produced no plan, no budget, and gave no thought to how much capital this venture would require. Their pies were indeed great and with little effort they built a customer base of individuals and restaurants that wanted the best and were willing to pay $12-15 per pie. Rob and Joan rented a kitchen from a catering firm that they could use during the caterer's off hours. With the new facility they could bake 100 pies per day. Their revenue was soon running at a pace of $500,000 per year with monthly sales of 3,000 pies at an average price of $14.

The success they were enjoying and the encouragement they received from customers and friends made them think of expanding their distribution regionally, creating a brand name, and adding other products. But these expansions required taking on significant new expenses. It was time to make a haphazard venture into an expansive venture with a bankable business plan.

With revenues of $500,000 per year and renting the kitchen from the caterer, they had profits of about $200,000 per year (they paid themselves no salaries.) The Variable Costs per pie were $4, and their Fixed Costs including staff, kitchen rental, and two delivery vehicles were approximately $160,000 per year. BEP=$160,000/10=16,000; current volume is 36,000.

Over a few months Rob and Joan developed the outline of a business plan:

- There was a closed restaurant that they could buy and equip as a commercial bakery. The parking lot could accommodate delivery trucks and employees' vehicles. The total cost of buying and equipping this new facility was $1 million.

- A bank agreed to lend them $500,000 at 7% per annum and the owner of the building offered to give them a second mortgage for the other $500,000 at 10% per annum. The total yearly interest cost would be $85,000 with principal payments of $50,000 beginning in the third year.
- The new location would allow them to triple production and keep Variable Costs at the same $4 per pie.
- The fixed costs after the move to the new facility would increase to $700,000 per year not including interest or principle payments, covering advertising, a full-time salesperson, and the operation of the bakery. Rob or Joan would still not be salaried.

Rob and Joan need to do some financial analysis of this deal. They want to know what impact this deal will have on their profits. Will it change their Break-Even Point? Is this new deal riskier? Is the upside much greater? How could they change the proposed deal to make it work better for them? In sum, would moving to this new facility give Rob and Joan a bigger piece of the pie?

End of Chapter Questions

1. How should an entrepreneur make the decision about how much debt and how much equity to use in the mix of financing? What are the plusses and minuses of each form of financing?
2. It is very common for entrepreneurs to underestimate the amount of financing their ventures will need. Why do think this is so?
3. What is a break-even analysis and why is so important?
4. What methods are available to obtain average financial comparisons for new and start-up ventures? Why might this be important in your business plan?

NOTES

1. Controller of the Currency, "Community Developments," Summer 2002, pp.1–3.
2. Interview with John Tear, Senior Vice President, Community Capital Bank, June 1, 2004.

CHAPTER 10

ISSUE 10: DEMONSTRATE THE ENTREPRENEUR'S ABILITIES AND QUALIFICATIONS

Now that you have completed nine of the twelve essential issues in creating your bankable business plan, you must establish that you, as the entrepreneur, as well as the others on your team, have the abilities and qualifications to make this venture a success. Financial supporters invest in people more than they invest in ideas. It is critical to convince potential funders of the good match between the needs of the business and the qualifications of management. For business plans that call for a management team, all of the members' roles must be defined and their qualifications presented.

The text of your business plan and your attached resume must state clearly who you are, what you have done, what you *can* do, and what you *will* do. Think of these elements of your business plan as a personal sales pitch about your qualifications to start your business and guide it to success. You must demonstrate that you are as bankable as your business plan.

Your qualifications make your plan credible, assuring readers that your goals are reasonable and attainable. Your skills are just as important as the right marketing strategy or your competitive advantage because *you* must implement the plan and make the business profitable. Prices don't select themselves and customer service doesn't evolve without strong leadership from an exacting manager. An effective marketing strategy, a superior competitive advantage, and stellar sales efforts are useless without *you* and your abilities.

Stressing your enthusiasm alone is not the most effective way to indicate to potential investors and lenders that you have the skills, savvy and determination to be successful.

The part of your business plan that stresses your credentials has the same purpose as the resume you attach to your appendix, but each is achieved through quite different means. A resume should be short and easy to read, so potential supporters can see a quick overview of the experience, training and education you bring to your venture. The text of your plan is where you can elaborate on the skills you brought to each of your previous positions and the areas of expertise that you developed on each job. The resume provides the bare bones of your experience; the text supplies the muscle. Both need to be strong.

Let's take a more detailed look at how your resume and the text of the plan help create a convincing case that you are the best person to start and run your business.

Focus on Research: How a Resume Leads to an Interview

Just as a bankable business plan leads to an in-person meeting with potential funders, the main purpose of a resume is to lead to an in-person job interview. If both the plan and your resume are effective, you have a better chance of garnering a face-to-face discussion about your venture with potential funders. Although this entire book is about creating a powerful, convincing plan, it is also important to know which resume characteristics increase the chances of being asked to move to the next step. Professor Peg Thoms and her colleagues at Penn State University at Erie ran an experiment to uncover the most essential qualities of an effective resume.[1]

The researchers created seven sets of four resumes that were almost identical. They used only first and middle initials and English last names to minimize possible ethnic, racial, or gender bias and they created fictitious colleges and universities to eliminate opinions based on schools. The graduation dates, majors, and work experience were closely matched. No personal information about family or hobbies was included.

But within each set of four matched resumes, two resumes had one characteristic that the other two did not. These differences were used to test which resume characteristics affected being selected for an interview. The seven sets of resumes were then reviewed by 64 business professionals who picked their first and second choices from each group of four to schedule follow-up interviews for a hypothetical position as a management trainee. Six of the seven variations were found to be very important in influencing the readers of the resumes to rank the candidate as a high choice for an interview:

These differences were:

- One page or two pages in length.
- The use or omission of an objective statement.
- The use of a specific objective statement (seeking entry-level management position in the private sector) or a general one (seeking a stimulating job in a growing company.)
- The listing of specific, relevant course work or its omission.
- The inclusion of a GPA of 3.0 or no GPA.
- The presence of a GPA of 3.5 or one of 2.75.
- The use or omission of statements of accomplishments for each position.

The seven sets of resumes were then reviewed by 64 business professionals who picked their first and second choices from each group of four to schedule follow-up interviews for a hypothetical position as a management trainee. Six of the seven variations were found to be very important in influencing the readers of the resumes to rank the candidate as a high choice for an interview:

- One page resumes worked better than two page resumes.
- Specific statements of objectives were preferred over general ones.
- Listing the relevant coursework was a positive.
- Listing a grade point average of 3.0 was better than not providing a grade point average.
- Having a grade point average of 3.5 had a strong positive effect on being selected for an interview when compared to a grade point average of 2.75.
- Detailing specific accomplishments with each position was much better than not listing any.

Of the seven variables that Thoms and her colleagues tested, only the use of a general objective statement when compared to no objective statement was found not to make any difference in rates of selection. This study did not address questions about the interaction of these changes, such as whether accomplishments balance a low GPA, nor does it state the best way to prepare a resume for every type of position. There may also be different conclusions for positions that are heavily dependent on specific skills or experience such as computer programming or having worked in a printing factory. While the study cannot provide rigid rules about how to prepare every resume, it does offer some valuable guidelines, especially if you are creating your business plan and resume for course work and are still in school, or if you are a recent graduate and trying to start your own venture in the real world.

Your Resume

Your resume should be organized to emphasize your skills, experience, education and training. Do not just slip your standard professional resume into the appendix of your business plan. Write a new one from scratch that stresses the credentials that make you absolutely the best person to start and grow your business.

Creating an effective resume is an art. Like your overall business plan, your resume must be neat, well designed, and free of spelling errors. It should have enough white space to make it easy to read and it should employ bullets, boldface, or underlining to emphasize important elements, such as the names of your previous employers and your job titles.

This is not the place for you to list every job you've ever had, or to proclaim unrelated professional or personal skills. You may have had the best baseball card collection in your neighborhood or bowled 300 20 times in your league last year, but if these accomplishments have no bearing on your ability to start and grow a particular business, leave them out. However, if you do have an interest that may not have appeared on a previous resume, but which adds to the case you're making about your qualifications, include it now.

The airline pilot with the pancake restaurant may have earned money towards his college tuition by waiting tables in the school cafeteria, in addition to working in his father's deli during high school. His resume might also include the leadership-training workshop he recently completed. These experiences have no place on his pilot's resume, but they certainly indicate that he knows the food industry from the ground up and that he is committed to polishing his managerial skills.

Here are some finer points of resume creation:

Be simple: Keep it to one page. This is a quick overview to remind readers of your basic skills and experience. Even if you feel compelled to list every one of the 155 weddings that your band played at to establish your ability to start your DJ service, don't do it here. Name a couple of the well-known brides and grooms and list the total number, but if potential investors want a more complete list, attach it to your appendix, or mail it to them later. Don't try to be slick or snazzy by using special paper or fancy fonts. A resume should impress people first and foremost with its content, neatness and readability, not by multicolored headings or a typeface that looks like calligraphy.

Be clear: Choose the right format for your resume that expresses your experience in the most powerful way possible. The organization of your skills and expertise must emphasize the qualities you wish to highlight for your readers. There are three basic formats to follow:

- **The chronological format** lists your work experience from the most recent job, placed first, back to your first job, which is placed last. It also includes the specific lengths of time you worked at each position. This is the most common type of resume, but it may not stress the skills you wish to emphasize to potential funders. It's a good exercise to create a resume in this format, so you can scan your complete employment history on one page and choose which experiences you want to highlight in a more effective version.
- **The functional format** organizes your experience and employment under particular headings according to the type of positions you held. This format allows you to group related skills, even if they were acquired during part-time jobs or from purely personal interests. Dates are not usually included in this format. Compiling your background by function enables you to present your skills in a more interesting and compelling manner.
- **The targeted format** focuses even more closely on the specific skills needed for your particular venture. If all of your past experience has been in the same field, and each position has moved you higher on the professional ladder, and starting your own business is simply a culmination of your entire career, you probably won't need either the chronological or the functional format; the targeted design will work best for you.

Be consistent: Keep the style similar to the tone and language of your business plan text. Use parallel construction in verbs so you describe your duties in each of your jobs with similar tenses. If you use the past tense under one position, such as "coordinated travel schedules for a touring tuba band," don't employ the present tense in another job description—unless you are still in that position, such as "analyzing customer service staff effectiveness." However, when you mention in your resume the business you founded that failed, all you have to do is list the information without discussing the outcome.

Be animated: Use action verbs and an active voice to describe your duties at each of your jobs. Words such as "achieved," "devised," or "pioneered" express power and accomplishment more than passive verbs such as "held the position of" or "served as." Phrases describing your duties should be short and to the point. Never use complete sentences or paragraphs. Omit professional abbreviations or jargon that potential funders might not recognize. Avoid the first person completely in your resume; never refer to yourself by using "I" to discuss your skills and accomplishments.

Be careful: Check your grammar, spelling, indents and layout. Then check them again, and one more time. Then give your resume to someone else, preferably an English teacher or a person with excellent editing skills, to make sure you haven't committed some terrible error that will ruin your credibility in an instant—or in a punctuation mark.

Be honest: Your resume should be scrupulously truthful. It is standard practice for many funding sources to check statements made on resumes. Don't say "Vice President" if you were "Assistant Vice President, or "supervised staff of 12," when it was actually 10. An aspiring entrepreneur had a major deal derailed because he claimed on his resume to have graduated from Princeton when he had not. His funders, who were ready to write a check, liked him, his idea, and his references. Nothing on his resume would have changed their minds—except a lie.

Remember that you are selling potential investors and lenders on you and your abilities, not just your business idea. You must impress people you want to support your venture that you—and your team—are uniquely qualified to establish this company and make it profitable. This is not exaggerating; this is the way to reassure funders that you have the background, talent, and enthusiasm to make your enterprise successful.

Let's look at two sample resumes for the same person, Lance Lindbergh, the entrepreneur who wants to open the restaurant featuring squid-flavored pancakes. The first example is his professional pilot's resume. As you can see, it follows all of the rules for good resume writing, but it contains language, abbreviations and other references that are far too technical to include in a resume supporting his business plan.

Figure 10.1
Sample Chronological Resume

Lance Lindbergh

2333 Air Pioneer Boulevard
Jeppesen, NY 10100
(247) 746-6337

OBJECTIVE: To obtain a position as a Flight Officer with JJ Montgomery Airways

EDUCATION

Bachelor of Arts, Orville University, 1995
Major: Art History Minor: Physics
Commercial Pilot Course, Wilbur Aviation Academy, 1997

FAA PILOT CERTIFICATE

Airline Transport Pilot, Airplane Multiengine Land, 1997
Type Ratings: B-737, EMB-145, EMB-120
Commercial Privileges, Single Engine Land

FLIGHT HOURS

TOTAL: 5054	**Turboprop:** 2171	**Jet:** 1661
Total PIC: 3916	**PIC E-145/135:** 1634	**PIC E-120:** 1249
Instructor: 897	**Night:** 763	**Instrument:** 348

PROFESSIONAL FLIGHT EXPERIENCE

CHANUTE AIRLINES, 1998-2001
Captain: EMB-145
Captain: EMB-120
First Officer: EMB-120

LILIENTHAL AVIATION ACADEMY, 1997–1998
FAR Part 141 Check Pilot
Performed Part 141 Stage Checks within the CFI section
Flight and Ground Instructor-CFI section
Provided airline oriented flight instruction to students in pursuit of their CFI, CFII, and MEI Ratings

FLIGHT AWARDS

Passenger Satisfaction Award, CHANUTE AIRLINES, 1998, 1999, 2000, 2001
Awarded for most comfortable landings and take-offs
Flight Instructor of the Year Award, LILIENTHAL AVIATION ACADEMY, 1997
Awarded for exceptional skill in aircraft control while teaching flight maneuvers, excellent knowledge of Federal Aviation Regulations and Flight Instructor responsibilities, and outstanding ability in stall and spin entries and recoveries

ADDITIONAL EMPLOYMENT

Peace Corps Volunteer, Calamari Island, Pusit, 1989–1991

ACADEMIC AWARDS AND HONORS

Recipient of Wilbur Aviation Academy's Right Stuff Award, 1997
Recipient of Orville University's Outstanding Senior Award, 1995
Recipient of Future Pilots of America Recognition, 1993, 1994

REFERENCES AVAILABLE UPON REQUEST

Now let's look at the resume our pilot created to accompany his actual business plan.

Figure 10.2
Sample Functional Resume

Lance Lindbergh

2333 Air Pioneer Boulevard
Jeppesen, NY 10100
(247) 746-6337

OBJECTIVE:
To obtain $300,000 in financing to open Lance's Squid Pancake Restaurant.

EXPERIENCE:

Peace Corps Volunteer, Calamari Island, Pusit, 1995-1997
Built fledgling native squid harvesting into an effective, profit-making industry. Designed and implemented native run and operated squid cooperative by creating legal entity, convincing individual squid fishers to join, and training native managers. Established international marketing plan which grew from a single foreign customer to ten foreign markets in two years, making Pusit the third largest squid exporting country in the world. Instituted supplemental squid farming to prevent over-harvesting of natural squid population. Prepared business plan to be followed by subsequent PCVs to grow profits and markets and to establish squid cooperatives in other Pusit islands.

Licensed Pilot, Since 1997 to Present
Captain, JJ Montgomery Airways, 2002-2007
Captain and First Officer, Chanute Airlines, 1998-2001.
Winner of Chanute Airlines Passenger Satisfaction Award in 1998, 1999, 2000, 2001.
Logged over 10,000 flight hours in various aircraft, including night and instrument flying.
Award-winning flight instructor at Lilienthal Aviation Academy, 1997-1998.

ADDITIONAL QUALIFICATIONS

Purchaser, Lindbergh Deli, 1991–1995
Supervised all bulk orders for successful delicatessen serving over 3,000 customers weekly. Negotiated contracts with suppliers, oversaw shipping schedule, and managed deliveries, including staff of three stocking personnel.

Short-order Chef, Lindbergh Deli, 1986–1991
Managed grill and produced 300 dishes during peak evening hours; Worked closely with wait and stock staff as well as management to keep orders and supplies operating smoothly. Maintained constant customer contact while preparing food.

EDUCATION
Bachelor of Arts, Orville University, 1995
Major: Art History Minor: Physics
Commercial Pilot Course, Wilbur Aviation Academy, 1997
Fluent in Tagalog

ACADEMIC AWARDS AND HONORS
Leadership Training Certificate, Newton Business Programs, 2007
Recipient of Wilbur Aviation Academy's Right Stuff Award, 1997
Recipient of Orville University's Outstanding Senior Award, 1995

REFERENCES AVAILABLE IN APPENDIX A

As you can see, Lance has completely revamped his resume, although he's maintained the basic qualities and design elements. He's kept it to a single page with plenty of bolds, underlinings and white space to make the information accessible, but he's emphasized the skills that potential funders will find most important. His education is less significant than his Peace Corps work, so he has moved it to the bottom of the page, while his years on Calamari Island have received far more prominence than they did in his pilot's resume. Lance has employed a combination of a functional and targeted resume format, but he made certain to include all of the dates of his work and educational experiences.

The way Lance describes his Peace Corps experience on his bankable business plan resume indicates how he has honed his problem-solving skills and his ability to inspire others to be good workers. It is also clear that he has planned for the long-term in preparing guidelines for future PCVs in Pusit. His years of working in his father's delicatessen after school never appeared on his professional pilot's resume, but this expertise will be invaluable in assuring investors and lenders that he knows how to buy food in bulk and run a grill.

How Resumes Are Checked and How to Prepare to Be Checked

Banks and other funding sources routinely perform background checks on the entrepreneurs who submit business plans. Be sure that your resume can stand up to close scrutiny. Here are some key areas to focus on:

Education: Degrees and honors awarded can be checked with schools. Resumes that say "Toupee State College, Business, 2004" are red flags to experienced resume readers. There is no degree given. So this could mean the person took one course or even just attended one class. At best it is incomplete. At worst, it is an attempt to mislead.

References: References who are friends, classmates, or peers have less credibility than those who are employers or supervisors. Many companies have the policy only to confirm employment, not to provide any judgments about the people. So before giving references, you should find out what their policies are and try to choose some references who will say specific, positive things about you. Note that Lance has indicated in his business plan resume that his references can be found in an appendix.

Employment History: Many people who will read your resume will treat gaps in your employment history or periods of self-employment with suspicion. If you are only presenting past employment that you regard as relevant then you should say so, listing employment history under a section called "Relevant Employment History." If you have periods of self-employment, your resume should point out some specific accomplishments or positives that resulted from those experiences.

Skills: If you refer to specific skills, you must do so in an entirely accurate, non-exaggerating way. If your resume states, as Lance's does, that you speak fluent Tagalog, you had best ask yourself what happens if the interviewer starts talking to you in Tagalog? Accurately describing your level of skills is obviously a requirement, but your resume might also discuss some benefits you produced for your company with particular software, what problems you solved for your employer using the software, or some particular specialties you have.

The Web: Both employers and funding sources now routinely check people's credentials on the Web. You may have posted profiles about yourself on myspace, facebook or other Web sites. It is critical to make certain that any facts available about you on the Web are accurate and consistent with your resume. Any information you have posted on Web sites must reinforce the message that you are a professional who deserves the support of investors and lenders. A good first step is checking what comes up about you through Google or other search engines as well as through the Web sites of organizations you are active in or to which you belong.

The Entrepreneur in the Text of the Business Plan

The body of your business plan is where you can elaborate on talents and skills that are not obvious from the work record listed on your resume. Although most potential supporters of Lance Lindbergh's business will gather that he has a deep understanding of the squid harvesting process from his resume, they need to know how this will help him run Lance's Squid Pancake Restaurant. Lance will have to explain in the text that he has maintained close ties with all the subsequent Peace Corps Volunteers in the island country of Pusit and that as a result, he will be able to negotiate an excellent price for continuous supplies of fresh squid. He must also emphasize in his text that in order for squid to be delivered as freshly as possible, he plans to train pilots in Pusit before he opens his restaurant, a piece of crucial information that cannot be deduced from his resume alone. His pilot's resume listed his professional citations for customer satisfaction with his airline, which indicates that Lance is goal-oriented and takes pride in the service he provided his passengers—and will undoubtedly offer his restaurant patrons. However, only in the text can he explain how being a pilot will enable him to train his staff to maintain their composure when a grease fire starts in the kitchen and he needs to reassure his diners to remain calm.

The information you provide in the text of your business plan will help you expand on your resume and convince others that you have acquired particularly useful skills that will make your business a success. For example, Amelia C. Ader is a Peace Corps Volunteer Lance knows well. She is about to finish up her Peace Corps stint in Pusit and is willing to stay on Calamari Island to supervise squid harvesting and shipping for Lance's restaurant. Her entire resume may not be needed in the business plan, but a paragraph stating her skills, her fluency in Tagalog, and her expansion of the program Lance instituted will add further credibility to the team and is worthy of mention in the text or perhaps in the Appendix.

Here are some additional points to follow in describing the skills and experience of you and your potential colleagues:

Style: Most business plans use the third person in discussing the qualifications of the entrepreneur seeking financial support. The pilot will probably refer to himself throughout his plan by his last name only, after introducing his full name near the beginning of the text. Employing the first person "I" in the body of the text is, however, a growing trend. The advantage is that it reinforces your role as the key person in your venture's success. However, if you have one or more partners in the business, stick to the third person and last names, which indicates that you will be working as a balanced, well-coordinated team in which each person's role is well defined.

Honesty: Be honest about your skills, but don't oversell or undersell yourself. You are not boasting when you claim particular talents or expertise. Stressing your strengths reassures potential funders that you have the ability and experience to succeed, but if you go overboard, you will raise serious doubts about your honesty. Even if you began a business that failed, it is far better to mention it in your plan in a positive light, than to hide the fact and have it emerge later.

Many successful entrepreneurs have failed in earlier attempts to start a business, but they learned from their experiences. Milton Hershey of chocolate bar fame, founded several candy companies that went belly-up before he settled on his unique and successful process of combining milk with chocolate. Even if an earlier venture failed, emphasize what you learned about running a business, hiring employees, attracting funding sources, being a boss or figuring out the right recipe. If your new business builds on what you've learned, negative experiences won't appear negative at all.

What Were They Thinking? Sunbeam Pays the Price for Not Checking the Facts

In 1996, Sunbeam Corporation, the appliance maker, faced declining financial fortunes. With its stock trading at about $12 per share, financier Ronald Perelman and mutual fund manager Michael Price, who both controlled large blocks of Sunbeam shares, were very unhappy. They needed to do something dramatic to boost the stock. They decided to hire Al Dunlop, nicknamed Chainsaw Al, a high-profile CEO with a reputation for taking fast and dramatic action. While they knew his reputation, they didn't know the full facts of his background and they never checked.

Just the announcement of Dunlop's appointment took the stock up more than 50% in one day. Things were off to a good start. Dunlop, who earned his reputation by slashing jobs, was well known for his previous turnaround at Scott Paper, where the stock price more than doubled in the 18 months of Dunlop's tenure, ending in a sale of Scott to Kimberly-Clark. Dunlop had also worked at American Can, Lily Tulip, and Crown Zellerbach. It later came to light that he had previously worked at two companies in the 1970s from which he had been fired, facts he had misrepresented to Sunbeam management and that Sunbeam had not checked.

Within six months of becoming CEO at Sunbeam, Dunlop fired more than half of Sunbeam's 12,000 workers and closed 12 of its 18 manufacturing plants. In October 1997, less than 18 months after becoming CEO, Dunlop hired investment bankers Morgan Stanley to explore a sale of the company as well as possible acquisitions. In March 1998, Sunbeam announced purchases of the Coleman Company that makes camping gear, First Alert that makes smoke alarms, and Signature Brands that makes Mr. Coffee coffee makers. Like a gambler with a plane to catch, Dunlop was racing to place his bets.

The acquisitions and continued good news of sales growth propelled Sunbeam stock up to a high of $52 per share in March 1998. Then the real story began to explode onto the front pages of the newspapers. Dunlop was slashing prices and giving incredibly generous payment terms to get Sunbeam products into the hands of retailers. Sometimes he made deals to put products into the warehouses of distributors for shipping to retailers later, but he would immediately book revenue as if the products had been bought by the retailer. This practice, while not illegal, made that period's financial results look better than they really were and auditor Arthur Andersen & Co. let it stand.

Dunlop had actually put in place a slash-and-burn short-term strategy that had as its cornerstone the creation of a false appearance of positive performance: Do anything to make Sunbeam's sales look better now and then hope that another company will buy Sunbeam, or that Sunbeam will be able to raise more money on Wall Street to buy other companies. If all this took place before the truth emerged about Sunbeam's core appliance business, Dunlop and the Sunbeam shareholders would make a big score because their shares in Sunbeam would skyrocket. Dunlop raced against time, but time won.

Dunlop had so severely cut the workforce that morale was low and many of the remaining workers were searching for new jobs. The departure of key executives, combined with weak profits, began to tip off some people on Wall Street that things were not as good as Dunlop claimed. By 1998, Dunlop had not brought either the purchase of other businesses or the sale of Sunbeam to fruition. The Board of Directors realized that the company was rapidly exhausting its cash reserves. Sunbeam would soon be in default of its $1.7 billion bank loan. Finally, the Board stepped in, firing Dunlop and eventually declaring bankruptcy. When Sunbeam emerged from bankruptcy in 2001, the Board felt the company name was so damaged by the debacles under Dunlop's leadership, that they dropped the Sunbeam name and renamed the company American Household, Inc. They probably do background checks on potential employees much more carefully now.

The Entrepreneur's Toolkit: Turn a Chronological Resume into a Functional Resume

Your resume is an important tool in selling potential investors and lenders on the specific abilities you bring to your venture. You must impress the people you want to support your business plan that you—and your team—are uniquely qualified to establish this company and make it profitable. This is not gloating or boasting; this is the best way to reassure funders that you have the background, talent and enthusiasm to make your enterprise successful.

An effective way to analyze your skills is by creating a chronological resume first and then transforming it into a functional resume. This will enable you to determine which work experiences and abilities are the strongest to emphasize when crafting your business plan.

Earlier in this Chapter are the examples of Lance Lindbergh's chronological and a functional resumes. Before you try to write similar chronological and functional resumes describing your own background and work experience, please look at these two resumes carefully. Do they have important stylistic components by employing bolds, underlining and white space to emphasize important information and make the resumes readable? Are both only a single page? Do they use active verbs to describe the jobs and responsibilities?

Remember how our pilot, Lance Lindbergh, moved his educational information to the bottom of his bankable business plan resume? For someone whose education is more recent and on target with the purpose of the resume, it is better for the education section to be placed near the top of both the chronological and functional resumes.

Creating Your Own Resume

Now create your own resume, keeping in mind that it will be included in your business plan and must support your contention that you are the right entrepreneur for this business. Start with the chronological format, which will be the easiest. Place your name and contact information at the top, your business plan objective next, followed by your educational background, if it is recent. Now list your jobs in *reverse* order, with the most recent one first. Clearly state your position, the years you served in that capacity and the duties you performed.

If your educational background includes training in a completely unrelated field, you might consider placing it last, at the bottom of your resume. For example, being an archeology major may not be significantly important to someone buying an ice cream store franchise so it probably shouldn't be prominent in that person's resume. But potential investors and lenders will still want to know the person's educational background.

Now convert your chronological resume into a functional resume by choosing those skills, experiences, and qualifications that are most important to your ability to lead your business.

STEPHEN HALL WRESTLES WITH HIS RESUME

Stephen Hall is a 25 year-old with an entrepreneurial dream and an eclectic background. His dream is to start a travel agency that specializes in sports-related trips. These would include travel packages to attend professional sports events throughout the world and multi-country tours that are built around specific sporting competitions. Stephen knows there are travel agencies that already do this, but he feels it is a growing market and his knowledge of sports and his ability to work well with customers should help him be successful. He estimates he needs $150,000 to start this business, most of which will go into marketing expenses. His father has agreed to give him $50,000 and now he is writing a plan to show to potential investors.

Stephen's background includes interest and experience in many sports. He was an excellent wrestler in high school and college where he majored in computer science and graduated with a 2.8 grade-point average. After graduating, he worked at a storefront travel agency that had no particular specialty. He currently is a customer-service rep for a regional airline at the major airport near his home. While in high school and college, Stephen held many part-time jobs including running the deep-fat fryer in a fast food restaurant, working for a moving company, and being a security guard at a movie theater.

Without overstating his qualifications, Stephen wants to point out his knowledge, relevant work experience, and personal skills that will make potential investors confident in supporting his venture. But he feels somewhat defensive talking about his background. His school career was not stellar and his jobs have been largely minimum wage and clerical.

Stephen is considering not including a resume in his plan and avoiding discussion of his own background in the text of his business plan. He also wonders if there is some way to define his business strategy that would better match his qualifications or if he can describe his experience and skills in the best light without exaggerating.

End of Chapter Questions

1. Playing the role of a potential investor, what do you consider Stephen's strengths and weaknesses?
2. What kind of resume should Stephen prepare?
3. Write a one paragraph description of Stephen that stresses how his qualifications and abilities could make this venture successful.

NOTES

1. Peg Thoms, Rosemary McMasters, Melissa R. Roberts, and Douglas A. Dombkowski, "Resume Characteristics as Predictors of an Invitation to Interview," *Journal of Business and Psychology*, Vol. 13, No. 3, (Spring 1999), p. 339.

CHAPTER 11

ISSUE 11
PRESENT THE PLAN ON PAPER

By now all the pieces of your bankable business plan are in place—or at least somewhere on your desk. You have created a comprehensive, high quality, compelling business plan, except for putting the sections together. As you have covered the issues outlined in this book, you should have accomplished the following:

- Refined and revised your business concept into one that works for you, your investors, bankers, and all the other people whose participation is needed to make your business a success.
- Addressed the needs of all these people and are prepared to answer their questions.
- Created a plan that makes reasonable assumptions about issues such as expenses, the time required to achieve your revenue goals, and the schedule your plan envisions for the growth of your business.

Now you must put the pieces together in a cohesive, easy-to-follow business plan which will motivate readers to take the actions you need them to take, whether as investors, lenders, or partners.

What Do You Want the Reader to Remember? Develop a Simple and Cohesive Message

Ask a friend who just saw a film what it was about and he will likely summarize it in less than a minute. *Titanic* is a love story set on a sinking ship with great special effects. *The Wizard of Oz* is about a young girl's trip through a fantasy land with witches, wizards, and talking lions, trees, and scarecrows that also has good songs. Of course, your friend remembers more details, but the central points are at the core of how he experienced the film. Business plans are similar.

You may have a 100-page business plan, but there will be a few main points that stand out to readers. Here are examples of the central points that could have been made about some well-known businesses while they were still growing and seeking funds:

- **Office Depot:** It is just like Staples but will open in places Staples hasn't reached yet.
- **Burger King:** It is just like McDonald's but will open in places that McDonald's hasn't reached yet.
- **eBay:** It will create a Web site on which people can sell and auction items directly to each other.
- **Starbucks:** Comfortable places with a variety of expensive coffee drinks.

What is the central message you want people to remember from your plan? Ideally, it should include a clear and accurate statement of what the business is, why it should be successful, and how qualified you are. It should fit into one or two sentences—a length that can be easily remembered and repeated to others. Write the one or two sentences you want everyone to remember. If this seems impossible, please note that a 30-second commercial, which can be extremely convincing and memorable, has about 50 words.

Table 11.1 reveals some potential core messages about two current well-known entrepreneurs and two historical figures:

TABLE 11.1
CREATE A SHORT, CENTRAL MESSAGE ABOUT YOU AND YOUR BUSINESS

The Facts	Michael Dell	Donald Trump	Bonnie and Clyde	You
About the Entrepreneur	Smart, ambitious, knows quite a bit about computers	Brash, rather strange-looking fellow who inherited hundreds of millions from his father	Bold couple who can shoot well and drive fast	
What the business is	Assembling PCs one at a time to meet customer specs	Turning his name into a brand with the hundreds of millions of dollars he inherited	Pointing a gun at bank employees and asking them for money without filing a proper application	
Why it will be successful	Low fixed investment and low inventory, customized product; can incorporate new technology quickly	He inherited hundreds of millions of dollars from his father and will happily put his name on any building or product	People prefer handing over money to being shot; not counting jail time, cost of sales is low	

Organize the Plan and Create an Outline

It is important to create an outline before you start pulling everything together for your final business plan. Outlines for simple and complex plans are provided in the Appendix, but remember that these are just guidelines. You are building a case for someone to take action and not all potential funders care about the same issues. A good outline makes that case for action as clear and compelling as possible. For example, lenders focus on having their principle recouped and their interest paid on time. Therefore, growth is not as important to them as security. Investors are more focused on the growth potential because much of the upside in your company's value will go to them. Some items on the sample outlines may be totally irrelevant for your plan. If you make a product, such as specialized software to sell only to telephone companies, you probably don't need to provide extensive research on primary, secondary, and tertiary markets. You can simply list the potential customers and describe how they will use your product.

You should place materials that are not essential to the main concept, such as background information, newspaper articles, staff resumes, and financial detail on your competitors, in an appendix. You can state the conclusion of the appended materials in the body of the plan and then refer the reader to the appendix for more detail.

When you write, discuss general issues first and then move to specific points:

- **Begin with an overview of the business,** the reason an opportunity exists, and what you need in terms of support.
- **Then discuss the business environment,** such as consumers' needs, the market, the industry, and the competition.
- **Identify the strategy for the product,** service, or business concept that will allow you to beat the competition.
- **Describe the implementation of your concept** through management, organizational structure, marketing, sales, and key staff members.
- **Finally, add financial materials,** such as Projected Income Statements, Balance Sheets, Cash Flow Statements, comparisons to RMA or other industry comparables, and Returns Analysis.

Don't follow this book's outlines to the letter or let a computer program for business plans dictate the content or structure of your plan. If you do, the resulting plan will look canned and will waste people's time by not addressing each reader's specific interests.

Write It Clearly and Simply

Now you can start filling in the outline, remembering that you should feel free to place detail or information that may not be important to all your readers in an appendix. Keep the language simple and to the point, but use active, animated verbs to add spark and movement to your prose.

Don't fall into the trap of using jargon, the technical and sometimes short-hand language of a specific field that can create a separation between the group that uses it and everyone else. Doctors call symptoms by their Greek names, such as presbyopia, when speaking with each other, but by their English names, such as nearsightedness, when talking to patients. Engineers create a blizzard of initials and numbers when they speak with each other that is impenetrable and off-putting to outsiders. Using jargon in your business plan or when speaking to potential investors does the same: It creates social and professional separation between you and others, a very poor idea when you are trying to forge a business relationship. Here is an example of a sentence of jargon taken from a Wall Street analyst's report followed by its translation:

What the Analyst Said

"Most analysts project a decline in ROEs of about 100 basis points in the QSR Industry through the next seasonal cycle. However, most CEOs, COOs, and CFOs of top-tier companies have projections of high-trajectory revenue producing enhancements."

The Jargon Explained

- ROE—Return on Equity, i.e. returns to shareholders
- Basis Points—one-hundredth of a percent
- QSR—Quick Serve Restaurants, i.e. fast food restaurants
- CEO—Chief Executive Officer
- COO—Chief Operating Officer
- CFO—Chief Financial Officer
- Top-tier—large
- High-trajectory—rapid

What the Analyst Meant

Wall Street sees a 1% decline of returns in the fast food industry over the next few months. The leaders of the large companies in the industry disagree.

Create a Time Line

A time line is a useful tool for planning, budgeting, managing, and presenting your business plan. Depending on the complexity of your plan, your time line could be a simple list of key dates or it could be a complex schedule of thousands of steps all linked together by a computer program. A time line can help you:

- **Develop a realistic schedule**. Creating a time line will force you to establish the amount of time it will take you to complete each step in starting your business. Many entrepreneurs have a tendency to gloss over the details of organizing a successful venture in a "build it and they will come" phenomenon. It may be true that customers will beat their way to your door once the business is ready, but just opening that door is usually preceded by many time-consuming steps such as receiving zoning approvals, licenses, and financing. Establishing a simple one person office requires, at a minimum, negotiating a lease, ordering furniture and equipment, and having a phone installed.

- **Design an accurate budget**. The process of creating a time line will help you produce a detailed and accurate budget. Budgets and financial projections all have a time dimension. A time line can include the dates for required expenditures such as when items need to be ordered, payments made, employees hired, and fees paid, all of which will help you keep track of your cash balances. On the revenue side, the time line can include items such as when funding from banks and investors will arrive, or when fees from clients can be expected.

- **Establish a system to monitor progress**. Once you have created your time line, you will have benchmarks against which to compare your actual operation and performance. The time line will keep you constantly apprized of what you need to focus on next, or tell you which steps are holding up your progress. No business follows its plan precisely. With a time line in place, you can easily see when you need to revise your business plan.

- **Demonstrate your professionalism**. Chapter 10 discusses how the plan has to demonstrate your abilities and qualifications. Providing a detailed and realistic time line clearly shows your readers that you know how to build and run your business, step by step.

- **Provide feedback to your investors**. Just as the time line works for you as a means to track progress, it will work for your investors in judging your performance. You will be asked many times,

"How are you doing compared to plan?" The time line provides a straightforward method for you to show your investors, bankers, employers, and suppliers precisely how well you are doing compared to plan.

- **Create an operational plan that can be adjusted**. As the time line examples provided later in this Chapter under The Entrepreneur's Toolkit indicate, activities often take longer than expected. A time line, especially one created with project software, provides an easy and fast way to update your schedule as adjustments are required.

A list of the steps you must take and the time required for each task is an essential part of creating a bankable business plan. A clear time line can help you develop a realistic schedule, design an accurate budget, establish a system to monitor progress, provide feedback for your investors and create an operational template for your business. Some types of time lines can also help you identify the *critical path* of activities, each of which must stay on schedule in order for the entire plan to stay on schedule. There are three basic formats for creating effective time lines. They are presented here from the most basic to the most sophisticated: A Simple Time Line, a Gantt Chart, and a PERT Chart.

A Simple Time Line

The simplest time line is a list of activities with start dates, the amount of time they will take to complete, and the tasks that must be finished before each activity can begin. On the next page is an actual time line that Luke Mangal produced prior to his decision to open a franchised real estate agency in Floral Park, New York.

Figure 11.1
Mangal Real Estate Agency:
Simple Time Line for Pre-Opening Activities

Name	Duration (Work Days)	Start Date	Finish Date	Revised Duration (Work Days)	Revised Start Date	Revised Finish Date
Evaluate Franchise Options	59.00	1/3/05	3/24/05	59.00	1/3/05	3/24/05
Purchase Franchise	30.00	3/25/05	5/5/05	30.00	3/25/05	5/5/05
Search for Location	70.00	5/6/05	8/11/05	70.00	5/6/05	8/11/05
Set up LLC	10.00	3/25/05	4/7/05	10.00	3/25/05	4/7/05
Obtain Renovation Estimates	40.00	8/12/05	10/6/05	40.00	8/12/05	10/6/05
Renovate Office	20.00	10/7/05	11/3/05	20.00	10/7/05	11/3/05
Evaluate Furniture Options	15.00	8/12/05	9/1/05	15.00	8/12/05	9/1/05
Furniture Delivered	1.00	8/12/05	8/12/05	1.00	8/12/05	8/12/05
Evaluate Telephone Systems	15.00	9/16/05	10/6/05	15.00	9/16/05	10/6/05
Negotiate and Sign Office Lease	25.00	8/12/05	9/15/05	25.00	8/12/05	9/15/05
Design Store Sign	10.00	9/16/05	9/29/05	10.00	9/16/05	9/29/05
Submit Sign for Town Approval	5.00	9/30/05	10/6/05	5.00	9/30/05	10/6/05
Obtain Town Approval of Sign	30.00	10/7/05	11/17/05	30.00	10/7/05	11/17/05
Obtain Bids on Sign	15.00	11/18/05	12/8/05	15.00	11/18/05	12/8/05
Order Sign	2.00	12/9/05	12/12/05	2.00	12/9/05	12/12/05
Receive and Install Sign	40.00	12/13/05	2/6/06	40.00	12/13/05	2/6/06
File for State Business License	10.00	4/8/05	4/21/05	10.00	4/8/05	4/21/05
Establish Bank Account	1.00	5/6/05	5/6/05	1.00	5/6/05	5/6/05
Obtain State Tax ID Number	5.00	4/8/05	4/14/05	5.00	4/8/05	4/14/05
Obtain Federal Tax ID Number	5.00	4/8/05	4/14/05	5.00	4/8/05	4/14/05
Evaluate Business Insurance Options	20.00	5/6/05	6/2/05	20.00	5/6/05	6/2/05
Purchase Business Insurance	10.00	6/3/05	6/16/05	10.00	6/3/05	6/16/05
Decide on Telephone and Internet Service	4.00	10/7/05	10/12/05	4.00	10/7/05	10/12/05
Install Phones	30.00	10/13/05	11/23/05	30.00	10/13/05	11/23/05
Find Graphic Designer	30.00	5/6/05	6/16/05	30.00	5/6/05	6/16/05
Find Web site Designer	30.00	6/17/05	7/28/05	30.00	6/17/05	7/28/05
Research Printers	30.00	6/17/05	7/28/05	30.00	6/17/05	7/28/05
Order Design of Print Materials	5.00	6/17/05	6/23/05	5.00	6/17/05	6/23/05
Obtain and Approve Designs of Printed Materials	20.00	6/24/05	7/21/05	20.00	6/24/05	7/21/05
Order Web site	3.00	7/29/05	8/2/05	3.00	7/29/05	8/2/05
Web site Development	30.00	8/3/05	9/13/05	30.00	8/3/05	9/13/05
Order Printed Materials	20.00	7/22/05	8/18/05	20.00	7/22/05	8/18/05
Attend Franchise Training	6.00	5/6/05	5/13/05	6.00	5/6/05	5/13/05
Take Course to Obtain Broker License	40.00	4/22/05	6/16/05	40.00	4/22/05	6/16/05
Obtain Real Estate License	15.00	6/17/05	7/7/05	15.00	6/17/05	7/7/05
Advertise and Interview for Receptionists	10.00	7/8/05	7/21/05	10.00	7/8/05	7/21/05
Hire Receptionist	5.00	7/22/05	7/28/05	5.00	7/22/05	7/28/05
Apply for and Join Board of Realtors	15.00	7/8/05	7/28/05	15.00	7/8/05	7/28/05

Even a seemingly very simple business can easily require many steps that have to be performed in succession. A delay in any one of them has the potential to derail the entire project. Here is an activities list for a small, part-time business selling cotton candy for a few weeks during the local county fair:

FIGURE 11.2
ACTIVITIES LIST FOR COTTON CANDY BUSINESS AT THE COUNTY FAIR

Activity	Dates	Expenditures Required
File with Fair Manager to Obtain Permit and Be Assigned Location	October 23	$50 fee
Obtain Permit	December 15	none
Order Trailer and Cotton Candy Making Machine	December 16	$3,000 deposit
Accept Delivery of Trailer and Cotton Candy Making Machine	March 1	$5,000 payment required
Take Trailer for Customized Paint Job	March 10	$750 deposit required
Pick up Painted Trailer	March 22	$2,000 payment required
Order Candy-Making Supplies	April 20	$600 payment required
Supplies Delivered	May 1	none
Test Trailer and Candy-Making Machine at the Little League Games	May 15-17	$300 for workers, but expect $500 in revenue
Set up at County Fair	June 3	none
Fair Week	June 6-13	$1,200 for workers, but expect $7,000 in revenue

A Gantt Chart

A Gantt chart is similar to the simple time line presented above, but with a graphic presentation of each activity. An engineer, Henry Laurence Gantt, developed this format in the 1910s as a way to coordinate and manage large industrial and construction projects. The major advantage of a Gantt chart is that it is easy to see whether the various activities listed are running sequentially, parallel to each other, or if they overlap. Gantt charts can be created using word processing programs such as Word or WordPerfect, spreadsheet programs such as Lotus or Excel, or with specialized programs such as Microsoft Project.

A Gantt chart enables you to visualize activities more clearly because you can:

- Fill in or color over the lines that represent each task as it is completed.
- Draw a line across all the tasks to see how many are running longer than projected.
- Create "subtask lists" that show all the underlying components of any one task on the chart. This can happen automatically if you use project management software.

Figure 11.3 shows the same project for the real estate office previously shown as a simple time line now produced as a Gantt Chart:

Figure 11.3
Mangal Real Estate Agency:
Gantt Chart of Pre-Opening Activities

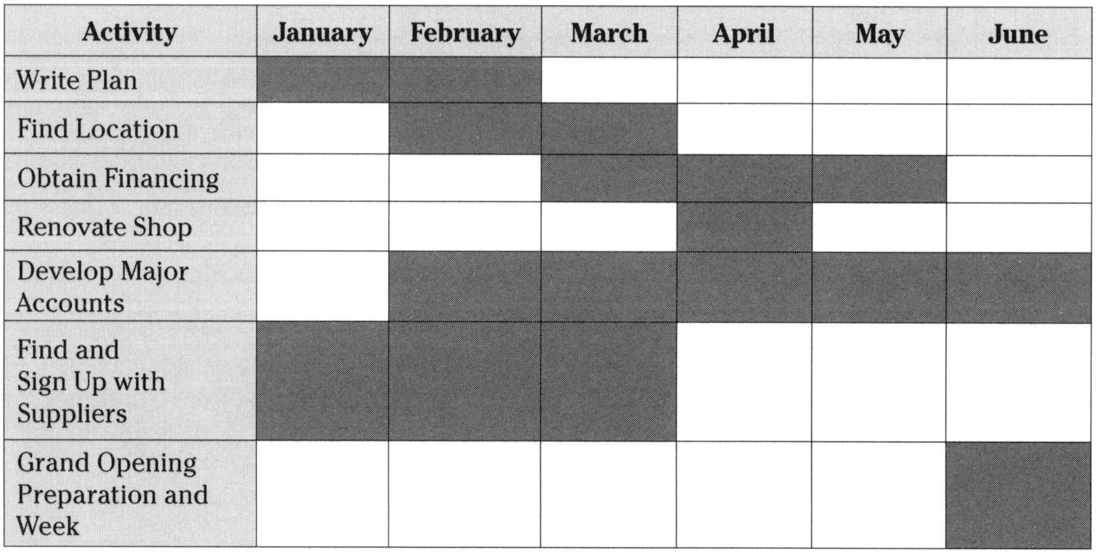

Activity	January	February	March	April	May	June
Write Plan						
Find Location						
Obtain Financing						
Renovate Shop						
Develop Major Accounts						
Find and Sign Up with Suppliers						
Grand Opening Preparation and Week						

A PERT Chart

The most sophisticated time line can be created with a PERT chart, which stands for Program Evaluation and Review Technique. PERT charts are most useful for projects that are very complex with many interdependent steps, and where the cost of delay can be crippling. Construction projects, for example, often use PERT charts. With a PERT chart it is possible to determine the critical path, which is the precise sequence of activities which must be completed on time or the project will be delayed. For simpler projects, you may also be able to calculate the critical path from Gantt charts or simple activities lists.

Like the simple time line or the Gantt chart, a PERT chart is produced by creating a list of all the activities that must be accomplished in order to bring your plan to fruition, along with an estimate of how long each activity will take. However, on a PERT chart, you need to list the immediate prerequisites for each activity as well. For example, you can't sign the contract to construct the factory until the bank loan is approved and the zoning variances are granted. When you have listed all the activities and their immediate prerequisite, you can create a chart similar to the one below shown in Table 11.4.

To figure out which activities are on the critical path, you can either look backwards from completion and find the shortest path, or estimate the earliest and latest completion times for each activity and find the path that minimizes the waiting time, called slack time, between activities. For the most complex projects, you can employ software that does this calculation automatically.

It is difficult to make a time line by hand that includes more than 20 activities. Over 20 and it is hard to fit the chart on a single page and difficult to design without a computer. Project management software can produce PERT charts printed on multiple sheets that can be placed next to each other to provide the most complete picture of your time line requirements.

Here is the same Mangal Real Estate office project shown as a PERT chart with the critical path indicated. The shortest time required to open the business is 13 months. Any delays in activities along the critical path and the necessary amounts of time will increase. By spending effort and money to reduce the length of time for any activity along the critical path, the 13 month period until the business opens can be reduced.

In the case of Mr. Mangal's real estate agency, renovations began during exceptionally cold weather and work was delayed because frozen pipes required repairs, adding 60 days to the job. The 30 days expected for town approval of the store sign actually took twice as long because the town rejected two proposals before finally granting a sign license for the third submission. Because these two activities occurred along the critical path, the entire project took 90 days longer than expected.

FIGURE 11.4
PERT CHART

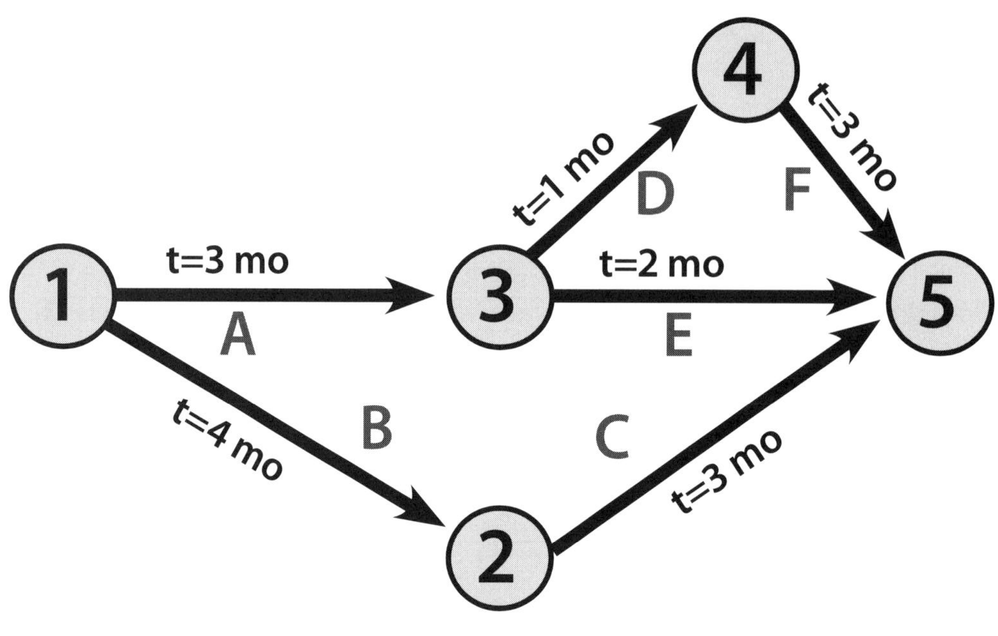

KEY
Activities: A-F
Time Required: t
Benchmarks: 1-5

Write a Compelling Executive Summary

An Executive Summary is ideally a one page—or shorter—overview of your plan, which presents a concise and convincing argument for the success of your business concept. More than just a simple explanation of your idea, the Executive Summary is the hook that must grab and hold the attention of your readers. If the people reading your plan do not like what they see in the Executive Summary, they rarely read any further, and your beautifully crafted plan based upon your brilliant concept will be tossed on to the already sky-high pile of rejects. Bankers, venture capital firms, and other investors see hundreds of plans every year. If your Executive Summary doesn't immediately assert that your plan merits their attention, or if it's unprofessional, poorly presented, or incomplete, you're history.

The Executive Summary should *briefly* cover all of the first ten esstential issues, each of which you addressed in the Chapter of the corresponding number:

1. **Business definition:** What will your business accomplish?
2. **Feasibility:** In analyzing your initial needs you answered the question: What will be required to start your business?
3. **Strategy:** How will you distinguish your product or service from competitors?
4. **Market analysis:** Who will want what you are selling?
5. **A marketing campaign:** How will you reach your potential customers and what will you say to them?
6. **A sales effort:** How will you attract customers and make sales?
7. **Company organization:** What will be the legal and management structure? How will you hire and organize your workforce?
8. **Potential funding sources:** Where will you obtain the required financing?
9. **Financial projections:** How will you convince others that your plan merits their support? How do your projections compare with industry averages?
10. **The entrepreneur's abilities and qualifications:** Why are you the right person to bring this to reality?

Not every business plan requires the discussion of all of the first ten essential issues. For example, if you are starting a single person venture and do not contemplate hiring anyone, you don't need to cover Issue 7. If there are no industry averages available for your business, then some information related to Issue 9 cannot be provided.

Here are four short, but complete, Executive Summaries adapted from actual plans. Each one covers all the necessary ten issues and addresses the interests of a particular funding source. To clarify which issue is being covered, the following Executive Summaries have corresponding numbers in parathenses.

- **The Sunny City Budget Motel** (written for investors and lenders). The Sunny City hotel/motel market is generally underbuilt and represents an opportunity for new hotels and motels (1). Compared to industry standards for hotel/motel rooms relative to the volume of travelers on the adjacent interstate highway, the city's population, and jobs in the market, there is unmet demand for hotel and motel rooms (3,4). Since there is no budget hotel or motel within the Sunny City metropolitan area, the market has a sizeable niche available (3, 4). A location has been identified that is adjacent to the interstate highway within two miles of downtown that can be purchased for the construction of a hotel or motel (1,4). The XYZ national budget hotel chain is willing to sell a franchise for this location to its former Assistant Manager, Harry Johnson, who has lived in Sunny City for five years (2, 8,10). The franchisor will provide a national reservation service (5,6), management and employee training, and a detailed operations manual (7). The cost numbers for the land and construction are below XYZ's national averages, while room rates are projected to be at or above average (9). Financial projections show that $2 million in equity investment will earn 21% returns and that $8 million in debt can be repaid in 8 years (2,9). Johnson will be providing $200,000 in collateral along with his ten years of management and employee history in the budget motel industry (2,10).

- **The LawnRider Company** (written for investors only). The riding lawnmower industry has grown three fold in the last 15 years with a strong trend toward adding features without raising prices (4). The LawnRider Company is being formed to become a major player in this market with a specially designed line which adds features to midpriced riding lawnmowers that previously have only been found on high end machines (1,3,4). LawnRider founder and CEO Julius Greengrass has negotiated a contract with a Korean company to manufacture the machines and give LawnRider the low cost advantage in this market (2,3,7). Greengrass has also approached the largest home center company in the U.S. market, which has agreed to carry LawnRider exclusively in its 1,200 stores (5,6,7). Both agreements have been negotiated by Greengrass , a lawyer and former suburban real estate developer (2,7,10). The key remaining element for LawnRider's success is for the company to market the product by building brand awareness among consumers. Towards that end, a detailed marketing plan has been created (3,4,5,6). LawnRider is seeking $4 million in investment, which is projected to earn a 32% average annual return over the next three years (8,9).

- **Mom's Restaurant** (written for a bank loan). Mom's has been a successful and well-known family restaurant with more than $2.5 million in annual revenue and profits of more $80,000 annually for the last nine years (1,3,5,9). The land, building, and contents are appraised at $425,000 (9). Janet Wise, the founder and manager of Mom's, is looking to sell. My Restaurant Corp. is a company formed by Bob Wyler, who has been the head chef at Mom's for six years, and his wife, Sylvia Wyler, who has managed Mom's for the past four years (2,7,10). My Restaurant has negotiated the purchase of Mom's restaurant, including the land on which the restaurant and parking lot stand, for $350,000 (2,9). The Wylers are investing $100,000 and are looking to obtain a bank loan for the balance of $250,000 to be secured by an SBA guarantee, the building, and the land (2,8,9). Mom's performs within industry standards according to the RMA data for similar restaurants (9,10). The Wylers have an excellent personal credit record (7,8,9,10) and there are no outstanding claims or liabilities against Mom's (9). The economy of the neighborhood, based on employment, housing prices, and new construction, is strong (1,3,4,6,9).

- **Bug-Be-Gone Corporation** (for investors) is seeking to raise $10 million in equity capital from individuals who will invest at least $1 million each (2, 8) to develop and market a unique line of fruit-scented insecticides that are nontoxic to humans and pets (1, 3, 4, 5). Bug-Be-Gone is owned and managed by Roger Roach, whose 20 years of experience in the insect extermination business will enable him to hire the most knowledgeable entomologists and the most precise bug sprayers in the industry (2,7,10). The company has already received preliminary orders from the three major firms that supply 80 percent of the California market, which consumes 50 percent of all insecticides in the United States (4, 5, 6). The financial projections show the company achieving higher than average profit margins (9) and that equity investors will receive returns in excess of 35 percent annually by the third year of operation (9).

Elevator Pitches

Elevator pitches are the short oral presentations sometimes requested by funding sources and at business plan competitions. Called "elevator pitches" because they represent an entrepreneur's business pitch during a brief elevator ride, they can also be delivered during informal meetings, phone calls, and even actual elevator rides. Think of an elevator pitch as a response to the question,"What are you up to?" More formal in-person presentations generally run from three to ten minutes; informal presentations, of course, are usually much less.

An elevator ride from the lobby of the Empire State Building to the observation deck requires two elevators and takes two minutes. Regardless of the setting or the precise length, an elevator pitch is a very useful tool for an entrepreneur, an oral equivalent of an Executive Summary. Since most people speak at the rate of two words per second, even the longest Executive Summary example above can be spoken aloud in under three minutes. The challenge is how to interest someone in your company when you may have only 30 seconds or less. In this case, you have about 50 words to deliver your message and will probably only be able to get through the first three essential issues that comprise your Executive Summary:

1. **Business Definition:** What will your business accomplish for others and yourself?
2. **Feasibility:** What will you require to start your business?

3. **Strategy:** How will you distinguish your product or service from competitors?

For Bug-Be Gone, the following would be the elevator pitch covering these three points plus potential returns:

> *Bug-Be-Gone is developing and marketing a line of fruit-scented insecticides that are non-toxic to humans and pets. We have already received some major orders and we are seeking to raise $10 million in equity and expect to provide returns above 35%.*

This elevator pitch is only 40 words long.

The Physical Qualities of a Bankable Business Plan

The look of your business plan will create an indelible first impression — negative or positive. People often make the mistake of creating a presentation that overshadows the content of the plan. Many entrepreneurs commit a great deal of effort and expense to designing an eye-catching written presentation. Some plans are true works of art—slickly produced with fanciful graphics and expensive, glossy paper. Others cobble together a sloppy business plan mixed with both original and photocopied pages generated by different computers and printed in mismatching fonts.

In all of these cases, even the most persuasive text was completely eclipsed by the physical presentation. Such artfully or poorly produced business plans give the impression that these entrepreneurs either have more flash than substance or are too disorganized and incompetent to start their own companies. The physical qualities of your plan should demonstrate that you took exceptional care to produce it and that you are a competent, meticulous, enthusiastic, and knowledgeable professional.

Neatness counts

If your business plan represents you, think about the impression you would make entering a potential investor's office with your shoelace flopping and your tie splattered with the pea soup you had for lunch, or with your slip showing and your silk blouse missing a beautifully embossed button. A disheveled appearance sends an instantly negative, and often unalterable, message about you to the other person. So does a messy business plan.

Some plans look as if they had been pecked out on 1937 Underwood typewriters by major holders of White-Out stock. An actual plan for a financial consulting venture had words in the typed text crossed out, with handwritten changes squeezed between the single spaced lines. The columns of numbers in the fiscal sections weren't lined up properly, so the subtotals and totals weren't clear. The content of the plan was actually rather impressive, but it's appearance was messy and amateurish. Any reader of this plan will ask, "What kind of product or service will these people be able to produce for their customers?"

Another actual plan was meticulous and persuasive, but left off a contact name, address, and telephone number. Another failed to include a heading with the name of her company and page numbers on each sheet. Both omissions could spell disaster if the order of the pages became jumbled, or the investors wanted to call to arrange a meeting.

Speaking of spelling disaster, misspellings, incorrect financial numbers, inconsistent text fonts, or pages that fall out easily, all reflect badly on you. Your plan must be neat, accurate, well proofread, and generated on a computer, so that changes and updates can be made easily. If you know how to use a spreadsheet program, do so, but a clean, clear list of financial figures produced on a quality printer will work well, too.

A business plan has sections and subsections. Using different fonts, lists, and indenting helps the reader to see when major new subjects are introduced and to find items in the plan easily. Establish a hierarchy of headings each with its own style and stick to it.

Color printing can be effective, but is not essential. Have your plan spiral-bound at your local copy store, with a clear top sheet and an opaque back sheet to further protect it during what you hope will be extensive reading and handling. Spiral binding also keeps the pages in order and allows your plan to be opened flat for easy reading. With a neat, accurate presentation, you will greatly increase your chances of convincing investors not only to read about your potential business, but to support it as well.

Decent paper is proper

Be sure the quality of paper you choose for printing is good enough so it stands up to multiple readings, but not too contrived or elaborate that you actually send the wrong message to your investors. An actual plan for a Christmas tree ornament store printed on alternating red and green paper was not only overly precious, it also rendered the text extremely difficult to read. A business plan printed on glossy card stock was also hard to read and the card stock made flipping back and forth between the pages virtually impossible. Using stock that is difficult to read, or inordinately expensive, may indicate that you're not very serious about your business plan or that you're a spendthrift who enjoys squandering money. Needless to say, none of these qualities will encourage potential investors to support your endeavor. Standard 24 lb. paper, commonly used in laser printers, is the best choice.

EXCESSIVE LENGTH EQUALS LONG-WINDEDNESS

Coming to the point quickly and effectively is important in both speaking and writing. Do not be fooled into believing that the longer and more detailed your plan, the more impressive it will appear to potential investors. Being excessively wordy implies that you do not value the small amount of precious time readers have to evaluate your written business plan. Take a look at the four sentence executive summary for Bug-Be-Gone. Four sentences should not necessarily be your goal, but if you strive for a statement this distilled, you should be able to cover all ten essential issues with very few words.

The same is true for the text of your business plan. You want to keep your statements clear, pithy, and highly readable. William Strunk, Jr. and E.B. White, in their famous 1,300 word book *The Elements of Style,* emphasize rule 13: "Omit needless words." As the authors explain, "This requires not that the writer make all his sentences short, or that he avoid all detail, but that every word tell." Chances are your first business plan draft will have many needless words. Find them and eliminate them.

ADDITIONAL MEDIA IS NOT A MUST

In this era of Palm Pilots, PowerPoint projections, iPhones, and other innovative communication techniques, it's tempting to employ cutting-edge technology in presenting your business plan. Some technology can be eye-catching and make a memorable impression, but it should only supplement your written plan, not replace it or overshadow it. In fact, many of those who read your plan will never meet you, see an in-person presentation, or look at supplemental material such as videos or DVDs. They will base their decision solely on the written plan, which must achieve your purpose on its own.

An actual plan for a commercial fishing venture was presented as a slick videotape showing boats, large catches of fish, and happy consumers enjoying elaborate seafood dinners. It was quite impressive, but apparently the authors of this plan thought it too mundane to include a few pieces of paper outlining their capabilities or projected returns to their potential investors.

The Actual Layout

Banks, loan institutions and professional investors review dozens of business plans every day. They want to grasp the business concept easily and evaluate the numbers quickly. To make sure their staff time is spent effectively, most financial institutions and investors prefer that all business plans conform to a particular format. Although there may be individual variations from one firm to another, which you must determine in advance, most formats are fairly standard and include the following five components in this order:

- **A cover page** that is cleanly designed and contains all the right information.
- **A table of contents** that is short and to the point.
- **An executive summary** that is a concise paragraph, but touches on all of the ten essential issues from the first ten chapters of this book.
- **A text** that is well edited and describes the ten issues in detail.
- **An appendix** with a complete set of exhibits.

The cover page is the first impression of your business plan. It must be neat and legible, and contain all the basic information so reviewers can contact you quickly and easily—that is, if they want to schedule an in-person meeting. Readers don't want to thumb through the entire plan to find your name, the title of your company, or its purpose.

The cover page should display the following:

- **The name of your company** in large type near the top of the page.
- **A single phrase** describing what your company does, directly beneath the company name.
- **The names of the founder** or partners involved, half-way down the page.
- **The name of the primary contact person,** near the bottom of the page.
- **The contact information** for reaching this person, including telephone number, fax number, e-mail address, and mailing address, directly beneath the contact person's name.

The following, Figure 11.5, is an example of a clear, clean cover page:

FIGURE 11.5
SAMPLE COVER PAGE

Bug-Be-Gone

A Company that Manufactures Non-toxic, Fruit-scented Bug Spray

Ralph Roach
Founder and Chief Executive Officer

Contact: Ralph Roach
Telephone: 888-BUG-BEGONE (212-284-2343)
Fax: 888-284-1245
E-mail: bugbegone@aol.com
Mailing Address:
Ralph Roach
Bug-Be-Gone
123 Silver Fish Lane
Insect, Indiana 12345
Date: August, 2007

The Table of Contents is helpful, even if your plan is fairly brief, and necessary if your plan is still lengthy after numerous edits. Place the table of contents directly after the cover page, so investors can turn to any specific section quickly. You may also consider attaching identifying tabs to each of the sections, so readers can locate them more readily.

Appendices of exhibits should consist of detailed information that would break up the flow of the text, such as market studies or copies of your partners' resumes, or data you may wish to be kept confidential, such as partnership agreements. Interleaving these documents into the actual text of your business plan will only slow the reader down. It's better to footnote the text with a phrase such as "detailed market studies are available on request," or "see appendix for partners' resumes."

If you have information that you will be giving only to certain readers, it's important to bind your appendices of exhibits separately from the main body of your text, so that you can provide it on an as-needed basis to your readers. The cover page of each appendix should mirror the cover page of the plan with the word *Appendix* clearly displayed. If your plan has multiple appendices, it is traditional to assign them consecutive letters, beginning with A.

Remember that all tables and exhibits must be completely self-explanatory. You must spell out what the information is, where it comes from, and any underlying assumptions you have made in projections. Think about people reading your bankable business plan on an airplane or in the middle of the night. They can't reach you to ask their questions, so the plan needs to supply all the answers.

Have Outsiders Read Your Plan

When you have finished writing your plan, ask friends or colleagues with business experience to read it and offer brutally honest comments about its clarity and persuasiveness. You may eventually want to follow their advice about tearing down the restaurant you want to buy and putting up a car wash in its place, but at this point, you primarily need to know if your plan is clear and complete.

Give It a Rest (Time Permitting)

You will find it useful to put the plan in a drawer for a few days or a week before you read it again. This little bit of perspective will help reveal weaknesses and flaws in the plan that you might not have noticed before. A fresh effort can clarify faulty thinking and polish the language.

Entrepreneur's Toolkit: Common Writing Mistakes to Avoid

There are several common writing mistakes that appear rather often in business plans.

Affect or Effect?

As verbs, affect means to influence something, but implies nothing about the size or direction of that influence and effect means to cause something to happen in one clear direction:

Boring teachers barely affect their students. Really boring teachers effect snoring levels in their classes.

As nouns, affect means a false front and effect means result:

He has the affect of an English gentleman. The effect of this is to make people laugh.

Invaluable and Valuable

Valuable means worth a great deal. Invaluable means valuable beyond measure. Very few business elements are beyond measure, so use invaluable sparingly. *Your business is valuable; the affection your goldfish gives you is invaluable.*

Buyout/Buy-out/Buy out

Any of these forms is fine, but stick with one throughout your plan.

Book and Article Titles

Book titles are either underlined or in italics (not both):

Six-Second Business Plans - or -

The Best Bankable Business Plans of the Middle Ages

Article titles are italicized or put in quotes:

"The Sordid Truth about Business Plans" or

Student Locked in Computer Lab over Spring Break Writes Brilliant Business Plan

Titles of Financial Statements

The titles of financial statements such as Income Statement or Statement of Sources and Uses are written with the first letter of each word, except articles and prepositions, capitalized.

Defined Financial Terms

Cash Flow, Net Earnings, or Short Term Liabilities are defined terms and are therefore capitalized.

Initials

If you want to use initials for the name of a business throughout your plan, write out the full name the first time you use it and put the initials in parentheses directly after it. From then on, you can just use the initials. *Success, Wizardry, Optimism, and Triumph, Inc. (SWOT) is a company dedicated to the promotion of the core values of entrepreneurship.*

Referring to People throughout a Document

You can refer to people you know well by their first names. Those you don't know well should be referred to with a title (Mr. Ms. Dr.) or by their last names.

Web site or Website or website or web site

All are fine, but choose one and always use it.

Fewer or Less

Fewer refers to things you can count (almost always plural) and less refers to things you can measure (almost always singular):

Cheerleaders start fewer entrepreneurial ventures with less enthusiasm than any other group.

Less is often used when fewer is correct such as at the Express Line at the supermarket for customers with ten items or less (it should be ten items or fewer.)

Fewer Words Are Always Better

Your plan, like any other document, will be more effective (not affective) at raising capital if you use as few (not less) words as possible. The sentence:

As to whether most everyone will, if asked, agree with her point about the importance of sauces derived from tomatoes on ground beef sandwiches is something that can hardly be argued with.

Can be replaced with:

People like catsup on their hamburgers.

Very Unique Is too Common

Unique means "one-of-a-kind." Something can't be "very one-of-a-kind." So just say unique.

Hyphens

Two-word adjectives such as the phrase "beauty-contest winner" are hyphenated because they modify the word "winner." Two-word nouns such as "beauty contest" are not hypenated.

Numbers

One through ten and zero are written out as words when used in text.
11 and above are written in numeral format.
Above 999,999 numbers that only have two digits or fewer that are not zeros are written as $5 million or $3.2 billion.

End of Chapter Questions

1. What type of time line will you use in your plan? Why?
2. Draft your Executive Summary and check that all ten required essential issues are included.
3. What are the most important points that you want every reader of your plan to remember? How are they related to the purpose of the plan?

CHAPTER 12

ISSUE 12
PRESENT THE PLAN IN PERSON

Despite of all the electronic communication available today, nothing is more effective than an in-person meeting. In fact, it is unlikely that you will raise funds from investors or a bank without meeting them in person. An in-person meeting gives you the chance to reinforce key points of your plan, respond to questions and objections, learn what did not come across well in the plan, and demonstrate the personal characteristics that lenders and investors want to see in an entrepreneur before writing a check.

As you prepare for an in-person presentation of your bankable business plan, keep in mind that you will need to understand and manage the Three Cs of any business meeting: *the Context, the Content,* and *the Code.*

The Context

The most productive meetings occur when the atmosphere, or context, is conducive to having an open, honest discussion about mutually beneficial goals. The presentation of a business plan is not a one-sided performance; it is a meeting to determine if you and potential backers will be able to work together to create a mutually beneficial venture. You can help establish the right context for a presentation by concentrating on your attitude, listening skills, and the physical setting.

Attitude. Your individual perspective, or point of view, that you bring to every meeting is an important factor in establishing a productive context. Being well prepared and knowing that you are well prepared will put you in a positive frame of mind. This will help build your confidence that your plan is strong and that your business can benefit the people listening to your presentation. You must be open to answering questions—and to asking questions—so you can understand the funders' or investors' goals.

Listening. A critical element of creating an effective context revolves around thoughtful and attentive listening. By being a good listener, you allow others to feel comfortable about sharing information openly and confident that their concerns will be addressed. This enables you to uncover their professional concerns more readily and respond to them effectively. The presentation of a business plan is not a one-sided performance; it's a meeting to determine if you and the potential investors or funders want to work together to produce to a mutually beneficial venture.

Physical Setting. Since you will probably be meeting in the bankers' or investors' offices, you will have minimal control over your physical surroundings. However, there are ways you can enhance the setting. First of all, arrive on time. No matter how compelling your business plan is, if you're late, you have made an irrevocably bad impression and set a poor tone for the meeting. If you're too early, don't hang around the waiting room looking like a person with nothing else to do. It is better to wait in your car or a nearby coffee shop. When you are ushered into the meeting room, try to choose a seat which enables you to make eye contact with others in the room, even if you have to adjust your chair. Take out your cell phone and turn it off to indicate your willingness to concentrate on the matters at hand.

When you have the right attitude, create the best physical setting, and listen fully, you are establishing a strong context and demonstrating that you are worthy of other people's time and attention.

The Content

The content, or subject, of your presentation should always be focused on the issues that are most crucial to your audience. Whether you are meeting with bankers or potential investors, you must address their separate and measurable goals in your presentation. This includes being able to pay back a bank loan with interest within a certain time period, or projecting the return on an investor's stake—in other words, how your business will make money for them.

Making these crucial issues the crux of your presentation moves the in-person meeting forward; talking about anything else stalls the conversation and reduces the chances of coming to an agreement to work together. Many entrepreneurs waste the opportunities intrinsic to an in-person presentation by concentrating solely on their own goals rather than focusing on the bankers' or investors' objectives.

Beyond a brief ice-breaker, the content of a presentation should not include topics such as the weather or sports. Brief discussions about relevant business issues, your credentials, and your experience are necessary to demonstrate that you are knowledgeable and credible, but the bulk of your presentation should focus on the other people's goals and objectives.

Start Strong and End Strong. Research shows that people tend to form opinions based on what they hear at the beginning and the end of any meeting. These tendencies, called the *primacy* and *recency* effects, are powerful tools. Be sure to put what you believe is your strongest point first in a presentation and to conclude with the same point or an equally strong message. Having a clear, simple, short statement that describes your business and explains the benefit of it to the people with whom you are meeting, sometimes called an *elevator pitch,* is essential for entrepreneurs. This is also why that all-important first impression is critical.

Customize Your Presentation. Don't waste bankers' time detailing the equity returns that your investors will earn, or bore your potential investors by describing your employees' stock options. These points may merit quick summaries in every presentation, but tailor the information for each group or individual with whom you meet. Carefully plan each presentation. Make a list of the issues that are most important to the specific audience you will be addressing and alter your outline and visual materials accordingly.

You're Not Mounting a Broadway Production. You do not need to create the proverbial "dog and pony" show with a high level of production values in order for your presentation to appear professional and credible. This may be true for the weak presenter who has little to say if the slide projector goes dim, but for someone who has created a quality bankable business plan there are several significant reasons to avoid complete dependence on these tools:

- The slide show or PowerPoint presentation can't be changed easily on the fly. It does not allow you to alter your presentation to incorporate new issues or a particular focus that might emerge through discussion with bankers or investors.

- Using these presentation tools discourages people from talking because they know that you are essentially following a script. You are, therefore, stifling one of the greatest assets of the opportunity to present in person—the ability to elicit productive dialogue, uncover your audience's issues, and discuss new concepts productively.
- Many people don't pay attention to presentations that aren't interactive. Dim the lights, turn on the projector, and most people will tune out. An interactive presentation can only occur if your audience is involved, not passively watching a performance.

Keep the exposition of your plan simple and flexible. Using PowerPoint slides or projections can work best if you are prepared to alter the order of the presentation, or skip some parts entirely. You can maximize the value of your in-person time with bankers or investors by focusing on the most important issues and skipping elements they have already agreed to or avoiding issues that you realize during the meeting have become irrelevant.

Leave Something Behind . . . the Right Something. It is great if you can leave your potential investors a copy of your plan, your financial projections, or even background materials on particular issues that were raised during your presentation. But it is better to leave nothing than to hand over a pile of relatively unimportant or even inaccurate documents.

Suppose you are presenting your plan to a bank for a loan. If you have prepared your financial projections under the assumption that the bank will lend 80% of your fixed asset valuation, but in the meeting you discover that they will actually lend 90%, it is better to revise your projections after the meeting and deliver the new figures a few days later. Inaccurate projections in your file can actually hurt your prospects.

Establish a Schedule for Follow-Up. It is crucial to establish a clear time table for tasks following the meeting. If you made a presentation to a bank, you must state when you will deliver revised financial projections, and what, if anything, you need from them, such as sample loan agreements, feedback on your financial projections, or references from people in whom they have invested.

Make sure the bank has everything they need to make their decision and ask them for a firm date by which you can expect an answer on your loan. Setting a fixed date later is more important than having a vague understanding about an early decision. A commitment for a specific date enables you to follow-up and remind them of the agreed upon time frame.

The Code

Nonverbal means of communication, such as facial expressions or body language that occur during an in-person meeting, comprise the code. During your presentation you will be sending and receiving innumerable transactions of this code. Misinterpreting this unspoken dialogue can lead to feelings of rejection that may interfere with your ability to make an effective in-person presentation and be disastrous.

Seeing is Not Always Believing. Many presentations are derailed because the presenters become unnerved by their audience's behavior and not by what they say. People coming and going, looking bored or angry, or taking on a challenging tone when asking questions, can make presenters feel that they have already failed. Interpreting body language alone is not always an accurate guide to a person's interests or intentions. There is a true story of a 20-minute sales presentation to a buyer who never once looked up from a game of solitaire on his computer. The presenter plugged along, befuddled by the buyer's rude and strange behavior. To the presenter's astonishment, the buyer agreed to purchase at the end of the presentation. The lesson to take from this example is that you should primarily focus on what people have to say rather than relying on interpreting their body language.

Don't Be Prejudiced. Don't prejudge your audience. The question you need to ask yourself is, "Would it be okay if these people liked my business plan and gave me the resources I need to create my company?" If the answer is "yes," as it should be, that you would be happy for their participation, then you need to work on understanding and controlling your prejudices.

Many presentations are made before individuals or groups who take a challenging tone as they probe for weaknesses in the plan and the presenter. Judges in business plan competitions and potential investors and funders often feel that by being as tough in tone and substance as possible that they are testing the mettle of the presenter. Many relatively inexperienced presenter are thrown off by this approach, interpreting this as dislike of the plan or its presenter. Some presenters respond by becoming challenging or aggressive as well. Others feel they have lost the interest of their audience. Both responses are usually wrong. Don't prejudge your audience. Assume that they are there to listen, are testing you, and that you should speak with conviction.

First Impressions Count. Your mother was right when she said you only get one chance to make a good impression. Research shows that within the first minute of meeting someone, people form lasting opinions. In studying the interviewing process, Oregon State University psychologist, Professor Frank Bernieri documented the extraordinarily rapid pace at which people form first impressions. Bernieri discovered that people who watched video clips of job applicants simply enter a room and shake hands with the interviewer reached virtually the same conclusions about that person as the trained and experienced interviewer did after a 15-minute interview. You can read more about this phenomenon in the Focus on Research section at the end of this chapter.

The impact of first impressions on presenting your plan is tremendous. That initial impression made in less than the first minute will largely determine what the other person thinks of you. You need to use that first 60 seconds to every advantage. You might be the most organized person in the world, but if you're late to an appointment because of unforeseen traffic and are forced to climb seven flights of stairs because the elevator is broken, you will walk into the other person's office sweaty and out of breath, creating a long lasting impression of being disorganized.

To improve that crucial first impression you make, be aware of it. Many people have no idea how they come across to others, and often impress people quite differently than they intended. People may feel they present themselves as aggressive or ambitious, but actually appear soft spoken and timid to others.

Ask some people who will be candid to the point of pain to participate in a exercise with you. Schedule meetings either at their offices or homes and ask them to describe your manner, your clothes, your posture, and your speech *one minute after your arrival*. An even more helpful demonstration is to videotape yourself in a similar business practice session so you can draw your own conclusions about the impression you make. And, if necessary, fix it!

Practice. If you are not too experienced in giving presentations, or you are worried about being nervous, or just want to be as well-prepared as possible, be sure to practice in front of friends, colleagues, the mirror, or that video camera you used for testing the first impression you made. This will help you master the flow and facts of your presentation, and you'll be able to focus on addressing the specific needs and interests of your audience. It is generally a good idea to keep an outline and a copy of your full plan in front of you so you don't skip any important points or can find your place if you get lost.

Just Be Yourself. Many entrepreneurs believe that in order to convince others to invest in their ventures they must be forceful and manipulative, even if those qualities are not part of their personalities. However, there is absolutely no reason to be anyone other than yourself while making an in-person presentation. You have probably written your plan with yourself in mind as the founder and president of your company, and the plan already has a section explaining your—and your team's—qualifications.

You don't need to be a Nobel Prize-winning scientist, an Olympic gold medalist, or the global entrepreneur-of-the-year. You don't even have to be a bulldozing salesperson; you just have to project a credible level of experience, knowledge, and professionalism.

Too many entrepreneurs try to be formal when they are usually relaxed, funny when they are essentially serious, or pushy when they are really quite unassuming. All they achieve is a level of discomfort in the role they are playing, which interfers with their ability to communicate their enthusiasm for their ventures. You simply need to demonstrate that you are the right person to start this company. Use that first 60 seconds to every advantage by being aware of the impression you make on others.

Focus on Research: How You and Your Plan Will Be Judged

We all want to be judged as individuals based on our skills, our knowledge, the merit of our ideas, and our accomplishments. Unfortunately, some studies indicate that this does not always happen. Professor Kimberly Elsbach of the University of California, Davis and Professor Roderick Kramer of Stanford University carried out a study that showed how objective standards can have little to do with the professional judgments people form of others[1].

Elsbach and Kramer studied how people with ideas for movies and television shows (the "pitchers") were judged by studio executives (the "catchers.") They observed presentations by the pitchers that typically took less than 20 minutes and then interviewed both the pitchers and the catchers. They discovered that catchers quickly categorized pitchers into one of several industry stereotypes based upon observations that seemed to have nothing to do with the quality of the pitcher's idea or any objective measure of the pitcher's creative potential. Instead, the catchers responded to each pitcher's appearance, manner, or way of speaking.

For example, pitchers who were quirky, unconventional, and unpolished were judged to be artists with high creative potential, but with weak business skills. Pitchers who acted naturally, were witty, charismatic, and passionate about their ideas were thought to be "show runners" who could manage a team and focus on the business aspects of the project. Pitchers who were charismatic, arrogant, and focused on business were perceived as deal makers with an interest in putting the project together, but not capable of being a creative force or of managing the production. The catchers made decisions about spending millions of dollars on television and movie projects based upon a few first impressions of the pitcher's personality and manner.

Elsbach and Kramer also found that catchers judged their interest in funding a pitcher's idea based on how well they felt they could collaborate with a pitcher. Positive emotional responses occurred when the pitcher was enthusiastic, a good listener, asked lots of questions, and contributed ideas to the dialogue.

Negative emotional responses occurred when the pitchers lectured to, argued with, or didn't pay attention to the catchers.

Although all potential funders may not be as limited as Hollywood moguls in their ability to judge an in-person presentation on its merits, this study provides some profound implications for anyone approaching backers for a bank loan or an investment.

When you make a presentation, keep in mind that:

- You might be judged in a very short time based on your behavior, manner, and appearance by catchers who will place you within a convenient industry stereotype.
- You will only get one chance to be pigeon-holed into a favorable category.
- You should listen, ask questions, and interact with the catchers as much as possible.
- It's best to focus on being knowledgeable, organized, concise, and enthusiastic.
- You must make sure your plan is the best it can be. Many potential investors will actually read it following your presentation.

A Presentation May Start a Negotiation

If your presentation creates interest among investors, lenders, partners, or anyone else you wish to participate in your business, you may find yourself at the start of a negotiation. Investors may ask how much of your company you are willing to sell, or if you would accept some changes to the terms you proposed. Bankers may ask how much collateral you have. Potential employees may want to know what salary and benefits you are offering. This is very good news!

Negotiating is the process of working out the terms after all the parties have expressed an interest in reaching an agreement, and negotiating well is an important entrepreneurial skill. If your presentation leads to a negotiation, you have probably done an excellent job. But you need to be ready by establishing a negotiation game plan in writing prior to your meeting. It should include the following elements:

Prioritize Your Objectives. What is most important to you? Is it more important that you control the business or that you get the business started even if someone else controls it? Are you willing to accept a financial proposal from funders that obligates you to high mandated payments or must you have significant flexibility? What are the "deal breakers" for you? For example, is there a valuation of the business, a salary for yourself, a share of equity for management, or the make-up of the Board of Directors that would encourage you to walk away from any deal?

Understand the Relative Sources of Leverage. The power relationships in a negotiation reflect the ability and willingness of each party to walk away. If you have to raise some capital or face dire personal consequences, your ability to hold firm to your position is greatly reduced. If you have six funding sources interested in investing in your business, you can expect to meet or exceed your objectives and are in a strong negotiating position. Many experienced negotiators feel that the most important part of their preparation is to prepare a "Plan B," or what they will do if they don't make the deal they expected. This might include a merger with another company, dipping into personal funds, or downsizing the company. While any Plan B is not ideal, it establishes manageable alternatives that will make you a stronger negotiator.

Styles Follow Relative Leverage. Your negotiating style signals a great deal to the other parties. You should decide on an appropriate negotiating style based on your estimate of relative leverage. The stronger your relative position, the more you can move to a "take it or leave it" style. The weaker your relative position, the more you should move to a flexible and cooperative style. Many people make the mistake of believing that negotiations are "zero-sum games," that anything one party wins comes at the expense of the other party.

Baseball and football are zero-sum games. Business is not. Business is a game at which everyone involved can and should win. A successful business deal enables all the parties to achieve their goals by working together to build a successful enterprise. Forcing onerous or impossible terms in a negotiation usually establishes the foundation for an adversarial relationship that makes business success unlikely.

Tactics that Support Your Negotiation

There are many effective negotiation tactics. Some people like to negotiate over a meal, while others only feel comfortable negotiating in their own offices. Here are some tactics that tend to support successful negotiations:

Set the Agenda. Before the negotiation starts, you should establish a list of all the issues you will cover and the order in which you will discuss them. Then obtain mutual agreement by all parties to this agenda.

Give Bad News First. If you have anything negative to discuss, address it right up front, otherwise you will seem to be hiding issues when they come up later, which will undermine your credibility.

Deal with Price Last. Often price is the most important issue in a negotiation, but it usually cannot be dealt with until the other terms are resolved. For example, how can you establish the price for your "100% cat hair socks" until you know the volume the customer wants and the delivery date?

Listen, Listen and then Listen Some More. It is absolutely key to listen to the needs, issues, goals, and preferences of others in a negotiation. Deals are made only after all the parties' needs have been met, so you must allow time for others to state their goals and you must listen attentively.

Matching the Other Party's Style. Some people believe that if you are negotiating with someone who fights over every detail, that you should assume the same style. They feel that if you don't, you may find yourself compromising quickly with someone who will not. Others insist that if you are negotiating with someone who focuses on the main issues and likes to move through a negotiation quickly, you may aggravate this person if you don't do the same. Of course, you may simply be most comfortable always following your own style without regard to the style of the person with whom you are negotiating. This is a decision you will have to make in the moment and your choice may be largely dependent on your estimate of the relative leverage of your position to the the other person's.

Negotiate Face-to-Face. Face-to-face interactions are less subject to interruption, provide all the parties with the greatest sense of the other person's issues, and demonstrate the greatest commitment to making a deal.

Never Make It Personal. Getting mad, acting hurt, or trying to be best friends is, at best, a distraction from the main issues. At worst, it is a reason for someone to decide not to do business with you.

Be Confident. If you have prepared your business plan and yourself thoroughly, you should be confident that you will bring the negotiation to its best possible outcome. Being unsure of yourself or timid can make others question whether they want to contribute resources to your venture.

Summarize Often. Summarizing what has been agreed to and what remains to be worked on, is a good way to keep everyone focused on the agenda.

Go to Contract Quickly. After you have reached an agreement, it is important to move ahead quickly to finalize and implement the agreement. The longer you wait to do so, the more likely something may change in the environment, in the business, or in the memory of one of the parties. If your agreement requires a contract, establish a deadline for its completion.

ENTREPRENEUR'S TOOLKIT: GOOD AND BAD SLIDES

Slides, presented through programs such as PowerPoint, can either enhance or interfere with your presentation. They can work for you or, if you are not careful, you will end up working for them. Here are some *bad* slides:

FIGURES 12.1 – 12.5
EXAMPLES OF BAD SLIDES

Don't Read Your Slides. Slides and visuals are there to support what you say, not be your script. If you need a script write one, but just use the slides to reinforce key points, unlike this slide:

Key Points

This one paragraph covers all 10 steps in four sentences:

Bug-Be-Gone Corporation is seeking to raise $10 million in equity capital from individuals who will invest at least $1 million each (2, 8) to develop and market a unique line of fruit-scented insecticides that are non-toxic to humans and pets (1, 3, 4, 5). Bug-Be-Gone is owned and managed by Roger Roach whose 20 years of experience in the insect extermination business will enable him to hire the most knowledgeable entomologists and the most precise bug sprayers in the industry (7). The company has already received preliminary orders from the three major firms that supply 80% of the California market, which consumes 50% of all insecticides in the United States (4, 5, 6). The financial projections show the company achieving higher than average profit margins (10) and that equity investors will receive returns in excess of 35% annually by the third year of operation (1, 9).

Offensive Images. Images that contain sexual innuendos, or pictures that present people or cultures as extreme stereotypes can be offensive. If you are not sure, avoid them.

Too Much on a Slide. Putting 200 numbers on a slide or ten years of detailed financials communicates nothing—unless your audience brought telescopes with them. The numbers are too small to read, it's impossible to see any patterns, and the slide is simply annoying.

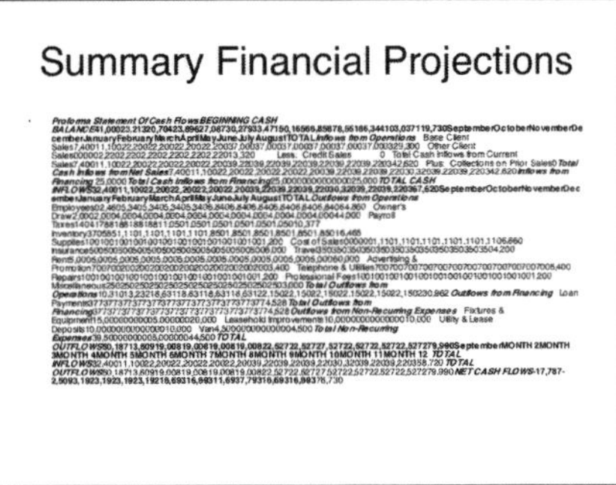

Too Little on a Slide. On the other hand, just a few words, or in the case of the example shown below, one word, is merely silly.

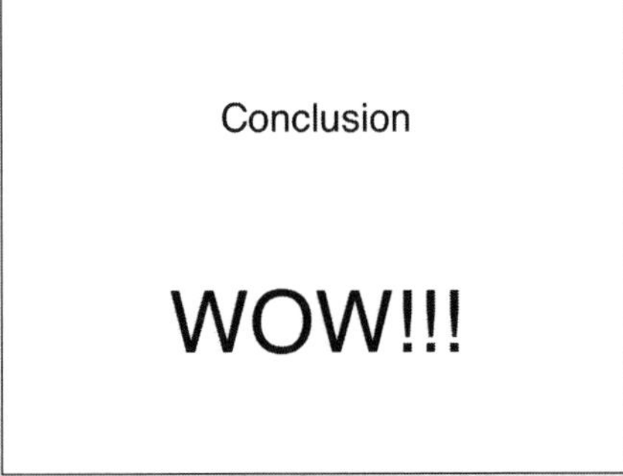

Make the Photographs Support Your Case. If you are talking about your spotless factory, a picture is much more effective at making the point than a slide that says "We have a spotless factory."

Distracting Images and Sounds. Cute sounds that play every time a line of text is displayed are distracting. Using it once or just a few times may be effective at providing emphasis, but constant use is a distraction. Similarly, images such as a plane that pulls every line of the slide into place are clever once, but not fifty times. Spinning the text when it is added makes most people dizzy.

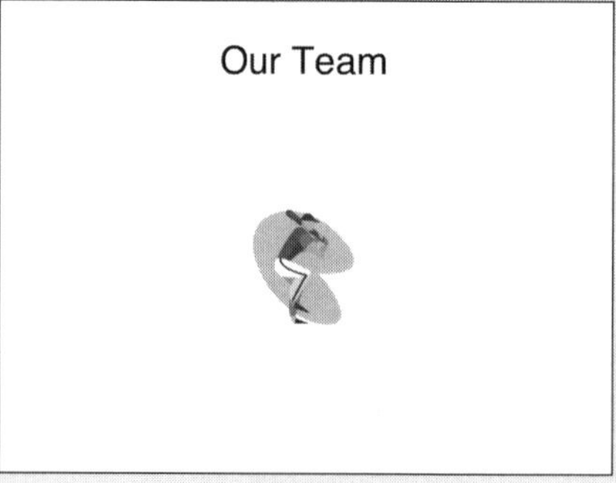

Use Reinforcing Images. Graphs and charts are good at showing trends, patterns, and comparisons, but they must be simple, clear and labeled. You don't want your audience to ask themselves, as they might with this slide, "what are we looking at?"

DR. PEPPER PREPARES FOR HER PRESENTATION

Dr. Penelope Pepper is a highly respected and experienced asthma specialist. Since graduating from medical school at the University of Chicago 22 years ago, she has specialized in lung diseases with a focus on asthma. A few years ago she realized that one of the problems in treating asthma is that patients usually don't recognize an asthma attack until it is full-fledged, at which point their medication is far less effective. Dr. Pepper wondered if she could find a way to alert patients to oncoming attacks even before they experienced debilitating symptoms, such as chest tightness and wheezing.

Seven years ago she was caring for a pregnant asthma patient in labor, which made her think about the fetal heart monitor the obstetrician was using during the birth. It contained a microphone that when placed on the mother's abdomen amplified the baby's heartbeat with much greater sensitivity and clarity than a stethoscope. Dr. Pepper wondered if such a device could be adapted for asthma patients so they could hear the beginning of an attack and treat it before they felt any symptoms. Dr. Pepper became obsessed with developing and commercializing her dream product.

Over the next seven years, Dr. Pepper spent nearly all of her $400,000 in savings, took significant time off from her practice, and had wandered down more blind alleys trying to build a prototype than she cares to remember. Now she feels it has all been worth the struggle. She has a working model that will cost $45 each to manufacture in lots of 10,000. She is confident that the product, which she has named the "Easy-Wheezy," can be sold for more than $250 each, and that insurance companies will gladly reimburse patients so they can reduce their total cost of asthma treatment.

Dr. Pepper has been invited to a conference of investors who specialize in medical products to present her business plan and recruit the $10 million she needs to run clinical trials and market the Easy-Wheezy. She will have a total of no more than 20 minutes to make her pitch and handle questions. Dr. Pepper has received the following advice:

Her lawyer told her to:

1. Not focus on financial projections because she can't guarantee definite returns.
2. Use all 20 minutes for her formal presentation and to not leave time for questions because she can't be sure what people will ask.
3. Explain what legal structure she anticipates using because this will let the potential investors know that she is business minded.

Her accountant told her to:

1. Present the financial projections in detail and have him join her to answer any particularly detailed questions.
2. Spend a lot of time at the bar in the hotel meeting potential investors one-on-one.
3. Make the profit-per-unit the conclusion of her presentation because the profitability is very high.

Her banker told her to:

1. Lower her expectations because such products are very risky.
2. Not come across as overly enthusiastic because that won't seem professional.
3. Include his name and that of the bank in the presentation because this will add credibility.

Her cousin Peter, who has started and run several businesses, told her to:

1. Focus on the ease of FDA approval.
2. Present detail on the size of the potential market in the U.S. and elsewhere.
3. Give a list of medical device companies that would want to add the Easy-Wheezy to their product line once it is a proven success.

4. Have him make the business presentation while she presents the medical and technical issues so that investors will see that she is business oriented and not just out to treat a disease.

Her mother told her to:

1. Be confident, relaxed, and try to smile.
2. Wear an expensive business suit.
3. Know that she will love her no matter what happens at the conference.

The conference is less than a month away and Dr. Pepper has to make some decisions about planning her presentation. Although these points seem to have merit, all this advice has made her so anxious about the presentation that she is even worrying about the impression her name will make because it always gets laughs whenever she is introduced.

Case Questions:

1. What advice do you think Dr. Pepper should take?
2. Write a 30-word elevator pitch for Dr. Pepper.

End of Chapter Questions

1. What are the context, content, and code of a conversation?
2. Why are first impressions so important and how should an entrepreneur try to make a good first impression?
3. What factors determine each party's relative leverage in a negotiation?
4. How should one prepare for a business presentation?

NOTES

1. Kimberley D. Elsbach and Roderick M. Kramer, "Assessing Creativity in Hollywood Pitch Meetings: Evidence for a Dual-Process Model of Creativity Judgments," *Academy of Management Journal*, Vol. 36, No. 3, (Fall 2003), pp. 283–301.

SAMPLE OUTLINES

Outline for a Simple Business Plan

Here is an outline for a simple plan. Of course, the exact headings of the subjects, or even whether these subjects exist, depends on the specifics of the business the plan is written about and the purpose of the plan.

Cover Sheet

Table of Contents

Executive Summary (less than 1 page)

- Statement of business opportunity
- Statement of what you are looking for such as loans or investment
- Purpose of plan
- Major reasons opportunity exists
- Expected financial results
- Cover first 10 Issues

Description of the Business

- Product/Service description and strengths
- For existing business, give history and financial performance.
- Organization of the business including information on management and ownership
- Legal structure

Market Overview

- Describe target market by geography, income, and demographics
- Competitive products and current buying patterns of the market

Industry Overview

- Competitors' history, products, and financial performance

- Trends such as product changes, technology adoption, or consolidation
- Projections for the future
- Regulatory issues

Business Opportunity

- Business strategy
- Product/service strengths
- Marketing and sales strategies
- Research to support projections
- Time line for business plan

Financial Projections

- Historical financial statements if business exists
- Projected Financial Statements:
- Income Statements
- Balance Sheets
- Cash Flow Statements
- Debt Service projections
- Comparisons to industry standards
- Returns Analysis

Appendices

- Newspaper, magazine, industry trade reports
- Resumes of key managers
- Leases and other key contracts
- Historical financials
- Research done to support projections

Outline for a Complex Business Plan

This outline is a listing of subjects you *may* wish to include in your plan. It is meant to be a relatively comprehensive list from which you can select the topics that relate to your business. It repeats some topics in more than one place if it is possible that the topic could fit in more than one place, but generally repeating topics within the body of the plan is not necessary.

I. Cover Sheet

II. Table of Contents

III. Executive Summary

A. The Purpose of the Plan

1. Obtain a bank loan
2. Attract investors
3. Document an operational plan for controlling the business
4. Test the financial feasibility of a business concept
5. Attract partners, vendors, or suppliers

B. The Company

1. Overview of the needs company will meet
2. The products or services you will offer to meet those needs
3. Legal structure

C. Market Analysis

1. The characteristics of your target market (demographic, geographic, etc.)
2. The size of your target market

D. Market Research

1. Market research that you have carried out to test and prove key elements of your plan including product or service characteristics, location viability, pricing, packaging, or target market acceptance

E. Product or Service Research and Development

1. Major milestones in product development and progress in meeting them

F. Marketing and Sales Activities

1. Marketing strategy
2. Sales strategy
3. Keys to success in your competitive environment
4. Sales and marketing efforts to date

G. Organization and Personnel

1. Key managers, owners, directors, advisors, and employees
2. Organizational structure

H. Financial Data

1. Funds required and their use
2. Historical financial summary
3. Prospective financial summary (including a justification for prospective sales levels)
4. Projected returns for equity investors
5. Debt coverage levels

IV. Company Description

The Company Description section provides an overview of the operational elements of your company without going into detail. It is meant to give an overview of how you will accomplish the company's operational goals.

A. Nature of Your Business
   1. Marketplace needs to be satisfied
   2. Method(s) of need satisfaction
   3. Key specific customers or market niches

B. Your Distinctive Competences and Competitive Advantages (primary factors that will lead to your success)
   1. Elements of superior customer need satisfaction
   2. Cost advantages such as production/service delivery efficiencies
   3. Personnel
   4. Distribution
   5. Marketing program
   6. Sales organization
   7. Patents, copyrights, brand names that you own
   8. Location strengths
   9. Experience, knowledge, or reputation

C. Operational Strategies
   1. Organizational structure
   2. Key financial incentives for employees, partners, distributors, market reps, and your sales force
   3. Control and feedback structures to ensure that goals are being accomplished
   4. Accountants, lawyers, consultants, directors and expertises they provide

V. Market Analysis

A. Industry Description and Outlook

1. Description of industry and primary competitors
2. List of competitors including their financial information, strategy, history, competitive strengths and weaknesses, products, and pricing.
3. Size of the industry, currently, history, and projections.
4. Industry characteristics: history and trends
    a. Technology changes
    b. Life cycle (Is industry growing, maturing, consolidating, shrinking?)
        1. historically
        2. presently
        3. in the future
    c. Major customer groups
        1. businesses
        2. governments
        3. consumers

B. Target Markets

1. Description and characteristics of target markets.
    a. critical needs to be filled
    b. extent to which those needs are currently being met
    c. demographics characteristics such as age, gender, race, ethnicity
    d. geographic location
    e. purchase decision-makers and influencers
    f. seasonal/cyclical trends

2. Primary target market size
   a. Number of prospective customers
   b. annual purchases of products or services meeting the same or similar needs as your products or services
   c. geographic area
   d. demographic characteristics
   e. anticipated market growth
3. Market penetration goals
   a. market share
   b. number of customers
   c. geographic coverage
   d. rationale for market penetration estimates including research, testing, and competitors' experiences
4. Pricing/gross margin targets
   a. price levels
   b. gross margin levels
   c. discount structure (volume, prompt, payment, etc.)
5. Methods by which specific members of your target market can be identified
   a. directories
   b. trade association publications
   c. government documents
6. Media Plan
   a. publications
   b. radio/television broadcasts
   c. sources of influence/advice
   d. specific media plan including budgets, sample ad copy, and plan to monitor ad results

7. Purchasing cycle of potential customers

8. Key trends and anticipated changes within your primary target markets

9. Secondary target markets and key attributes

   a. needs

   b. demographics

   c. significant future trends

C. Market Test Results

1. Potential customers contacted
2. Information/demonstrations given to potential customers
3. Reaction of potential customers
4. Importance of satisfaction of targeted needs
5. Test group's willingness to purchase products/services at various price levels

D. Lead Times (amount of time between customer order placement and product/ service delivery)

1. Initial orders
2. Reorders
3. Volume purchases

E. Competition

1. Identification (by product line or service and market segment)

   a. existing

   b. market share

   c. potential (How long will your "window of opportunity" be open before your initial success breeds new competition? Who will your new competitors likely be?)

   d. direct

   e. indirect

2. Strengths (competitive advantages)
   a. ability to satisfy customer needs
   b. market penetration
   c. track record and reputation
   d. staying power (financial resources)
   e. key personnel

3. Weaknesses (competitive disadvantages)
   a. ability to satisfy customer needs
   b. market penetration
   c. track record and reputation
   d. staying power (financial resources)
   e. key personnel

4. Importance of your target market to your competition

5. Barriers to entry into the market
   a. cost (investment)
   b. time
   c. technology
   d. key personnel
   e. customer inertia (brand loyalty, existing relationships, etc.)
   f. existing patents and trademarks

F. Regulation

1. Customer or governmental regulatory requirements
   a. methods of meeting the requirements
   b. timing involved in meeting the requirements
   c. cost of meeting the requirements

2. Anticipated changes in regulatory requirements

3. Positives of regulations
   a. barriers to entry for potential competitors
   b. patent, copyright, trademark protection
   c. government support of industry
   d. trade protections for industry

VI. Products and Services

A. Detailed Product/Service Description (from the users' perspective)
   1. Specific benefits of product/service
   2. Ability to meet needs
   3. Competitive advantages
   4. Present stage (idea, prototype, small production runs, etc.)

B. Product Life Cycle
   1. Describe the product/service's current position within its life cycle
   2. Factors that might change the anticipated life cycle
      a. lengthen it
      b. shorten it

C. Copyrights, Patents and Trade Secrets
   1. Existing or pending copyrights or patents
   2. Anticipated copyright and patent filings
   3. Key aspects of your products or services which cannot be patented or copyrighted
   4. Key aspects of your products or services which qualify as trade secrets
   5. Existing legal agreements with owners and employees
      a. non-disclosure
      b. non-compete agreements

D. Research and Development Activities

1. Activities in process at this time.
2. Future activities (include milestones)
3. Anticipated results of future research and development activities
    a. new products or services
    b. new generations of existing products or services
    c. complimentary products or services
    d. replacement products or services
4. Research and development activities of others in your industry
    a. direct competitors
    b. indirect competitors
    c. suppliers
    d. customers

VII. Marketing and Sales Activities

A. Overall Marketing Strategy

1. Competitive advantages
    a. pricing
    b. delivery Time
    c. service
    d. product features
    e. brand name
    f. reputation
    g. status

2. Market penetration strategy
   a. high profitability
   b. significant market share
   c. growth strategy
      1. internal
      2. acquisition
      3. franchise
      4. horizontal (providing similar products to different users)
      5. vertical (providing the products at different levels of the distribution chain)

4. Distribution channels (include discount/profitability levels at each stage)
   a. original equipment manufacturers
   b. distributors
   c. retailers

5. Communication
   a. promotion
   b. advertising, including detailed media plan
   c. public relations
   d. personal selling
   e. printed materials (catalogs, brochures, etc.)

B. Sales Strategies
   1. Sales force
      a. internal vs. independent representatives (advantages and disadvantages of your strategy)
      b. size
      c. recruitment and training
      d. compensation

2. Prospecting
   a. identifying prospects
   b. prioritizing prospects
   c. qualifying prospects (separating prospects from suspects)
3. Sales activities
   a. number of sales calls made per period
   b. average number of sales calls per sale
   c. average dollar size per sale
   d. average dollar size per reorder

VIII. Operations

A. Production and Service Delivery Procedures
   1. Internal
   2. External (subcontractors)

B. Production/Service Delivery Capacity
   1. Internal
   2. External (subcontractors)
   3. Anticipated increases in capacity
      a. investment
      b. new cost factors (direct and indirect)
      c. logistics (Will the expansion force you to slow or stop production for a time?)
      d. timing

C. Operating Competitive Advantages
   1. Techniques
   2. Experience
   3. Economies of scale
   4. Lower direct costs

D. Suppliers

1. Identify suppliers of critical elements of production
   a. primary
   b. secondary
2. Lead time requirements
3. Evaluate risks of critical element shortages
4. Describe existing and anticipated contractual relationships with suppliers

IX. Management and Ownership

A. Management Staff Structure

1. Management staff organization chart
2. Narrative description of the chart

B. Key Managers (complete resumes should be presented in an appendix to the business plan)

1. Name
2. Position
3. Primary responsibilities and authority
4. Primary responsibilities and authority with previous employers
5. Unique skills and experiences that add to your company's distinctive competences
6. Compensation basis and levels

C. Planned Additions to the Management Staff

1. Position
2. Primary responsibilities and authority
3. Requisite skills and experience
4. Recruitment process

5. Timing of employment
6. Anticipated contribution to the company's success
7. Compensation basis and levels (be sure that they are in line with the market)

D. Legal Structure of the Business

1. Corporation
    - a. C corporation
    - b. S corporation
    - c. Limited Liability Corp.
2. Partnership
    - a. general
    - b. limited
    - c. Limited Liability Partnership
    - d. Sole Proprietorship

E. Owners

1. Names
2. Percentage ownership
3. Extent of involvement with the company
4. Form of ownership
    - a. common stock
    - b. preferred stock
    - c. general partner
    - d. limited partner
5. Outstanding equity equivalents
    - a. options
    - b. warrants
    - c. convertible debt

6. Common stock
    a. authorized
    b. issued

F. Board of Directors
    1. Names
    2. Position on the board
    3. Extent of involvement with the company
    4. Background
    5. Contribution to the company's success
        a. historically
        b. in the future

X. Organization and Personnel

A. Complete Organization Chart
    1. Positions
    2. Reporting relationships
    3. Narrative description of the organization chart

B. Brief Position Descriptions
    1. Primary duties
    2. Recruitment and training
    3. Staffing levels

4. Compensation
    1. Method
    2. Level

5. Anticipated Human Resource Requirements
    1. Organization chart
    2. Staffing levels by position
    3. Changes in compensation levels and/or methods

XI. Funds Required and Their Uses

A. Current Funding Requirements
   1. Amount
   2. Timing
   3. Type
      a. equity
      b. debt
      c. mezzanine
   4. Terms

B. Funding Requirements Over the Next Five Years
   1. Amount
   2. Timing
   3. Type
      a. equity
      b. debt
      c. mezzanine
   4. Terms

C. Use of Funds
   1. Capital expenditures
   2. Working capital
   3. Debt retirement
   4. Acquisitions

D. Impact of the New Funds on the Company's Financial Position

   1. Dilution of ownership

   2. Change in leverage levels (debt to equity ratio)

E. Long-Range Financial and Exit Strategies

   1. Going public

   2. Leveraged buyout

   3. Acquisition by another company

   4. Debt service levels and timing

   5. Liquidation of the venture

XII. Financial Data

A. Historical Financial Data (past three to five years, if available)

   1. Annual summaries

      a. income statement

      b. balance sheet

      c. cash flow statement or statement of changes in financial position

      d. comparison to industry standards such as RMA data

   2. Level of CPA involvement (and name of firm)

      a. audit

      b. review

      c. compilation

B. Prospective Financial Data (next five years)

   1. Next year (by month or quarter)

      a. income statement

      b. balance sheet

      c. cash flow statement

d. capital expenditure budget

e. returns analysis

f. debt service schedule

2. Final four years (by quarter and/or year)

a. income statement

b. balance sheet

c. cash flow statement

d. capital expenditure budget

e. returns analysis

f. debt service schedule

3. Summary of significant assumptions

4. Type of prospective financial data

a. forecast (management's best estimate)

b. projection ("what if scenarios")

XIII. Appendices or Exhibits

A. Resumes of Key Managers

B. Pictures of Products

C. Professional References

D. Market Studies

E. Pertinent Published Information

1. Magazine Articles

2. References to books

F. Patents

G. Significant Contracts

1. Leases
2. Sales contracts
3. Purchases contracts
4. Partnership/ownership agreements
5. Stock option agreements
6. Employment/ compensation agreements
7. Non-compete agreements
8. Insurance
    a. product liability
    b. officers' and directors' liability
    c. general liability
9. Financial Commitments
    a. letters of intent from funding sources
    b. bank commitment letter
    c. letters of interest from potential customers

SAMPLE PLANS

Sample Business Plan for a New Business

A plan for a new business is based entirely on projections. An existing business has a history and, therefore, some financial elements that are closely related to its existing reality. A new plan requires assumptions for everything from rent to revenue. To make the plan more credible and to give the readers—whether they be investors or lenders—confidence in the projections, it is wise to anchor projections to careful research. The plan for S & J Advertising is strong because the founders focus on their ability to bring clients to their proposed agency and on the market conditions that create a market niche for their business.

S & J Advertising
A New Agency for the New Toledo
Sonica Smith and Sally Jones
Co-founders

Contact: Sonica Smith
Telephone: 419-123-4567 • Fax: 419-419-4199
E-mail: esseandjay@verizon.net

Mailing Address:
Sonica Smith
444 Advertising Road
Toldeo, OH 43605

Date: March 2007

Executive Summary

The purpose of this plan is to establish a strategy for the creation of S & J Advertising, a new agency that will be based in Toledo, Ohio. Sonica Smith and Sally Jones are the co-founders of S & J and between them bring 19 years of experience in the Toledo advertising market to this venture. Their relationships with current advertisers will result in at least 5 clients coming to the firm at its inception. These 5 clients have given S & J letters stating their intent to join the firm as clients.

The co-founders' experience as professional and proven advertising executives will insure that their current clients will be satisfied and that additional clients will join the S & J roster. Moreover, recent changes in the Toledo media market have created the need among advertisers for a firm of this caliber and expertise.

S & J expects to be profitable within its first year of operation, but seeks $50,000 in bank debt for working capital and the construction of production facilities. The owners expect to personally guarantee this debt and to put in $50,000 of their own capital. The projections show that the company's cash flow will exceed debt service by a ratio of more than 5 to1 in the first year and that the debt can be repaid within 5 years.

The Market

Toledo is an economically healthy and diverse market of more than 600,000 people located in northeastern Ohio. Major employers include Daimler Chrysler, Libbey Glass, Dana Corporation, and General Motors. There are more than 50,000 students enrolled in local institutions of higher learning including Bowling Green College, the University of Toledo, and Owens Community College. For the last five years, unemployment has been consistently below 5%. Toledo has an opera company, a symphony orchestra, an art museum, a zoological society, a minor league baseball team, and a regional airport.

The Advertising Market

The local advertising market has more than $150 million in annual revenue and includes 7 television stations, 1 local newspaper, and 20 radio stations. According to the 2001 Duncan Radio Market Guide, the market revenues break down as follows:

Radio	$ 29 million
Television	$ 56 million

Newspaper	$ 54 million
Outdoor Advertising	$ 7 million
Cable Television	$ 4 million
TOTAL	$ 150 million

Advertising Agency Competition
There are currently 3 advertising agencies in the Toledo area:

Bob Williams Advertising is a one-man shop that has been in business for 12 years and has three clients: a large local bakery, a car dealer, and a local bank.

Global Agency has been in business for 5 years, has 6 employees, and about 15 clients including 2 car dealerships, a few restaurants, and a local college. They have video production capacity.

The Kryzyki Group has been in business for 8 years, has 3 employees and 10 clients who mostly require copy writing services and print ad production. Clients are generally non-profits and educational institutions including the opera company, the symphony orchestra, the zoo, and a chain of day care centers.

The Current Opportunity

Radio Consolidation: Over the last 6 years the radio industry has gone through a major consolidation. As a result, two companies now have more than 90% of the radio revenue, with each owning 8 stations. To make this consolidation work, the radio companies have cut back on their production staffs and the number of advertising representatives. The remaining representatives no longer have enough time to work with local advertisers on the creative and media planning aspects of their advertising expenditures. Production is more rushed, and sometimes is even issued from remote, centralized facilities which slows down the process and results in frequent mistakes, such as the mispronunciation of local proper names.

Media Service Reductions: In addition to radio stations, local television, newspaper, and cable companies have all reduced the level of service to local advertisers, apparently as they push for higher profitability or respond to weak national trends in advertising.

The Rise of the Internet: Although the Internet has not proven itself as a mass advertising force, many businesses have Web sites and e-commerce strategies. Generally, local businesses rely upon computer-oriented people to build these Web pages and do a poor job of integrating their Internet strategy with their overall advertising.

The opportunity that Smith and Jones have identified is the existence of many local advertisers who need and want higher levels of service, including the development and implementation of Internet strategies.

The Management Team

Sonica Smith holds a degree in Advertising from Ohio State University and worked as an Account Representative for a local radio station for 5 years before becoming Sales Manager, a position she has held for the past 4 years.

Sally Jones was a local radio personality in Findlay, Ohio for 7 years, which included responsibility for producing advertisements. She moved to Toledo 10 years ago and became the advertising manager for a local bank. In that capacity she dealt with all the local media, developed the bank's Web site and completed courses in computer science and programming at the University of Toledo.

Smith and Jones are prepared to invest $25,000 each in the agency and to work at minimal salaries to keep the agency's break-even point low until S&J produces adequate profits to compensate them additionally.

Sales and Marketing Strategies

The sales and marketing strategies have already been established by commitments from 5 sizeable advertisers to engage S & J as their advertising agency. These clients include the bank where Sally Jones currently works, a local nightclub, 2 car dealerships, and a large outlet store. In the previous 12 months, these five businesses spent $1.1 million on advertising, not including Web site expenditures.

Smith and Jones have a target list of 23 additional advertisers that they know personally and believe will sign up as clients. They are currently meeting with each of these potential customers to tell them their plans and try to obtain a commitment to join their roster of clients. In addition, Smith and Jones have identified an additional 135 potential clients in Toledo with advertising expenditures of $75,000 or more annually.

Company Structure

S & J will be an LLC so income will pass through to the two owners without being taxed at the company level and to afford personal liability protection to both owners. Smith and Jones are currently working with a lawyer to draft the papers for the organization of the company, including an agreement between each of them to cover all contingencies in case one wishes to leave or in the unlikely event that their working relationship deteriorates.

Capital Requirements

The Appendix details the projected expenditures, including estimates from vendors, but Smith and Jones foresee the following basic capital requirements:

Computer Hardware:	$ 7,500
Computer Software:	$ 1,500
Audio Production Studio:	$ 12,500
Video Editing Equipment:	$ 8,000
Office Furniture:	$ 5,000
TOTAL	$ 34,500

Financing Requirements

Smith and Jones are seeking $50,000 in bank debt as working capital to help build offices and production studios. They are willing to personally guarantee this loan. The attached tables show that the company will be profitable in the first year and capable of handling this amount of debt.

Financial Projections

The attached projected financial statements make conservative assumptions for both revenue and expenses. They show S & J having an income of $23,485 in year 1 and earning $32,325 and $65,040 in years 2 and 3. The revenue projections assume that the company adds a net of 8 new clients in year 2 and 10 in year 3. Given that 5 clients have already signed up and the company has a prime target list of 23 clients and an additional target list of 135 clients, this is also conservative. If, for any reason, the company does not meet its Cash Flow and Profit targets, the principals are prepared to reduce their salaries.

The Operating Cash Flow projections show that the company will end it first year of operation with a cash balance of $72,951, which is nearly six months of operating expense. The projections also show that the company will comfortably service debt, including repaying $10,000 in loan principal, at the end of year 1.

The Ratio Analysis and Comparison with the RMA Data shows that the company is within the range for the average advertising agency, with the exception of having more cash than the average. It also has fewer short term liabilities than the average agency. This is likely due to the fact that the typical agency does much more expensive production than S & J expects to handle. S & J plans to focus more on time buying, which will result in a positive cash flow because time will not be ordered until S & J has received payment from the client. This focus also results in lower fixed asset percentages than the average agency. The Quick Test ratio comprised of cash and net receivables divided by current liabilities similarly shows S & J to be more financially secure than the average agency.

The projections show that S & J Advertising will be able to repay the loan in the 5th year.

3 Year Projections

S & J Advertising

Start-up Expenses

Computer Hardware	7,500
Computer Software	1,500
Production Studio Construction	12,500
Video Editing Equipment	8,000
Audio Production Equipment	6,000
Office Furniture	5,000
Office Rent Deposit	3,000
Phone Deposit	1,200
Stationary, etc.	600
Misc.	4,500
TOTAL	49,800

S & J Advertising

Monthly Expenses

Fixed Expenses	
Rent	1500
Phone	500
Travel and Entertainment	1500
Office Manager	3000
Jones Salary	1000
(Salaries go up as possible)	
Smith Salary	1000
Employee Fringe (35%)	1750
Insurance	400
Variable Expenses	
Studio Producers 10 hours/week @$30	1,300
TOTAL EXPENSES	11,950

S & J Advertising

Proforma Statement Of Cash													
BEGINNING CASH BALANCE	25,000	65,084	54,554	42,999	34,510	28,888	26,332	27,098	30,563	36,727	45,590	57,153	71,414
	September	October	November	December	January	February	March	April	May	June	July	August	TOTAL
Inflows from Operations													
Base Client Sales	5,000	7,500	10,000	12,500	15,000	17,500	20,000	22,500	25,000	27,500	30,000	32,500	225,000
Other Client Sales	1,200	2,000	2,800	3,600	4,400	5,200	6,000	6,800	7,600	8,400	9,200	10,000	67,200
Less: Credit Sales	6,200	9,500	12,800	16,100	19,400	22,700	26,000	29,300	32,600	35,900	39,200	42,500	
Total Cash Inflows from Current Sales	0	0	0	0	0	0	0	0	0	0	0	0	0
Plus: Collections on Prior Sales		6,200	9,500	12,800	16,100	19,400	22,700	26,000	29,300	32,600	35,900	39,200	249,700
Total Cash Inflows from Net Sales	0	6,200	9,500	12,800	16,100	19,400	22,700	26,000	29,300	32,600	35,900	39,200	249,700
Inflows from Financing	100,000												100,000
Total Cash Inflows from Financing	100,000	0	0	0	0	0	0	0	0	0	0	0	100,000
TOTAL CASH INFLOWS	100,000	6,200	9,500	12,800	16,100	19,400	22,700	26,000	29,300	32,600	35,900	39,200	349,700
	September	October	November	December	January	February	March	April	May	June	July	August	TOTAL
Outflows from Operations													
Employees	4,936	4,936	8,068	8,068	8,068	8,068	7,838	8,168	8,498	8,828	9,158	9,488	94,122
Owner's Draw	1,500	1,500	1,500	1,500	1,500	1,500	1,500	1,500	1,500	1,500	1,500	1,500	18,000
Payroll Taxes	660	660	1,013	1,013	1,013	1,013	987	1,024	1,061	1,098	1,135	1,172	11,849
Cost of Sales	310	475	640	805	970	1,135	1,300	1,465	1,630	1,795	1,960	2,125	14,610
Supplies	100	100	500	500	500	500	500	500	500	500	500	500	5,200
Insurance	300	300	300	300	300	300	300	300	300	300	300	300	3,600
Rent	3,750	3,750	3,750	3,750	3,750	3,750	3,750	3,750	3,750	3,750	3,750	3,750	45,000
Truck lease	1,200	1,200	1,200	1,200	1,400	1,400	1,400	1,400	1,400	1,400	1,400	1,400	16,000
Truck operation costs	750	750	750	750	750	750	750	750	750	750	750	750	9,000
Advertising & Promotion	500	500	500	500	500	500	500	500	500	500	500	500	6,000
Telephone & Utilities	650	650	650	650	650	650	650	650	650	650	650	650	7,800
Professional Fees	100	100	100	100	100	100	100	100	100	100	100	100	1,200
Miscellaneous	300	300	575	644	713	781	850	919	988	1,056	1,125	1,194	9,444
Total Outflows from Operations	15,056	15,221	19,546	19,779	20,213	20,447	20,425	21,026	21,627	22,227	22,828	23,429	241,824
Outflows from Financing													
Loan Payments	1,509	1,509	1,509	1,509	1,509	1,509	1,509	1,509	1,509	1,509	1,509	1,509	18,111
Total Outflows from Financing	1,509	1,509	1,509	1,509	1,509	1,509	1,509	1,509	1,509	1,509	1,509	1,509	18,111
Outflows from Non-Recurring Expenses													
Fixtures & Equipment	25,850	0	0	0	0	0	0	0	0	0	0	0	25,850
Leasehold Improvements	3,750	0	0	0	0	0	0	0	0	0	0	0	3,750
Utility & Lease Deposits	3,750	0	0	0	0	0	0	0	0	0	0	0	3,750
Base Inventory	10,000	0	0	0	0	0	0	0	0	0	0	0	10,000
Realtor	0	0	0	0	0	0	0	0	0	0	0	0	0
Licensing	0	0	0	0	0	0	0	0	0	0	0	0	0
Advertising	0	0	0	0	0	0	0	0	0	0	0	0	0
Total Non-Recurring Expenses	43,350	0	0	0	0	0	0	0	0	0	0	0	43,350
TOTAL OUTFLOWS	59,916	16,731	21,055	21,289	21,722	21,956	21,934	22,535	23,136	23,737	24,338	24,938	303,286
	September	MONTH 2	MONTH 3	MONTH 4	MONTH 5	MONTH 6	MONTH 7	MONTH 8	MONTH 9	MONTH 10	MONTH 11	MONTH 12	
TOTAL INFLOWS	100,000	6,200	9,500	12,800	16,100	19,400	22,700	26,000	29,300	32,600	35,900	39,200	349,700
TOTAL OUTFLOWS	59,916	16,731	21,055	21,289	21,722	21,956	21,934	22,535	23,136	23,737	24,338	24,938	303,286
NET CASH FLOWS	40,084	-10,531	-11,555	-8,489	-5,622	-2,556	766	3,465	6,164	8,863	11,562	14,262	46,414

S & J Advertising

Year One Projection of Income & Expense

Estimated Sales or Revenue	$292,200
Minus: Cost of Goods Sold	$14,610
Estimated Gross Profit	**$277,590**

Estimated Operating Expenses

Employees	$94,122
Owner's Draw	$18,000
Payroll Taxes	$11,849
Supplies	$5,200
Insurance	$3,600
Rent	$45,000
Truck lease	$16,000
Truck operation costs	$9,000
Advertising & Promotion	$6,000
Telephone & Utilities	$7,800
Professional Fees	$1,200
Miscellaneous	$9,444
Interest	$6,636
Depreciation	$3,693
Total Estimated Operating Expenses	**$217,771**
Estimated Net Profit or Loss	**$59,819**

Year Two Projection of Income & Expense

Estimated Sales or Revenue	$321,420
Minus: Cost of Goods Sold	$16,071
Estimated Gross Profit	**$305,349**

Estimated Operating Expenses

Employees	$98,828
Owner's Draw	$18,000
Payroll Taxes	$13,034
Supplies	$5,720
Insurance	$3,960
Rent	$45,000
Truck lease	$17,600
Truck operation costs	$9,900
Advertising & Promotion	$6,600
Telephone & Utilities	$8,580
Professional Fees	$1,320
Miscellaneous	$9,444
Interest	$6,636
Depreciation	$3,693
Total Estimated Operating Expenses	**$248,315**
Estimated Net Profit or Loss	**$57,034**

S & J Advertising

Year Three Projection of Income & Expense

Estimated Sales or Revenue	$353,562
Minus: Cost of Goods Sold	$17,678
Estimated Gross Profit	**$335,884**

Estimated Operating Expenses

Employees	$108,711
Owner's Draw	$19,800
Payroll Taxes	$14,337
Supplies	$6,292
Insurance	$4,356
Rent	$45,000
Truck lease	$19,360
Truck operation costs	$10,890
Advertising & Promotion	$7,260
Telephone & Utilities	$9,438
Professional Fees	$1,452
Miscellaneous	$10,388
Interest	$6,636
Depreciation	$3,693
Total Estimated Operating Expenses	**$267,613**
Estimated Net Profit or Loss	**$68,271**

Sources and Uses of Funds

	Uses			Sources
Fixtures & Equipment	25,850		Long Term Loan	100,000
Leasehold Improvements	3,750			
Utility & Lease Deposits	3,750			
Base Inventory	10,000			
Realtor	0			
Licensing	0			
Advertising	0	43,350	Equity	25,000
Working Capital	81,650	81,650		
		125,000		**125,000**

S & J Advertising

Opening Balance Sheet

Current Assets		Current Liabilities	
Cash	81,650	Current Portion Long Term Debt	11,475
Inventory			
Total Current Assets	81,650	Total Current Liabilities	11,475
Fixed Assets		Long Term Debt	88,525
Fixtures & Equipment	25,850		
Leasehold Improvements	3,750		
Utility & Lease Deposits	3,750		
Base Inventory	10,000		
Realtor	0		
Licensing	0		
Advertising	0	Total Debt	100,000
Total Fixed Assets	43,350	Equity	25,000
Total Assets	125,000	Total Liabilities + Equity	125,000

Balance Sheet – Year Two

Current Assets		Current Liabilities	
Cash	70,175	Current Portion Long Term Debt	12,304
Inventory			
Total Current Assets	70,175	Total Current Liabilities	12,304
Fixed Assets		Long Term Debt	76,221
Fixtures & Equipment	25,850		
Leasehold Improvements	3,750		
Utility & Lease Deposits	3,750		
Base Inventory	10,000		
Realtor	0		
Licensing	0		
Advertising	0	Total Debt	88,525
Total Fixed Assets	43,350	Equity	25,000
Total Assets	113,525	Total Liabilities + Equity	113,525

S & J Advertising

Loan Calculator

Loan Amount	$100,000.00
Annual Interest Rate	7.00%
Loan Period in Years	7
Start Date of Loan	9/1/04

Scheduled Monthly Payment	$1,509
Scheduled Number of Payments	84
Total Interest	$26,779

Month	Payment Date	Beginning Balance	Scheduledt Payment	Principal	Interest	Ending Loan Balance
1	September	$100,000.00	$1,509	$926	$583	$99,074
2	October	99,074.07	$1,509	$931	$578	$98,143
3	November	98,142.73	$1,509	$937	$572	$97,206
4	December	97,205.96	$1,509	$942	$567	$96,264
5	January	96,263.73	$1,509	$948	$562	$95,316
6	February	95,316.00	$1,509	$953	$556	$94,363
7	March	94,362.74	$1,509	$959	$550	$93,404
8	April	93,403.92	$1,509	$964	$545	$92,440
9	May	92,439.51	$1,509	$970	$539	$91,469
10	June	91,469.47	$1,509	$976	$534	$90,494
11	July	90,493.78	$1,509	$981	$528	$89,512
12	August	89,512.39	$1,509	$987	$522	$88,525
13	September	88,525.28	$1,509	$993	$516	$87,532
14	October	87,532.41	$1,509	$999	$511	$86,534
15	November	86,533.74	$1,509	$1,004	$505	$85,529
16	December	85,529.26	$1,509	$1,010	$499	$84,519
17	January	84,518.91	$1,509	$1,016	$493	$83,503
18	February	83,502.67	$1,509	$1,022	$487	$82,480
19	March	82,480.50	$1,509	$1,028	$481	$81,452
20	April	81,452.37	$1,509	$1,034	$475	$80,418
21	May	80,418.24	$1,509	$1,040	$469	$79,378
22	June	79,378.07	$1,509	$1,046	$463	$78,332
23	July	78,331.85	$1,509	$1,052	$457	$77,280
24	August	77,279.51	$1,509	$1,058	$451	$76,221
25	September	76,221.04	$1,509	$1,065	$445	$75,156
26	October	75,156.40	$1,509	$1,071	$438	$74,086
27	November	74,085.54	$1,509	$1,077	$432	$73,008
28	December	73,008.44	$1,509	$1,083	$426	$71,925
29	January	71,925.05	$1,509	$1,090	$420	$70,835
30	February	70,835.35	$1,509	$1,096	$413	$69,739
31	March	69,739.29	$1,509	$1,102	$407	$68,637
32	April	68,636.83	$1,509	$1,109	$400	$67,528
33	May	67,527.94	$1,509	$1,115	$394	$66,413
34	June	66,412.59	$1,509	$1,122	$387	$65,291
35	July	65,290.73	$1,509	$1,128	$381	$64,162
36	August	64,162.32	$1,509	$1,135	$374	$63,027
37	September	63,027.34	$1,509	$1,142	$368	$61,886
38	October	61,885.73	$1,509	$1,148	$361	$60,737
39	November	60,737.46	$1,509	$1,155	$354	$59,582

S & J Advertising

Loan Calculator (cont'd)

Month	Payment Date	Beginning Balance	Scheduledt Payment	Principal	Interest	Ending Loan Balance
40	December	59,582.49	$1,509	$1,162	$348	$58,421
41	January	58,420.79	$1,509	$1,168	$341	$57,252
42	February	57,252.31	$1,509	$1,175	$334	$56,077
43	March	56,077.01	$1,509	$1,182	$327	$54,895
44	April	54,894.86	$1,509	$1,189	$320	$53,706
45	May	53,705.81	$1,509	$1,196	$313	$52,510
46	June	52,509.83	$1,509	$1,203	$306	$51,307
47	July	51,306.87	$1,509	$1,210	$299	$50,097
48	August	50,096.89	$1,509	$1,217	$292	$48,880
49	September	48,879.85	$1,509	$1,224	$285	$47,656
50	October	47,655.72	$1,509	$1,231	$278	$46,424
51	November	46,424.44	$1,509	$1,238	$271	$45,186
52	December	45,185.98	$1,509	$1,246	$264	$43,940
53	January	43,940.30	$1,509	$1,253	$256	$42,687
54	February	42,687.35	$1,509	$1,260	$249	$41,427
55	March	41,427.09	$1,509	$1,268	$242	$40,159
56	April	40,159.48	$1,509	$1,275	$234	$38,884
57	May	38,884.48	$1,509	$1,282	$227	$37,602
58	June	37,602.04	$1,509	$1,290	$219	$36,312
59	July	36,312.11	$1,509	$1,297	$212	$35,015
60	August	35,014.67	$1,509	$1,305	$204	$33,710
61	September	33,709.65	$1,509	$1,313	$197	$32,397
62	October	32,397.02	$1,509	$1,320	$189	$31,077
63	November	31,076.74	$1,509	$1,328	$181	$29,749
64	December	29,748.75	$1,509	$1,336	$174	$28,413
65	January	28,413.02	$1,509	$1,344	$166	$27,069
66	February	27,069.49	$1,509	$1,351	$158	$25,718
67	March	25,718.13	$1,509	$1,359	$150	$24,359
68	April	24,358.88	$1,509	$1,367	$142	$22,992
69	May	22,991.71	$1,509	$1,375	$134	$21,617
70	June	21,616.56	$1,509	$1,383	$126	$20,233
71	July	20,233.39	$1,509	$1,391	$118	$18,842
72	August	18,842.15	$1,509	$1,399	$110	$17,443
73	September	17,442.79	$1,509	$1,408	$102	$16,035
74	October	16,035.27	$1,509	$1,416	$94	$14,620
75	November	14,619.54	$1,509	$1,424	$85	$13,196
76	December	13,195.56	$1,509	$1,432	$77	$11,763
77	January	11,763.26	$1,509	$1,441	$69	$10,323
78	February	10,322.61	$1,509	$1,449	$60	$8,874
79	March	8,873.56	$1,509	$1,458	$52	$7,416
80	April	7,416.06	$1,509	$1,466	$43	$5,950
81	May	5,950.05	$1,509	$1,475	$35	$4,475
82	June	4,475.49	$1,509	$1,483	$26	$2,992
83	July	2,992.33	$1,509	$1,492	$17	$1,501
84	August	1,500.51	$1,509	$1,501	$9	$0
			$126,779	**$100,000**	**$26,779**	

S & J Advertising

Ratios

S No.	Type	
1	Current	7.12
2	Quick	7.12
3	Sales / Receivables	6.88
4	Cost of Sales / Inventory	1.46
5	Cost of Sales / Payables	0.00
6	Sales / Working Capital	3.58
7	EBIT / Interest	7.33
8	Net Profit + Depr.,Depr Amort/ Cur.Mat L/T/D	5.53
9	Fixed / Worth	1.73
10	Debt / Worth	4.00
11	% Profit Before Taxes / Tangible Net Worth	239.28
12	% Profit Before Taxes / Total Assets	47.86
13	Sales / Net Fixed Assets	6.74
14	Sales / Total Assets	2.34
15	% Depr.,Dep.,Amor. / Sales	0.01
16	% Officers',Directors',Owners' Comp / Sales	38.37

Sample Plan for Creating a New Venture Within an Existing Business

If you buy an existing company, your plan will likely focus on one or more growth initiatives while leaving the core business relatively unchanged. Writing a plan for a new venture within an existing company combines the challenges of a start-up with the acquisition of an existing business.

Your plan must demonstrate that the new initiative will be successful by generating profits greater than the necessary investments. You also need to show that the core business will continue to do well and even improve. Many readers of your plan will be concerned that your initiatives may distract management from the existing parts of the business, move the company's focus away from its main customers and products, or take customers from your current products or services. So your plan should emphasize how your business will benefit from what you are proposing while not risking what you already have.

Picasso Pizza
Plan for Expansion
Ralph Williams
Owner

Contact: Ralph Williams
Telephone: 415-987-6543 • Fax: 415-924-9923
E-mail: Ralph@picassopies.com

Mailing Address:
123 First Street
San Francisco, CA 94105

Date: March 2007

Executive Summary

Ralph Williams has owned Picasso Pizza for seven years and has built it into a successful business with more than $400,000 in annual sales. Picasso has an excellent location in the growing SoMa area of San Francisco and focuses on providing healthy pizza made from whole wheat flour and organic vegetables and meats. The business has no debt and Ralph is the sole owner. An adjacent 600 square foot store has become available and with an investment of $173,000, Ralph believes he can significantly increase sales by expanding his seating area and adding a bar. The projections provided below are very conservative regarding increases in sales and provide for an ample margin of error for the cost of the expansion. Ralph is willing to invest $73,000 personally in this project. This plan is written in support of an application for a $100,000 loan without personal guarantees. Pre-tax profit, even under the conservative assumptions in this plan, covers interest payments by approximately three times.

Background

Ralph Williams opened Picasso Pizza in the SoMa (South of Market Street) area of San Francisco in 1997. The neighborhood was not as busy as many of San Francisco's more established neighborhoods, but Ralph saw residential development moving towards this area as well as the planned opening of SBC Park, the new home of the San Francisco Giants just a few blocks away. Ralph negotiated a 20-year lease on a 900-square-foot corner store at $2500 per month.

Ralph worked with Professor Barry Rosen, a marketing professor and expert in the restaurant industry, to develop a plan that would position Picasso Pizza in the crowded and highly-fragmented pizza market. They decided upon a healthy gourmet pizza that would appeal to the type of customers who prefer organic foods, count calories, enjoy something different, and—most importantly—love delicious pizza. This orientation allowed Picasso to charge premium prices and quickly earn a name and reputation in the market.

The 1997 plan worked out the details of financial investment, cost of goods, and operating expenses to calculate a breakeven point of $22,000 per month. Ralph exceeded that number in the fourth month and has since been growing in revenue and profitability. Today, Picasso Pizza has annual revenues of $410,000 and profits (after owner's salary) of $20,000.

The adjacent 600-square-foot store has now become available and the landlord has approached Ralph to see if he is interested in expanding. In his current store, there are seats for 12 and a stand-up counter in the window that can accommodate six. Based on very conservative revenue projections, the expansion project will cost \$173,000. Ralph will finance \$73,000 of this himself through an equity contribution to the business.

This plan will support Ralph's application for a bank credit line of \$100,000 without personal guarantees or collateral.

The Market

Picasso Pizza is a pizzeria dedicated to providing delicious "healthy pizza." Compared to the majority of existing pizzerias today, Picasso has targeted the niche market that is interested in healthier alternatives to typical pizza and in gourmet quality. The vast majority of pizzerias make pizza with tomato sauce, mozzarella cheese, and a choice of toppings such as sausage, pepperoni, or mushrooms. Speciality dine-in restaurants that serve gourmet pizza, such as brick-oven pizza or ultra-thin crust pizza, charge much higher prices than typical pizzerias.

Within an eight-block radius of Picasso's there are more than 25,000 residents with an average income of over \$41,000. There is no reliable statistic on the number of visitors to the SoMa area, but it is significant and growing. On days that the Giants play at SBC Park, more than 30,000 people visit the area.

Management

Ralph Williams is a graduate of the University of California, Santa Barbara, majoring in archeology. While a student, Ralph worked part-time at a large fast-food chain that specialized in pizza. Upon graduation, Ralph was offered a management position with training for further promotions. Over the next four years, Ralph served in various management positions and attended management training programs at the company's headquarters. Ralph was then promoted to Regional Manager with authority for 15 locations, a position he remained in for two years. In 1996, he decided it was time to start his own business and he began to work with Professor Rosen to develop a plan. Ralph's record at Picasso is very strong, having brought the start-up phase in on budget and exceeding his revenue and profit forecasts for the first five years.

Of the 23 people who work at Picasso either full or part-time, Ralph has identified two, Regina White and Bob Unterman, with strong management potential. He has since trained them and given them the opportunity to function in that role. Ralph is confident leaving the pizzeria under their supervision when he takes time off or, as he has done lately, when he is working on growth plans for the expanded Picasso.

Product Description

Pizza serves many functions: as a snack, lunch, or dinner at a dine-in restaurant, and a take-home or delivered product for family dinners or events with friends. A typical slice of cheese pizza has the following nutritional profile:

- 410 Calories
- 40 Grams of carbohydrates (39% of total calories)
- 23 Grams of protein (22% of total calories)
- 18 Grams of fat (20% of total calories)

Although many foods have profiles with more calories and fat than pizza, Williams believed that he could make a healthier pizza by following these guidelines:

- Use whole wheat flour rather than white flour
- Use low-fat cheese rather than full-fat mozzarella
- Use no additional oils except light olive oil where absolutely required
- Minimize the use of meat toppings and use fish, vegetables, and herbs instead
- Use no fried foods as toppings
- Use only fresh ingredients, avoiding the high salt content of canned products
- Use only locally grown, organic products

Among the most popular items at Picasso are:

- Mushroom pizza with fresh mushrooms, tomato sauce, parsley, oregano and basil
- Eggplant pizza with thinly sliced eggplant, tomato sauce, garlic and parsley
- Zucchini pizza with thinly sliced zucchini, low-fat processed white American cheese, egg, and low-fat mozzarella
- Potato pizza with thinly sliced fresh potatoes, egg, low-fat mozzarella, rosemary, and pepper

- A line of cold pizzas featuring fish, shrimp, or calamari along with fresh tomatoes and spices
- Stuffed spinach pizza with two crusts, fresh spinach, low-fat feta cheese, low-fat mozzarella, and egg whites
- Calzones with various fillings such as spinach, shrimp, cheese, and spices

Beverages include fruit juices, bottled iced teas, water, and a line of locally bottled root beer.

Prices run from $2 to $4 for one slice, and $12 to $19 for an entire pie.

Schedule of Operation and Staffing

Picasso Pizza is open seven days a week from 11a.m. to 1 a.m. The first shift arrives at 9 a.m. to accept deliveries and begin food preparation. It is closed only on Thanksgiving and Christmas Day. Picasso is usually staffed by teams of five people including

- Two servers
- One cashier who also takes phone orders
- One cook
- One assistant cook

Each team works an eight-hour shift of either 9 a.m. to 5 p.m. or 5 p.m. to 1 a.m. Some of the workers are part-time and others work six shifts per week. In total, Picasso's has 23 full and part-time employees.

Ralph has worked hard to hire people who have experience in the pizza business, but he has also tried to hire people who have the friendly, service-oriented attitude he wants Picasso to present to its employees and customers.

Competition

There are four pizzerias or restaurants serving pizza within a ten-block radius of Picasso, all of which seem to be generally busy:

- California Pizza Oven has gourmet pizza but is more expensive than Picasso and is generally perceived as a restaurant chain, not a locally-owned business.

- Paul's Pizza is a full-service restaurant with a full Italian menu. Pizzas are not sold by the slice and pies are made to order, which takes 20 minutes. It does not do take-out.
- Familia Pizza is a simple pizzeria with no seats and a traditional take-out only pizza menu.
- Anna's Deep Dish is a restaurant and bar that serves Chicago-style pizza that is made to order. It does take-out business, but does not deliver.

Among the existing four competitors there is no pizzeria that has taken both the "gourmet" and "healthy" positions.

Financial Performance

Picasso has sales in the last year of $410,000 and pre-tax profits of $20,000 (after owner's salary.) It has experienced an increase of 6% per year average sales growth.

Current Opportunity

The landlord has offered Ralph the opportunity to rent an adjacent store that could be combined with the current store. The 600-square-foot space could accommodate a full-service bar, a food preparation area for additional menu items, and seating for 20. After discussions with Ralph, the landlord offered to rent the adjacent space at $1,000 per month. A review of current rents has satisfied Ralph that this is below current market prices.

Marketing Strategy

When Picasso Pizza opened in 1997, the marketing consisted of neighborhood flyers, an ad in the Giants' scorecard, and the hiring of a public relations person to make sure that Picasso was listed in all the San Francisco restaurant guides. The flyers and print ads used 10% off coupons that helped Ralph establish the effectiveness of his various marketing efforts.

If the expansion takes place, Picasso will employ similar strategies but will increase the focus on getting restaurant reviews and receiving mentions in the local media. San Francisco is a city with a great reputation for restaurants and Ralph believes that word-of-mouth is exceptionally effective. But this also means that the food, service, and decor must be perfect.

In 1997, Picasso spent $3,000 on marketing efforts around the opening. To be conservative, after the addition is complete, Ralph is budgeting $20,000 in advertising and promotion during the first year.

Licenses

Picasso currently has a retail food service license and a license to operate a commercial oven. There is no limitation on the number of liquor licenses or their potential locations, but the process of obtaining one is time consuming and is estimated to take six months. Picasso has already filed its application and should have it granted prior to the opening of the expansion.

Break-Even Analysis for the Project

When the current location opened in 1997, the fixed costs per month were estimated to be approximately $25,000. The cost of goods sold were estimated to be about 30% of sales. With an average sale estimated very conservatively at $4 (one slice and a beverage), the average contribution to fixed costs of each sale was $2.80.

Doing a similar calculation for the new space yields the following results:

Fixed Costs of operation:

Rent: $1,000

Utilities: $500

Staff of five including a bartender who will also be the cashier, two servers, one cook, and an assistant cook for 13 hours every day or $1,950 estimated conservatively at an average of $7/hour = $13,650

Insurance and Other: $1,500

Total Monthly Fixed Costs for the New Space: $16,650

Assuming an average sale of only $10 (two slices and a beverage) with a variable cost of 30%, the average contribution to fixed cost per sale will be $7. In all likelihood, the average sale is likely to be closer to $15 as parties order full pies, appetizers, desserts, and alcoholic beverages. At $15 the contribution to fixed costs per sales would be $10.50. Reaching the break-even point will require about 50 sales per day, far below the space's capacity. While these numbers seem extremely conservative, the projections are even more conservative showing that the new space will add no sales in the first year, and $30,000 per year in sales over a two-year period—only about 12 meals per day.

Project Costs

Ralph estimates that the cost of renovating and decorating the new space will be $88,000, broken out as follows:

Renovations including hardwood floors, painting, electrical, and plumbing: $39,000

Fixtures including food preparation equipment, bar, tables and chairs, and lighting: $14,000

Marketing Campaign: $20,000

Operating Losses until break-even point reached: $100,000

Total Project Financing Required: $173,000

Ralph is seeking a line of credit of $100,000 and will fund the balance of the project personally.

Picasso Pizza

Income Statement Previous 12 Months

	Total
Revenue from In-Store Sales	409,000
Revenue from Delivery Sales	53,100
Net Revenue from Sales	462,100
Total Cost of Sales, 30% (Raw Food Ingredients)	138,630
Gross Margin, 70%	323,470
Operating Expenses:	
Salaries and Wages	162,624
Payroll Taxes	20,250
Lease/Rent	42,000
Telephone and Utilities	15,700
Depreciation (estimate)	3,204
Insurance	3,600
Supplies	6,000
Maintenance	3,600
Advertising and Promotion	13,500
Professional Fees/Licenses	6,500
Miscellaneous	16,000
Total: Operating Expenses	292,978
Other expenses:	
Interest (loan) 10.5%	10,500
Total: Other expenses	10,500
Total: All expenses	303,478
Net-Profit (Loss) pre-tax	19,992

Picasso Pizza

Projected Income Statements

	Year 2	Year 3
Revenue from in-store sales	441,720.00	477,057.60
Revenue from delivery sales	57,348.00	61,935.84
Net Revenue from Sales	499,068.00	538,993.44
Total Cost of Sales 30%	149,720.40	161,698.03
(Raw Food Ingredients)		0.00
Gross Margin 70%	349,347.60	377,295.41
Operating Expenses:		
Salaries and Wages	175,633.92	189,684.63
Payroll Taxes	21,870.00	23,619.60
Lease/Rent	42,000.00	42,000.00
Telephone and Utilities	16,956.00	18,312.48
Depreciation (estimate)	3,204.00	3,204.00
Insurance	3,888.00	4,199.04
Supplies	6,480.00	6,998.40
Maintenance	3,888.00	4,199.04
Advertising and Promotion	14,580.00	15,746.40
Professional Fees/Licenses	7,020.00	7,581.60
Miscellaneous	17,280.00	18,662.40
Total: Operating Expenses	312,799.92	334,207.59
Interest at 10.5%	10,500.00	10,500.00
Total: All expenses	323,299.92	344,707.59
Net-Profit (Loss) pre-tax	26,047.68	32,587.81

Picasso Pizza

Projected Balance Sheet

	Year 1	Year 2	Year 3
ASSETS			
Cash & Cash Equivalents	15,829	46,547	83,923
Accounts Receivable	4,234	4,573	4,939
Furniture & Equipment	55,500	55,500	55,500
Leasehold Improvement	230,000	230,000	230,000
Less Accumulated Depreciation	(26,197)	(29,401)	(32,605)
TOTAL ASSETS	279,366	307,219	341,757
LIABILITIES			
Accounts Payable	22,565	24,370	26,320
Short Term Bank Borrowing	100,000	100,000	100,000
Long Term Debt	0	0	0
SHAREHOLDERS EQUITY			
Common Stock	123,000	123,000	123,000
Retained Earnings	13,809	33,801	59,849
Earnings	19,992	26,048	32,588
Total stockholders' Equity	156,801	182,849	215,436
TOTAL LIABILITIES & STOCKHOLDERS' EQUITY	279,366	307,219	341,756

Plan for the Purchase of an Existing Business: Transylvania Transmissions, Inc.

Sometimes it's easier to buy a business than to start a new one. An existing business may be earning profits that will allow you to obtain financing more readily and it may also be less expensive than building a new enterprise from scratch. Buying an existing business is less risky if it has a solid reputation, a loyal group of customers, and well-trained employees.

There are many ways to find businesses for sale:

- **Business brokers match buyers and sellers of businesses.** They are usually paid on a reverse sliding scale following the purchase. A typical fee structure for a business broker is 5% to 6% of the first $1 million, and 2% to 3% on any sale over $5 million. Some brokers charge up-front fees, but this may express their lack of confidence in being able to make a deal.
- **Lawyers, accountants, and consultants who work in the industry often hear about businesses for sale.** Tell them you're interested in purchasing a business and they may be able to make a match. Some will charge a fee for this work. Others won't charge a fee but will expect you to become a loyal client if they make a successful match.
- **The Business Opportunities section of your local newspaper lists sales.** Many papers have a classified advertising section one or two days a week that will list business brokers, companies selling franchises, and individuals trying to sell their own businesses. Most industry newspapers and magazines also have sales sections.
- **Business owners themselves can be a great source of opportunities.** Don't be shy about sending letters, calling, e-mailing, or stopping by in person to make these connections. You will learn a great deal about your industry by talking to people active in the field.

Special Considerations for Business Acquisitions

A plan for the purchase of an existing business eliminates some of the problems of creating a plan for a start-up, but the challenges of demonstrating growth potential are much greater. Existing businesses have historical financial statements, sales data, market share information, and, most importantly, they may have a strong history of profitability. These all reduce the perception of risk among potential funding sources, partners, and other readers of the plan whose participation you hope to recruit in order to make your business a success.

Once a business has a proven track record of profitability it has a better chance of attracting lenders' money or raising equity investment. But the plan for the purchase of an existing business has its own challenges. First you must demonstrate the potential for growth. Investors, lenders, and you as the entrepreneur will all benefit from the growth of the business you acquire. Growth in most cases makes a business more profitable and, therefore, more valuable. Growth allows you to pay the interest on loans more easily, create more profits for distribution to your partners, invest in further growth initiatives, or increase the company's value if it is sold.

If the business you plan to purchase has existed for a while, the readers of your plan will want to know why you will be able to do a better job than the current ownership and managers of the company. You will have to demonstrate in your plan that you have specific and credible ways to create growth through strategies such as expanding markets or product lines, reducing costs, raising prices, or benefitting from the growth of the market your business serves.

Transylvania Transmissions, Inc.
Plan for Purchase By
Bill Gaxton

Contact: Bill Gaxton
Telephone: 773-897-1543 • Fax: 773-544-2388
E-mail: Gax234@TransylvaniaTrans.com

Mailing Address:
4550 West Cermack Road
Chicago, IL 60666

Date: March 2007

Transylvania Transmissions, Inc.

Executive Summary

The purpose of this plan is to create a financial and operational strategy for the purchase of Transylvania Transmissions for $1,000,000 by Bill Gaxton. Gaxton brings more than 25 years of experience in all aspects of the transmission-repair industry, including nearly 20 years of experience with Transylvania Transmissions. The business is currently profitable and growing—and Gaxton expects to be able to continue that trend. The company has a successful history of more than 80 years, strong market positions with retail and company fleet markets, an ongoing sales effort, and an expertise that cannot be matched by local competitors.

The purchase price represents less than five times current Cash Flow and slightly more than two times current revenue. In addition to the $500,000 of his own money that Gaxton will invest, the current owner is offering seller financing of $325,000. This plan is being presented to The Second National Bank of Chicago in support of an application for a bank loan of $325,000. The owner's equity and the loan from the bank will be used to make partial payment to the seller and to establish adequate working capital.

The bank will be given a senior position and the seller note will be subordinated to it. Ratio analysis that is presented in the Appendix shows that the company will always cover its loan payments easily and the financial projections are well within industry standards. If Gaxton sells the business for only 3 times Cash Flow (a reduction of 2 in the multiple he is paying), the equity returns will exceed 70% annually.

Company Background

In 1920, Laszlo Popescu, a thirty-year-old immigrant from Romania, opened a gas station on West Cermack Road in Chicago. As the city grew and car sales boomed, Laszlo's Gas Station grew to include three gas pumps, a repair facility, and a radio-dispatched tow truck. In 1958, Laszlo's son, Alexandru (Al), joined him and eventually took over operation of the business in 1970 when Lazslo retired. Once at the helm, Al felt that the company had too little space to compete with large gas stations. At the same time, he saw that cars were becoming more complex and repair shops were starting to specialize, creating tire shops, and repair shops that focused on brakes, mufflers, or windows. Given the space available, plus his extensive knowledge and his experience, as well as that of his staff, Al decided to specialize in transmission repairs.

In 1975, Laszlo's Gas Station closed, the pumps were removed and a new, larger repair facility was built that included six lifts, eight transmission rebuilding stations, a reception area, and offices for Al, a business manager, the shop manager, and a salesperson. In recognition of his family's origins, he named the new business Transylvania Transmissions.

In 1985, Al hired Bill Gaxton who had three years of experience at a nearby transmission franchise as a transmission rebuilder. In 1992, Bill was made shop manager and has served the role of Al's second-in-command ever since. In 2004, Al decided he would like to retire and was interested in selling Transylvania Transmissions.

The Market

The market for transmission repairs has grown along with the increase in complexity of automobile transmissions and the aging of the average car. Transmissions, which were entirely mechanical devices from their introduction, now usually have built-in computers or they connect to the car's computer controller. New hybrid engine vehicles that are more fuel efficient but more complex will continue this trend toward more complicated transmissions. Repairs by do-it-yourself mechanics are virtually impossible. In fact, most repair shops subcontract transmission work to businesses such as Transylvania. In 1985, the average age of a car on the road in the United States was 7.6 years. Today it is over nine years. Because the likelihood of a transmission failure a generally a function of time-in-operation, older cars represent better markets for transmission repair shops.

Transylvania Transmissions does no work under manufacturers' warranties because this work is done by dealers. In fact, the dealer generally does not repair the transmission but replaces it with a rebuilt transmission supplied by the manufacturer that comes from a centralized transmission repair facility. Transylvania will repair or replace the transmission on any type of car, van, or truck.

The primary markets for Transylvania include:

1. **Fleet operators** such as utilities and distribution businesses, government departments such as the police, and transportation companies such as cabs, school bus operators, and limousine services.
2. **Subcontracted business** from general auto repair shops within a ten-mile radius of Transylvania's location.

3. **Retail business** from individuals who bring in their own personal vehicles for repair.

The average price of a job is $1,000 with retail customers paying somewhat more and fleet operators who negotiate annual rates somewhat less. Trucks and buses average two to three times that amount, but represent less than 15% of Transylvania's revenue.

Competition

There are many competitors for the retail market including franchised shops such as Aamco and Cottman, three locally-owned transmission businesses within a five-mile radius of Transylvania, and two other large-scale transmission shops similar to Transylvania in the Chicago area. The closest one is eight miles away. Both have existed for more than ten years.

The Management Team

As mentioned above, Bill Gaxton has more than 25 years of experience in the transmission business. He started as an assistant, became a rebuilder, a salesperson handling retail and corporate clients, and, finally, manager. It is expected that the other people who currently work at Transylvania will remain. Key employees include:

Lynette Periwinkle, the business manager, who has a business degree from the University of Illinois and has been at Transylvania for nine years.

Rob Rondinello, who has been the salesperson handling fleet accounts for the last four years. Prior to that he worked as a rebuilder for five years.

There are four rebuilders who earn on average $800 per week, four installers who remove and replace the transmissions from the vehicles and earn on average $500 per week, three drivers who drive the tow truck or customer's vehicles that are being picked up or returned and earn about $350 per week, and two assistants who perform tasks such as aiding the installers and cleaning the facility and earn $300 per week.

When the sale takes place, Gaxton expects to promote one of the installers to fill the job of manager that he currently occupies. The salary for this job is $1,200 per week.

Sales and Marketing Strategies

Transylvania has for many years used the following marketing strategies:

- Calendars and desk items around the theme of Transylvania using bats, castles, and Count Dracula are distributed to vehicle fleet managers and repair shop owners.
- A quarter-page in the Chicago Yellow Pages.
- An annual Halloween party for neighborhood children has been run for nearly 30 years.
- A three-year warranty on all retail transmission repairs.

The company salesperson visits fleet-managers and repair shop operators throughout the area to keep Transylvania in people's mind. The salesperson is paid a salary but keeps track of new business that comes from the result of his efforts. The company never pays fees or kickbacks to fleet managers but does perform repair work on their personal vehicles for greatly reduced fees.

Growth Potential

Transylvania has a more than 80 year history of growth. Over the last ten years, sales have averaged 13% annual growth. To be conservative, Gaxton is projecting no increase in sales for the first year of his ownership and then 10% annual growth. Growth comes from the increased age of cars on the road, the complexity of transmissions, and the importance of skilled transmission specialists to repair or rebuild a modern transmission. Transylvania's practice of giving three-year warranties makes it unique among the competition.

In the future, the company could move into the repair of other complex components such as electrical or computer systems, but that decision is at least several years away.

Company Structure

Transylvania is currently an S Corporation with Al Popescu as the only shareholder. Mr. Popescu would like to structure the deal as a stock sale to eliminate any continuing legal liability he might have after selling the company. An environmental review is currently underway to determine if any oil or gasoline has leeched into the ground under the facility that could represent a major cost to remove. If this is not a problem, Mr. Gaxton will purchase the company's stock. If there are environmental liabilities, Mr. Popescu has agreed to either pay for the clean-up or retain the land and provide Mr. Gaxton a long-term lease at $1 per year.

Capital Requirements

The company requires no capital improvements. The projections assume $25,000 in one-time legal expenses for the transaction and $20,000 in one-time expenses related to changing the corporate name such as stationary, business cards, and promotional materials—although these are expected to cost much less than these estimates. The projections include capital requirements of $2,000 per month for new tools, equipment, computers, phone systems, and building improvements.

Transylvania Transmissions Purchase Plan

Proforma Statement Of Cash Flows

Beginning Cash Balance	25,000	130,025	145,050	156,925	168,799	180,474	189,449	198,424	207,399	216,374	225,349	234,323	243,298
	Sept	**Oct**	**Nov**	**Dec**	**Jan**	**Feb**	**Mar**	**April**	**May**	**June**	**July**	**Aug**	**TOTAL**
Inflows from Operations													
Base Client Sales	100,000	100,000	100,000	100,000	100,000	100,000	100,000	100,000	100,000	100,000	100,000	100,000	1,200,000
Other Client Sales	0	0	0	0	0	0	0	0	0	0	0	0	0
Less: Credit Sales	100,000	100,000	100,000	100,000	100,000	100,000	100,000	100,000	100,000	100,000	100,000	100,000	
Total Cash Inflows from Current Sales	0	0	0	0	0	0	0	0	0	0	0	0	0
Plus: Collections on Prior Sales	100,000	100,000	100,000	100,000	100,000	100,000	100,000	100,000	100,000	100,000	100,000	100,000	1,200,000
Total Cash Inflows from Net Sales	100,000	100,000	100,000	100,000	100,000	100,000	100,000	100,000	100,000	100,000	100,000	100,000	1,200,000
Inflows from Financing													
Bank Loan	325,000												325,000
Seller Financing	325,000												325,000
Gaxton Equity Investment	200,000												200,000
Total Cash Inflows from Financing	850,000	0	0	0	0	0	0	0	0	0	0	0	850,000
TOTAL CASH INFLOWS	950,000	100,000	100,000	100,000	100,000	100,000	100,000	100,000	100,000	100,000	100,000	100,000	2,050,000

Transylvania Transmissions Purchase Plan

Proforma Statement Of Cash Flows

	Sept	Oct	Nov	Dec	Jan	Feb	Mar	April	May	June	July	Aug	TOTAL
Outflows from Operations													
Employees	40,000	40,000	40,000	40,000	40,000	40,000	40,000	40,000	40,000	40,000	40,000	40,000	480,000
Owner's Salary	10,000	10,000	10,000	10,000	10,000	10,000	10,000	10,000	10,000	10,000	10,000	10,000	120,000
Payroll Taxes	5,200	5,200	5,200	5,200	5,200	5,200	5,200	5,200	5,200	5,200	5,200	5,200	62,400
Cost of Sales	15,000	15,000	15,000	15,000	15,000	15,000	15,000	15,000	15,000	15,000	15,000	15,000	180,000
Supplies	100	100	500	500	500	500	500	500	500	500	500	500	5,200
Insurance	300	300	300	300	300	3,000	3,000	3,000	3,000	3,000	3,000	3,000	22,500
Tow Truck Leases	1,200	1,200	1,200	1,200	1,400	1,400	1,400	1,400	1,400	1,400	1,400	1,400	16,000
Truck operation costs	750	750	750	750	750	750	750	750	750	750	750	750	9,000
Advertising & Promotion	500	500	500	500	500	500	500	500	500	500	500	500	6,000
Telephone & Utilities	1,650	1,650	1,650	1,650	1,650	1,650	1,650	1,650	1,650	1,650	1,650	1,650	19,800
Professional Fees	1,000	1,000	1,000	1,000	1,000	1,000	1,000	1,000	1,000	1,000	1,000	1,000	12,000
Miscellaneous	300	300	3,050	3,050	3,050	3,050	3,050	3,050	3,050	3,050	3,050	3,050	31,100
Total Outflows from Operations	76,000	76,000	79,150	79,150	79,350	82,050	82,050	82,050	82,050	82,050	82,050	82,050	964,000
Outflows from Financing													
Interest on Bank Loan	2,234	2,215	2,195	2,175	2,155	2,134	2,114	2,093	2,073	2,052	2,031	2,010	25,479
Principal Payments on Bank Loan	2,872	2,892	2,911	2,931	2,952	2,972	2,992	3,013	3,034	3,054	3,075	3,097	35,794
Principal Payment on Seller Note	3,869	3,869	3,869	3,869	3,869	3,869	3,869	3,869	3,869	3,869	3,869	3,869	46,429
Total Outflows from Financing	8,975	8,975	8,975	8,975	8,975	8,975	8,975	8,975	8,975	8,975	8,975	8,975	107,702

Transylvania Transmissions Purchase Plan

Proforma Statement Of Cash Flows

	Sept	Oct	Nov	Dec	Jan	Feb	Mar	April	May	June	July	Aug	TOTAL
Outflows from Non-Recurring Expenses													
Purchase of Assests	700,000												700,000
Legal Expenses for Purchase	25,000	0	0	0	0	0	0	0	0	0	0	0	25,000
Branding	20,000	0	0	0	0	0	0	0	0	0	0	0	20,000
Capital Expenditures	15,000												15,000
Total Non-Recurring Expenses	760,000	0	0	0	0	0	0	0	0	0	0	0	760,000
TOTAL OUTFLOWS	844,975	84,975	88,125	88,125	88,325	91,025	91,025	91,025	91,025	91,025	91,025	91,025	1,831,702
TOTAL INFLOWS	950,000	100,000	100,000	100,000	100,000	100,000	100,000	100,000	100,000	100,000	100,000	100,000	2,050,000
TOTAL OUTFLOWS	844,975	84,975	88,125	88,125	88,325	91,025	91,025	91,025	91,025	91,025	91,025	91,025	1,831,702
NET CASH FLOWS	105,025	15,025	11,875	11,875	11,675	8,975	8,975	8,975	8,975	8,975	8,975	8,975	218,298

Assumptions:

Sales for Year 1 remain at previous year level. After that they increase by 10% per year.

Bank provides $325,000 7 year loan at 8.25%

Seller provides $325,000 7 year note at 0% interest; Amortization payments only.

Sales and Expenses stay at previous year level for the first year, then grow at 10% per year.

Gaxton takes Popescu's salary and Gaxton is replaced with someone at same salary that he earned

Either the land is included in the sale or Popescu leases it to Gaxton for 25 years at $1 per year

Employee expense represents the current staff level of 15 as explained in the text.

Transylvania Transmissions

Projected Income Statements and Cash Flow (EBT)

	Year 1	Year 2	Year 3
Revenue	1,200,000.00	1,320,000.00	1,452,000.00
Minus: Cost of Goods Sold	180,000.00	198,000.00	217,800.00
Estimated Gross Profit	1,020,000.00	1,122,000.00	1,234,200.00
Expenses			
Employees	480,000.00	504,000.00	529,200.00
Owner's Salary	120,000.00	120,000.00	120,000.00
Payroll Taxes	62,400.00	65,100.00	67,935.00
Supplies	5,200.00	5,720.00	6,292.00
Insurance	22,500.00	24,750.00	27,225.00
Tow Truck Leases	16,000.00	16,000.00	16,000.00
Truck operation costs	9,000.00	9,900.00	10,890.00
Advertising & Promotion	6,000.00	6,600.00	7,260.00
Telephone & Utilities	19,800.00	21,780.00	23,958.00
Professional Fees	12,000.00	13,200.00	14,520.00
Miscellaneous	31,100.00	34,210.00	37,631.00
Operating Expenses	784,000.00	821,260.00	860,911.00
Interest	25,479.13	22,411.86	19,081.76
Depreciation	127,000.00	127,000.00	127,000.00
Total Expenses	936,479.13	970,671.86	1,006,992.76
Cash Flow/EBITDA	236,000.00	300,740.00	373,289.00
Retained Earnings	83,520.87	151,328.14	227,207.24

Assumptions:

Sales for Year 1 remain at previous year level. After that they increase by 10% per year.
Bank provides $325,000 7 year loan at 8.25%
Seller provides $325,000 7 year note at 0% interest; Amortization payments only.
Sales and Expenses stay at previous year level for the first year, then grow at 10% per year.
Gaxton takes Popescu's salary and Gaxton is replaced with someone at same salary that he earned
Either the land is included in the sale or Popescu leases it to Gaxton for 25 years at $1 per year
Employee expense represents the current staff level of 15 as explained in the text.

Transylvania Transmissions

Year One (Includes Purchase and One Year of Operation)
Statement of Sources and Uses of Funds

	Uses		Sources
Purchase of Assests	1,000,000.00	Bank Loan	325,000.00
Legal Expenses for Purchase	25,000.00	Owner's Investment	500,000.00
Branding	20,000.00	Seller Note	325,000.00
Capital Expenditures	15,000.00		
Working Capital	90,000.00		
TOTAL USES	1,150,000.00	TOTAL SOURCES	1,150,000.00

Transylvania Transmissions

At Purchase and Projected Balance Sheets

	At Purchase	Year 1	Year 2	Year 3
ASSETS				
Current assets:				
Cash & Cash equivalents	50,000.00	152,160.00	343,278.00	0.00
Accounts receivable	100,000.00	105,000.00	110,250.00	115,762.50
Other short-term assets				
Total current assets	150,000.00	257,160.00	453,528.00	115,762.50
Long Term Assets:				
Furniture & Equipment, cost	400,000.00	400,000.00	400,000.00	400,000.00
Goodwill	600,000.00	600,000.00	600,000.00	600,000.00
Equipment		25,000.00	25,000.00	25,000.00
Brand		20,000.00	20,000.00	20,000.00
Legal		15,000.00	15,000.00	15,000.00
Less accumulated depreciation		-127,000.00	-254,000.00	-381,000.00
Total fixed assets	1,000,000.00	933,000.00	806,000.00	679,000.00
Other assets:				
Other assets and miscellaneous investments				
Total Other assets	0.00	0.00	0.00	0.00
TOTAL ASSETS	1,150,000.00	1,190,160.00	1,259,528.00	794,762.50
LIABILITIES & STOCKHOLDERS' EQUITY				
Current liabilities:				
Accounts payable				
Short term bank borrowing		38,861.27	42,191.37	45,806.84
Other short term liabilities		0.00	0.00	0.00
Total current liabilities	0.00	38,861.27	42,191.37	45,806.84
Non current liabilities:				
Long term debt	650,000.00	528,916.16	440,296.22	348,060.81
Total Liabilities	650,000.00	567,777.43	482,487.59	393,867.65
Stockholders' equity:				
Common stock	500,000.00	500,000.00	500,000.00	500,000.00
Retained earning	0.00	0.00	83,520.87	234,849.01
Income	0.00	83,520.87	151,328.14	227,207.24
Total stockholders' equity	500,000.00	583,520.87	734,849.01	962,056.25
TOTAL LIABILITIES & STOCKHOLDERS' EQUIT'	1,150,000.00	1,190,159.56	1,259,527.97	1,401,730.73

Transylvania Transmissions

Debt Management Schedule

Loan Amount	325,000.00
Annual Interest Rate	0.08
Loan Period in Years	7.00
Start Date of Loan	38,231.00
Scheduled Monthly Payment	5,106.09

Month	Payment Date	Beginning Balance	Scheduledt Payment	Principal	Interest	Ending Loan Balance
1	September	325,000.00	5,106.09	2,871.72	2,234.38	322,128.28
2	October	322,128.28	5,106.09	2,891.46	2,214.63	319,236.82
3	November	319,236.82	5,106.09	2,911.34	2,194.75	316,325.48
4	December	316,325.48	5,106.09	2,931.36	2,174.74	313,394.12
5	January	313,394.12	5,106.09	2,951.51	2,154.58	310,442.61
6	February	310,442.61	5,106.09	2,971.80	2,134.29	307,470.81
7	March	307,470.81	5,106.09	2,992.23	2,113.86	304,478.58
8	April	304,478.58	5,106.09	3,012.80	2,093.29	301,465.77
9	May	301,465.77	5,106.09	3,033.52	2,072.58	298,432.26
10	June	298,432.26	5,106.09	3,054.37	2,051.72	295,377.88
11	July	295,377.88	5,106.09	3,075.37	2,030.72	292,302.51
12	August	292,302.51	5,106.09	3,096.51	2,009.58	289,206.00
13	September	289,206.00	5,106.09	3,117.80	1,988.29	286,088.20
14	October	286,088.20	5,106.09	3,139.24	1,966.86	282,948.96
15	November	282,948.96	5,106.09	3,160.82	1,945.27	279,788.14
16	December	279,788.14	5,106.09	3,182.55	1,923.54	276,605.59
17	January	276,605.59	5,106.09	3,204.43	1,901.66	273,401.16
18	February	273,401.16	5,106.09	3,226.46	1,879.63	270,174.70
19	March	270,174.70	5,106.09	3,248.64	1,857.45	266,926.05
20	April	266,926.05	5,106.09	3,270.98	1,835.12	263,655.07
21	May	263,655.07	5,106.09	3,293.47	1,812.63	260,361.61
22	June	260,361.61	5,106.09	3,316.11	1,789.99	257,045.50
23	July	257,045.50	5,106.09	3,338.91	1,767.19	253,706.59
24	August	253,706.59	5,106.09	3,361.86	1,744.23	250,344.73
25	September	250,344.73	5,106.09	3,384.97	1,721.12	246,959.76
26	October	246,959.76	5,106.09	3,408.25	1,697.85	243,551.51
27	November	243,551.51	5,106.09	3,431.68	1,674.42	240,119.84
28	December	240,119.84	5,106.09	3,455.27	1,650.82	236,664.57
29	January	236,664.57	5,106.09	3,479.03	1,627.07	233,185.54
30	February	233,185.54	5,106.09	3,502.94	1,603.15	229,682.60
31	March	229,682.60	5,106.09	3,527.03	1,579.07	226,155.57
32	April	226,155.57	5,106.09	3,551.27	1,554.82	222,604.30
33	May	222,604.30	5,106.09	3,575.69	1,530.40	219,028.61
34	June	219,028.61	5,106.09	3,600.27	1,505.82	215,428.33
35	July	215,428.33	5,106.09	3,625.02	1,481.07	211,803.31
36	August	211,803.31	5,106.09	3,649.95	1,456.15	208,153.36
37	September	208,153.36	5,106.09	3,675.04	1,431.05	204,478.32
38	October	204,478.32	5,106.09	3,700.31	1,405.79	200,778.02
39	November	200,778.02	5,106.09	3,725.75	1,380.35	197,052.27
40	December	197,052.27	5,106.09	3,751.36	1,354.73	193,300.91
41	January	193,300.91	5,106.09	3,777.15	1,328.94	189,523.76
42	February	189,523.76	5,106.09	3,803.12	1,302.98	185,720.64
43	March	185,720.64	5,106.09	3,829.26	1,276.83	181,891.38
44	April	181,891.38	5,106.09	3,855.59	1,250.50	178,035.79
45	May	178,035.79	5,106.09	3,882.10	1,224.00	174,153.69
46	June	174,153.69	5,106.09	3,908.79	1,197.31	170,244.90
47	July	170,244.90	5,106.09	3,935.66	1,170.43	166,309.24
48	August	166,309.24	5,106.09	3,962.72	1,143.38	162,346.52

Transylvania Transmissions

Debt Management Schedule (cont'd)

Month	Payment Date	Beginning Balance	Scheduledt Payment	Principal	Interest	Ending Loan Balance
46	June	174,153.69	5,106.09	3,908.79	1,197.31	170,244.90
47	July	170,244.90	5,106.09	3,935.66	1,170.43	166,309.24
48	August	166,309.24	5,106.09	3,962.72	1,143.38	162,346.52
49	September	162,346.52	5,106.09	3,989.96	1,116.13	158,356.56
50	October	158,356.56	5,106.09	4,017.39	1,088.70	154,339.17
51	November	154,339.17	5,106.09	4,045.01	1,061.08	150,294.16
52	December	150,294.16	5,106.09	4,072.82	1,033.27	146,221.33
53	January	146,221.33	5,106.09	4,100.82	1,005.27	142,120.51
54	February	142,120.51	5,106.09	4,129.02	977.08	137,991.50
55	March	137,991.50	5,106.09	4,157.40	948.69	133,834.09
56	April	133,834.09	5,106.09	4,185.98	920.11	129,648.11
57	May	129,648.11	5,106.09	4,214.76	891.33	125,433.35
58	June	125,433.35	5,106.09	4,243.74	862.35	121,189.61
59	July	121,189.61	5,106.09	4,272.92	833.18	116,916.69
60	August	116,916.69	5,106.09	4,302.29	803.80	112,614.40
61	September	112,614.40	5,106.09	4,331.87	774.22	108,282.53
62	October	108,282.53	5,106.09	4,361.65	744.44	103,920.88
63	November	103,920.88	5,106.09	4,391.64	714.46	99,529.24
64	December	99,529.24	5,106.09	4,421.83	684.26	95,107.41
65	January	95,107.41	5,106.09	4,452.23	653.86	90,655.18
66	February	90,655.18	5,106.09	4,482.84	623.25	86,172.34
67	March	86,172.34	5,106.09	4,513.66	592.43	81,658.68
68	April	81,658.68	5,106.09	4,544.69	561.40	77,113.99
69	May	77,113.99	5,106.09	4,575.94	530.16	72,538.05
70	June	72,538.05	5,106.09	4,607.40	498.70	67,930.66
71	July	67,930.66	5,106.09	4,639.07	467.02	63,291.58
72	August	63,291.58	5,106.09	4,670.96	435.13	58,620.62
73	September	58,620.62	5,106.09	4,703.08	403.02	53,917.54
74	October	53,917.54	5,106.09	4,735.41	370.68	49,182.13
75	November	49,182.13	5,106.09	4,767.97	338.13	44,414.16
76	December	44,414.16	5,106.09	4,800.75	305.35	39,613.42
77	January	39,613.42	5,106.09	4,833.75	272.34	34,779.67
78	February	34,779.67	5,106.09	4,866.98	239.11	29,912.68
79	March	29,912.68	5,106.09	4,900.44	205.65	25,012.24
80	April	25,012.24	5,106.09	4,934.14	171.96	20,078.10
81	May	20,078.10	5,106.09	4,968.06	138.04	15,110.04
82	June	15,110.04	5,106.09	5,002.21	103.88	10,107.83
83	July	10,107.83	5,106.09	5,036.60	69.49	5,071.23
84	August	5,071.23	5,106.09	5,071.23	34.86	0.00
			428,911.91	325,000.00	103,911.91	

Scheduled Number of Payments	**84.00**
Total Interest	**103,911.91**

Transylvania Transmissions

Loan Calculator

Loan Amount	325,000
Annual Interest Rate	0
Loan Period in Years	7
Start Date of Loan	38,231

Scheduled Monthly Payment	3,869
Scheduled Number of Payments	84
Total Interest	0

Month	Payment Date	Beginning Balance	Scheduledt Payment	Principal	Interest	Ending Loan Balance
1	September	325,000	3,869	3,869	0	321,131
2	October	321,131	3,869	3,869	0	317,262
3	November	317,262	3,869	3,869	0	313,393
4	December	313,393	3,869	3,869	0	309,524
5	January	309,524	3,869	3,869	0	305,655
6	February	305,655	3,869	3,869	0	301,786
7	March	301,786	3,869	3,869	0	297,917
8	April	297,917	3,869	3,869	0	294,048
9	May	294,048	3,869	3,869	0	290,179
10	June	290,179	3,869	3,869	0	286,310
11	July	286,310	3,869	3,869	0	282,440
12	August	282,440	3,869	3,869	0	278,571
13	September	278,571	3,869	3,869	0	274,702
14	October	274,702	3,869	3,869	0	270,833
15	November	270,833	3,869	3,869	0	266,964
16	December	266,964	3,869	3,869	0	263,095
17	January	263,095	3,869	3,869	0	259,226
18	February	259,226	3,869	3,869	0	255,357
19	March	255,357	3,869	3,869	0	251,488
20	April	251,488	3,869	3,869	0	247,619
21	May	247,619	3,869	3,869	0	243,750
22	June	243,750	3,869	3,869	0	239,881
23	July	239,881	3,869	3,869	0	236,012
24	August	236,012	3,869	3,869	0	232,143
25	September	232,143	3,869	3,869	0	228,274
26	October	228,274	3,869	3,869	0	224,405
27	November	224,405	3,869	3,869	0	220,536
28	December	220,536	3,869	3,869	0	216,667
29	January	216,667	3,869	3,869	0	212,798
30	February	212,798	3,869	3,869	0	208,929
31	March	208,929	3,869	3,869	0	205,060
32	April	205,060	3,869	3,869	0	201,190
33	May	201,190	3,869	3,869	0	197,321
34	June	197,321	3,869	3,869	0	193,452
35	July	193,452	3,869	3,869	0	189,583
36	August	189,583	3,869	3,869	0	185,714
37	September	185,714	3,869	3,869	0	181,845
38	October	181,845	3,869	3,869	0	177,976
39	November	177,976	3,869	3,869	0	174,107

Transylvania Transmissions

Loan Calculator (cont'd)

Month	Payment Date	Beginning Balance	Scheduledt Payment	Principal	Interest	Ending Loan Balance
40	December	174,107	3,869	3,869	0	170,238
41	January	170,238	3,869	3,869	0	166,369
42	February	166,369	3,869	3,869	0	162,500
43	March	162,500	3,869	3,869	0	158,631
44	April	158,631	3,869	3,869	0	154,762
45	May	154,762	3,869	3,869	0	150,893
46	June	150,893	3,869	3,869	0	147,024
47	July	147,024	3,869	3,869	0	143,155
48	August	143,155	3,869	3,869	0	139,286
49	September	139,286	3,869	3,869	0	135,417
50	October	135,417	3,869	3,869	0	131,548
51	November	131,548	3,869	3,869	0	127,679
52	December	127,679	3,869	3,869	0	123,810
53	January	123,810	3,869	3,869	0	119,940
54	February	119,940	3,869	3,869	0	116,071
55	March	116,071	3,869	3,869	0	112,202
56	April	112,202	3,869	3,869	0	108,333
57	May	108,333	3,869	3,869	0	104,464
58	June	104,464	3,869	3,869	0	100,595
59	July	100,595	3,869	3,869	0	96,726
60	August	96,726	3,869	3,869	0	92,857
61	September	92,857	3,869	3,869	0	88,988
62	October	88,988	3,869	3,869	0	85,119
63	November	85,119	3,869	3,869	0	81,250
64	December	81,250	3,869	3,869	0	77,381
65	January	77,381	3,869	3,869	0	73,512
66	February	73,512	3,869	3,869	0	69,643
67	March	69,643	3,869	3,869	0	65,774
68	April	65,774	3,869	3,869	0	61,905
69	May	61,905	3,869	3,869	0	58,036
70	June	58,036	3,869	3,869	0	54,167
71	July	54,167	3,869	3,869	0	50,298
72	August	50,298	3,869	3,869	0	46,429
73	September	46,429	3,869	3,869	0	42,560
74	October	42,560	3,869	3,869	0	38,690
75	November	38,690	3,869	3,869	0	34,821
76	December	34,821	3,869	3,869	0	30,952
77	January	30,952	3,869	3,869	0	27,083
78	February	27,083	3,869	3,869	0	23,214
79	March	23,214	3,869	3,869	0	19,345
80	April	19,345	3,869	3,869	0	15,476
81	May	15,476	3,869	3,869	0	11,607
82	June	11,607	3,869	3,869	0	7,738
83	July	7,738	3,869	3,869	0	3,869
84	August	3,869	3,869	3,869	0	0
			325,000	**325,000**	**0**	

Transylvania Transmissions

Ratios

Type	Year 1	Industry Avg.
Current	6.62	2.30
Quick	6.62	0.60
Sales / Receivables	11.43	13.90
Cost of Sales / Payables	NA	NA
EBIT / Interest	9.26	2.80
Fixed / Worth	NA	0.80
Debt / Worth	0.91	1.50
Sales / Total Assets	1.01	3.20
Owner's Comp/Sales	0.10	0.06
Return on Equity	0.40	NA

Transylvania Transmissions

Value of the Company – Year Three

Sales Price at 3 times EBITDA	1,119,867
Seller Note Repayment	325,000
Bank Debt Repayment	208,153
Net Sale Proceeds	586,713
Dividends (1)	806,988
Total Return (Div +Cap Gain)	1,393,702
Investment	500,000
Annual Average Return (Pre-Tax)	72%

IRR Calculation

Investment	400,000
Year 1 Dividend	200,206
Year 2 Dividend	300,740
Year 3 Dividend + Gain	920,605
IRR	72%

Note:
During the 3 years, the company can disperse its Earnings Before Depreciation but after principal payments on the notes.

Resources

There is a Web site with information and tools to supplement this book. It includes sample plans, links to other useful sites, a Web-based automated business plan writing system and other material: ***www.bankablebusinessplans.com***.

Chapter 4: Analyze Potential Markets

The Encyclopedia of Associations, published by Thomson, is available in book form or on the Web through libraries that subscribe to it. It is a good place to find your industry association that might publish industry background information.

The *Thomas Register of American Manufacturers* is similarly available in book form or free on the Web at www.thomasnet.com. If you need to locate possible suppliers for your business, it is an efficient place to begin.

Start Your Own Business, 4th Edition, by Rieva Lesonsky, Entrepreneur Press, 2007. This book is a comprehensive guide to the process of starting your business.

Entrepreneur magazine's site, www.entrepreneur.com, is also extremely useful.

Hoover's at www.hoovers.com, provides company and industry data and various useful links. Some information is provided at no charge; other data is on a fee basis.

Financial and Operating Results of Department and Specialty Stores, published by the National Retail Merchants Association, is an annual presentation of detailed financial information that can serve as useful guidance and comparison.

The U.S. Census Bureau, at www.census.gov is a source for literally billions of dollars of high-quality research on population, industries, employment, and ethnic groups, most of which is available for all localities throughout the United States. Industry reports compiled by the Census Bureau can be searched by NAICS code (see Chapter 9 for an explanation of the coding systems at www.census.gov). There is so much information, that it may take a while to sort through it all, but it's worth the time, and the price is right . . . it's free.

Other ways to search the vast array of government offerings include the Catalog of Federal Domestic Assistance at www.cfda.gov; the Government Printing Office at www.gpo.gov; FedStats at www.fedstats.gov; the National Associations of Counties at www.naco.org.

The Small Business Administration (www.sba.gov) is loaded with useful information, reports, financing worksheets, background on government programs, and many links. It is somewhat cumbersome to navigate, but worth the time. Some of the same information is available more directly through another SBA site, the U.S. Small Business Advisor (www.sba.gov/smallbusinessplanner/plan/index.html).

Information on public companies in your industry can provide good background or comparisons with your own plans. The Securities and Exchange Commission site, www.sec.gov/info/edgar.shtml, provides fast access to all public company filings.

Quicken and CNN, along with their Web sites, www.quicken.com and www.money.cnn.com, provide current and historical financial information for public companies.

Standard and Poor's has various industry reports at its site, www.standardandpoors.com.

General business background information is available through www.factiva.com, which is the site for searching the Reuters and Dow Jones business publications.

LexisNexis (www.lexis.com) offers data from public records, newspapers, and magazines.

Kompass at www.kompass.com provides product and contact information for 2 million companies throughout the world. Their Product/Services and Companies search engine is a valuable resource.

Moody's | Economy.com (www.economy.com/freelunch) offers links to nearly a million sources of economic and financial data on industries, consumers, and government statistics.

Many libraries offer information directly over the Web, or provide links to business references. Among the better ones are:

The Library of Congress (www.lcweb.loc.gov)

U.S. Public Libraries on the Web
(www.lists.webjunction.org/libweb/Public _ main.html)

The American Library Association guide to best business Web sites
(www.ala.org/rusa/brass/besthome.html)

The Librarian's Index to the Internet (www.lii.org)

Some Web sites such as Factiva, Standard and Poor's, and LexisNexis charge for their use, but many libraries subscribe to these services and make them available at no charge.

Chapter 5: Develop A Marketing Campaign

The Successful Marketing Plan, 3rd Edition, by Roman F. Hiebing, Jr. and Scott W. Cooper, NTC Business Books, 2003. This is a very clear and detailed explanation of the marketing aspect of a business plan.

The 33 Ruthless Rules of Local Advertising, by Michael Corbett with Dave Stilli, SummitView Publishing, 2001. No one understands the issues of marketing a small business better than Michael Corbett and Dave Stilli. This book is indispensable for businesses that need to rely on local advertising to be successful (www.33rules.com).

The Marketing Plan, 4th Edition, by William A. Cohen, John Wiley & Sons, 2004.

The Psychology of Persuastion: Influence, 2nd Edition, by Robert B. Cialdini, William Morrow, 1993.

The American Marketing Association (www.marketingpower.com) maintains a Web site with many reports, most of which are free, and useful links, all of which are related to marketing strategies.

For information about Internet marketing, including useful and free daily newsletters, you should try:

www.emarketer.com (some of its best content must be purchased)

www.imediaconnection.com

www.iab.net (Interactive Advertising Bureau)

Chapter 6: Build a Sales Effort

Getting to Yes: Negotiating Agreement Without Giving In, 2nd Edition, by Roger Fisher and William Ury, Houghton Mifflin, 1991.

You Can't Teach a Kid to Ride a Bike at a Seminar : The Sandler Sales Institute's 7-Step System for Successful Selling, 2nd Edition, by David H. Sandler, Bay Head, 2000.

The New Strategic Selling: The Unique Sales System Proven Successful by the World's Best Companies, Revised and Updated for the 21st Century, by Stephen E. Heiman and Diane Sanchez, Warner Business Books, 1998.

Chapter 7: Organize the Company

American Association of Franchisees and Dealers (www.aafd.org) has a very useful Web site that includes both free information and an online bookstore with publications about franchises.

Franchising 101, edited by Ann Dugan, Upstart Publishing Company, 1998. This is an excellent collection of articles by experts on various aspects of franchising.

Eight Things to Look for in a Franchise available through the American Association of Franchisees and Dealers (AAFD), www.aafd.org.

Ultimate Franchise Book, available through *Entrepreneur Magazine,* www.entrepreneur.com.

Also, www.businessfranchisedirectory.com is a directory of franchise offerings.

Chapter 9: Produce Financial Projections

Entrepreneurial Finance: Finance for Small Business, 2nd Edition, by Philip J. Adelman and Alan M. Marks, Prentice-Hall, 2001.

Venture Economics annually publishes *Pratt's Guide to Venture Capital Sources,* which provides a comprehensive list of venture capital companies, along with their investment criteria and areas of focus.

The National Venture Capital Association publishes a similar directory, *National Venture Capital Association Directory,* which is also available on the Web (`www.nvca.org`).

A useful site for information on bank lending, current rates and credit cards is Bank Rate.com (`www.bankrate.com`).

The Commerce Clearing House (CCH) Web site (`www.toolkit.cch.com`) has a great deal of useful and easy to find information including model spreadsheets, sample business plans, reports on topics of importance to small business, and legal and tax information.

Nolo (`www.nolo.com`) specializes in legal issues. Sample documents, such as contracts, are available for a fee, but most of their background material on legal issues is available at no charge.

The Edward Lowe Foundation (`www.edwardlowe.org`) is a service which promotes entrepreneurship. There is an extensive library of reports and numerous links to other business sites.

The Kauffman Foundation (`www.kauffman.org`) has a great number of resources for entrepreneurs. The reader is directed to an especially helpful site: `www.eVenturing.org`.

Accounting help, including break-even analysis, returns analysis, and creating statements, can be found in *Introduction to Management Accounting, 13th Edition,* by Charles T. Horngren, Gary L. Sundem and William O. Stratton, Prentice-Hall, 2004.

Salary.com, Inc. provides a useful site for all things related to salary (`www.salary.com`).

Additional Information Related to Financial Issues

Winning business plans from the **University of Texas MOOTCORP Competition**, like the ones presented in the Sample Plans section of the appendices, are available at their Web site, www.businessplan.org.

Accounting help including Break-Even Analysis, Returns Analysis, and creating statements, can be found in *Introduction to Management Accounting*, by Charles T. Horngren, Gary L. Sundem, and William O. Stratton, 12th Edition, Prentice-Hall, 2002.

Entrepreneurial Finance for New and Emerging Businesses, by James McNeill Stancill, Thomson South-Western, 2004.

Financial Planning for the Entrepreneur, by Donald E. Vaughn, Prentice-Hall, 1997.

Chapter 10: Demonstrate the Entrepreneur's Abilities and Qualifications

How to Say It in a Job Search: Choice Words, Phrases, Sentences, for Resumes, Cover Letters, and Interviews, by Robbie Miller Kaplan, Prentice Hall, 2001. A helpful guide to presenting your skills and background.

Chapter 11: Present the Plan on Paper
Create a Time Line

Project Management: A Systems Approach to Planning, Scheduling and Controlling, 9th Edition, by Harold Kerzner, John Wiley & Sons, Inc., 2005. A textbook that clearly and comprehensively covers project-management tools. For your own application, you will probably only need to refer to a few pages, so you may want to review it at a library.

The Fast Forward MBA in Project Management, 2nd Edition, by Eric Verzuh, John Wiley & Sons Inc., 2005. An overview of project-management tools, and will be helpful in determining which of these tools will be appropriate to your needs.

Teach Yourself Microsoft Project 2000, by Vickey L. Quinn, Hungry Minds, Inc., 2001. A good guide that will get you up and running quickly.

An Introduction to Management Science: Quantitative Approaches to Decision Making, 11th Edition, by David R. Anderson, Dennis J. Sweeney, and Thomas A. Williams, South-Western Publishing, 2004.

Operations Management: Processes and Value Chains, 8th Edition, by Lee J. Krajewski, Larry P. Ritzman, and Manoj K. Malhotra, Prentice Hall, 2006.

Chapter 12: Present the Plan in Person

The Entrepreneurial Conversation: The Powerful Way to Create Mutually Beneficial, Long-Term Business Relationships, by Edward G. Rogoff and Michael Corbett with Perry-Lynn Moffitt, Rowhouse Publishing, 2007. There is also a Web site: `www.thinklistenspeak.com`.

Getting to Yes: Negotiating Agreement Without Giving In, 2nd Edition, by Roger Fisher and William Ury, Houghton Mifflin, 1991.

Negotiation: Readings, Exercises, and Cases, 2nd Edition, by Roy J. Lewicki, David M. Saunders, John W. Minton and Bruce Barry. McGraw-Hill, 2002.

Index